GOD IS IN THE CROWD

CONTENTS

WITHDRAWN

GOD
IS IN THE
CROWD

Twenty-First-Century

Judaism

TAL KEINAN

SPIEGEL & GRAU SPIEGEL&GRAU NEW YORK

Published in the United States by Spiegel & Grau, an imprint of Random House, a division of Penguin Random House LLC, New York.

SPIEGEL & GRAU and colophon is a registered trademark of Penguin Random House LLC.

Library of Congress Cataloging-in-Publication Data
Names: Keinan, Tal, author.
Title: God is in the crowd / Tal Keinan.
Description: New York : Spiegel & Grau, [2018] | Includes bibliographical references and index.
Identifiers: LCCN 2018000337| ISBN 9780525511168 | ISBN 9780525511175 (ebook)
Subjects: LCSH: Jews—Identity. | Jews—Civilization. | Judaism—21st century. | Judaism and state—Israel.
Classification: LCC DS143 .K43 2018 | DDC 305.892/4—dc23
LC record available at https://lccn.loc.gov/2018000337

Printed in the United States of America on acid-free paper

randomhousebooks.com
spiegelandgrau.com

2 4 6 8 9 7 5 3 1

First Edition

Book design by Susan Turner

For my girls and their crowd

PROLOGUE

This book first took form as a diary. I used it to record my ambivalent thoughts on affiliation with a tribe, the Jews. I was born with membership but, in my early years, did not accept it as anything more than an option I would be unlikely to redeem. I was American. My interest in Judaism was, ironically, sparked by a Protestant minister at a New England prep school. It was not religion I was seeking. It was belonging. My parents had divorced when I was a child. I had changed schools every year or two since then. I wanted a home, and I discovered one in Judaism.

Membership in the Jewish tribe became the obsession that animated the most important, and the most reckless, decision of my young life. I moved to Israel and committed to an eight-year stint in the Israeli Air Force. I was nineteen years old and still knew very little about the membership I had claimed. The intensity of my military service left almost no time for contemplating Judaism. It was only toward the end of that service that I again began to question the specific value of membership in the Jewish People.

My relationship with Judaism has become more thoughtful in adulthood. I have been supported by teachers from the worlds of Jewish theology, Israeli politics, and American Jewish activism, and by some who have nothing to do with Jewish affairs. Most of my post–Air Force professional life has been at Clarity, an asset management firm. I have shuttled between Clarity's offices in the United States and Israel, the two countries that currently account for almost 90 percent of the world's Jews. I have the privilege of living in both. My Jewish associates at Clarity have hailed from six continents and have represented most of the spectrum of Jewish affiliation, including Reform, Conservative, and Modern Orthodox Judaism. Years of intimate intellectual engagement with my colleagues, in matters ranging from Jewish history to mathematics, have provided a framework for the prescriptive thinking behind *God Is in the Crowd*.

I wrote this book having read much of the existing literature on Jewish Peoplehood. I would consider it a great success if it inspired readers to seek a diversity of views on Jewish identity, and to examine alternative prescriptions for Jewish continuity. I hope for the book to open a personal window through which greater numbers of Jews, affiliated and unaffiliated, might be able to contemplate the value of their Judaism, to themselves as individuals, to their communities, and to humanity as a whole. I hope for the book to inspire these people to claim a role in defining this value, an act that does not require years of Jewish scholarship.

A common Hebrew proverb loosely translates as "It is the new guest who sees the home's faults." As I was spared the indoctrination implicit in much of structured Jewish education, my own approach to the home of Judaism was originally that of a guest. The questions I pose here emerge directly from my personal Jewish journey. My prognosis for the Jewish future is grim. The severity of that prognosis drives the aggressiveness of my prescription, a remedy that some have perceived as radical. The ideas behind *God Is in the Crowd* have already framed a debate within a small group of Jewish and non-Jewish thinkers. My ambition for the book is to draw a critical mass of the world Jewish community into this debate. I believe that only through the engagement of this critical mass, a population I describe as the Crowd, will the Jewish People claim control of its destiny.

Many of *God Is in the Crowd*'s early readers are Jewish leaders who have invested tremendous energy and immense financial resources in Jewish continuity. Organizations such as the Jewish Agency, and initiatives such as Birthright Israel, have shaped the course of recent Jewish history. But the Jewish reality continues to evolve. If we fail to recognize this evolution and adapt our approach, we will look back on these efforts one day and realize that they only bought us more time. If the Jewish People is to survive, in Israel, in the United States, and in the remnants of Diaspora, Judaism must reclaim its relevance to the individual by reestablishing its spiritual value. It must reclaim its relevance to the community by finding common cause among a critical mass of its individual adherents. This can happen only through the continued evolution of Jewish thought and practice. In an era of seemingly limitless personal options, our choice as a community is stark: Create meaning in Judaism or accept extinction.

PART
ONE

| Should There Be Jews? |

1

False Peaks

I awoke to the smell of ammonia. I was on my feet, but couldn't remember where. It was quiet and dark. I exhaled instinctively, to expel the fumes burning my throat, and held my breath for as long as I could. When the air rushed back in, the wet burlap hood fastened around my neck pressed against my cracked lips. I tasted urine, and the reality began flooding back. I was hunched low, in an underground cell, my shaved head scraping through the burlap against a jagged stone ceiling. My wrists were bound behind me with a thin cable. A metal rod wedged between my arms and my back, its ends grating inside grooves in the walls, prevented me from turning. I was barefoot, confined to one spot on a floor embedded with studs. I could straighten either my back or my legs, but not both. The silence around me was periodically pierced by a heavy water drop striking the floor somewhere outside my cell, its impact echoing against distant walls.

During the interludes, the pulse throbbed in my ears. My feet were swollen. I slid my soles along the wet stone in search of a smooth spot, but the studs were positioned too densely.

As the fog in my mind gradually dissipated, I began to take stock of my situation. I sensed the height of my cell. I could roughly judge its width but not its length. I could somehow picture chipped white paint on the iron bars at its entrance. I tried to remember when I might actually have seen those bars. I had no memory of being here without my blindfold and hood. It was possible I had imagined them. Memory and imagination had become fused together over the past few days. Old friends, from another universe, had visited me here several times. Their impressions were so distinct that I struggled to convince myself they were not real.

A quiver in my thighs signaled muscle spasms. The last time my legs seized up, I had gashed my head on the ceiling. That was real. I could taste the blood. Wide awake now, I felt a wave of dread beginning to break over me. I was alert enough to recognize the value in my awareness of the approaching panic. I knew how to use that awareness as a weapon in my battle for self-control. There were two fronts in that battle. On one, the external front, I fought for a sense of my surroundings. I would count my steps when I was hauled from room to room, trying to keep a mental map of the underground facility. I would try to identify the voices of different guards, and to monitor the passage of time by noting the rotations of their shifts. I would review a mental task list in a constant loop. It included debriefing recent interrogations, recalling and memorizing details of the stories I was manufacturing, planning strategy for approaching interrogations, taking stock of my body and my mental state. Holding the line on the external front was vital when the pace of events was fast. The fight provided orientation. It was my interlocutor and companion in the hostile void. It helped me to resist emotional engagement with my interrogators, who baited me with occasional poisoned kindness, dangling in front of me the dangerous illusion of a life raft.

The battle lines on the internal front were ambiguous, but their vulnerability was frighteningly clear in periods like this, when the pace of events was slow, during breaks between manipulative skirmishes with interrogators or guards, or with the occasional doctor. Here, the adversary was my own wandering thoughts. Uncontrolled, they would lead me through helplessness and panic to total and permanent defeat.

I returned to an exercise that had been successful before. I closed my eyes. I had not seen light through the hood for hours, maybe days, but my eyes were now shut by choice. I had to control those aspects of my reality that I could, even though they were small. I began narrowing my thoughts to my own breathing, gradually peeling through layers of distraction. I descended through the sting in my nostrils and the burning skin on my lacerated back, irritated by the swell of each breath I took. My breathing slowed. The muscles in my legs and back gradually relaxed. I was still conscious of physical pain, but it was becoming distant. My racing thoughts were quieting. Questions that had earlier undermined my confidence in my own narrative now faded in significance. How had I arrived here? How long had I been here? Was this still a training exercise, or had the missing links in the chain of my recent memory somehow obscured a grimmer reality? As I reached the zone I was seeking, even the present shrank to nothing. I lapsed into unconsciousness.

I awoke on my back. I could feel a needle in my arm and a pleasant cold running up my vein. My breathing was calm, my burning back soothed by the cool stone floor. My feet no longer ached. I must have been in this position for some time. It occurred to me to remain still beneath the damp hood. That might prolong the hiatus. I restarted my checklist. Orientation: I remembered that my dungeon cell was four stories underground. I had counted my steps over the days. I could faintly hear the echoes of angry curses issued in Arabic, iron doors slamming, beatings, and cries. They were likely coming from minus two, where I believed my teammates were being held. This was almost certainly minus three, where my previous interrogations had been conducted. I realized I was in line for a session. I moved to strategy. I refreshed my story, reviewing the last iteration of details as I remembered them. I imagined the ruses and traps that might be in store. They would insinuate that I had been betrayed by my teammates. One interrogator would beat me without restraint. Another, posing as his superior, might interrupt the beating with a kindly worded invitation to betray my comrades in return. I steeled myself for the battle of wits and finished my checklist with time to spare. I felt lucid. I was ready, but as far as the guards knew, I was still unconscious. I continued lying motionless.

As I savored my remaining moments of autonomy, I noticed that I was not defeated. As unlikely as it now seemed, I had reserves. My parents and siblings were half a world away.

Not a single member of the community that had raised me to adulthood knew where I was. I was more alone than I had ever been, but driven by a conviction that eclipsed my solitude. I could summon its energy almost effortlessly. I felt it now, throbbing in my limbs, firing my optimism. More trials lay ahead, but I welcomed them. This was the right place for me. This is what I was meant to be doing. I took a moment to recognize the absurdity of my gratitude at the threshold of the interrogation chamber, and caught myself smiling softly under the hood.

That conviction was born in high school. I was a junior, an "upper," at Phillips Exeter Academy in 1986. Exeter is an icon within the storied league of New England prep schools founded at the time of the American Revolution. John Phillips established Exeter and its sister school, Andover, in the tradition of the Congregational Church, the American colonial brand of Calvinism that originally took root in the Plymouth and Massachusetts Bay colonies in the 1620s. Having fled persecution in Europe, the Congregationalists celebrated the virtue of tolerance, an ideal that took root in much of colonial New England, and extended it to its Jewish population at the time. The academy, however, was a Christian institution, and it had remained closed to Jewish students during most of its first two centuries. It became a citadel of America's white Protestant elite, a link in the chain of exclusive institutions that shepherded bright young men through life, to Harvard and Yale and on to the prestigious banks and law firms of New York, Boston, and Philadelphia, or to careers in the officers' corps and the nation's political leadership.

My father had taken me on a visit for prospective students one year earlier. I was the sheltered product of a sleepy high school in Florida, provincial and naïve. I would have stayed in Florida had there been somewhere for me to stay, but my family had disintegrated. My father was newly married for the fourth time, and his efforts at building another life would have failed had he clung too closely to his previous one. My younger brother and I would willingly have stayed with him but understood there was no place for us in his new home. My mother was weathering a series of unsuccessful relationships. She struggled to find her own footing, and our presence kept her perpetually off balance. Ron and I took the initiative to apply to prep schools ourselves. We already knew that life. Our parents had sent us to elementary boarding schools several years earlier, during their divorce. We had come back to Florida for high school, but as our lives there became untenable, we began to see boarding school as our best alternative.

I had not appreciated the provinciality of my life in Florida until a magazine article about Exeter provided a comparison. The Exeter kids interviewed in the article viewed life from a higher vantage point than I did. Their world was bigger, wiser, and more pertinent. The smallness of my own unexamined life suddenly became apparent. The ignorance that confined me to it was suddenly unjustifiable. I was ashamed of it. Oblivious to the newness of my own eligibility as a Jew, I wanted in.

I brought up the rear on the campus tour. I stopped to read the flyers on message boards advertising student-run events and club meetings. Their names suggested sophisticated members, with knowledge and skills that were foreign to me. The Buddhist Meditation Society. The Fencing Club. The Squash Team. The Lamont Art Gallery. I knew I was out of my depth, but I understood the deal I could strike. Exeter was a privilege into which I could grow, but my transformation would have to be fundamental. The boy I was on the day of the tour would never be at home here. I would have to leave him behind. As we dispersed at the school bookstore and some of the other applicants crowded in to buy sweatshirts and hats, I stood to the side, drawing in the cold New England air, focusing my thoughts on the admissions interview scheduled to begin soon.

My father watched me from a deliberate distance, chatting with the student who had led the tour. LeRoy Wiener's generation had not had access to opportunities like Exeter. He had clawed his own way to every milestone he had ever achieved, without guidance from seasoned insiders. He could only imagine the dedicated teachers and expert coaches who would now escort me down the path to privilege. He had always been conscious of a line beyond which talent and grit could never take him. Screened out of the Ivy League by quotas and tuition, he went to City College. He shuttled across town four times a day, to predawn and late-night workouts, winning national swimming titles for the school. He climbed to the top of his class as a chemical engineer, landing a coveted spot as a member of Edward Teller's enrichment team on the Manhattan Project at the age of twenty. During the war, the urgency of that team's mission had endowed its members with resources and attention they had never known. LeRoy received a personal citation from Secretary of War Henry Stimson.

My father and I never discussed his relationship with his Jewishness, but I pieced it together on my own. It was clearly the motivation for his vicarious ambitions for me. His achievements early in life had been remarkable, but always within the context of a Jewish world. City College's engineering programs were probably 90 percent Jewish. Edward Teller's team on the Manhattan Project was also predominantly Jewish. My father's early social life, capped by a youthful romance with Bess Myerson, the beauty queen, was almost exclusively Jewish. He spent his first twenty-five years riding high enough to push against the Jewish glass ceiling, but never accumulated enough momentum to crash through it.

His entire generation knew that ceiling. When the war ended, the engineering team dissolved into a job market saturated with surplus defense industry employees and veterans coming home from the front. The prestige that had accompanied the team's successes suddenly evaporated, and LeRoy found himself kicked back to the streets of his childhood, facing the professional and social barriers he had almost succeeded in forgetting. He watched as cousins and classmates, returning from Europe and the Pacific, gradually corrected their own heady ambitions. Turned away from the prestigious Manhattan firms in which they would have been qualified to serve but for one wrinkle in their résumés, they founded neighborhood law practices or applied for government posts. LeRoy's once steady course began to meander, the professional path of least resistance forcing unlikely turns through Boston, Denver, and finally Miami. Having run uphill at full tilt since childhood, he was permanently spent by midlife. He never recovered the fight of his youth. The sons of his first three marriages would pick up where he had left off, becoming his vicarious shot at full admission to Club America.

To his sons' generation, however, membership was suddenly, finally, within reach. We were the first to have arrived, though we felt we had been here forever. Full membership came with the privilege of ignorance. We cruised the paved roads my father had never traveled, with oblivious nonchalance that he must have found at once gratifying and gallingly alien. Exeter was the smoothest of those roads. My talented father had missed it by just a generation. Fully aware of his timing, and inescapably mindful of his own parents' starting blocks, set even farther back than his own, he attached deep significance to his son's arrival. He wanted this opportunity for me, and I was determined to seize it.

My mother, Zipora, the third of my father's four wives, was the daughter of Central European Jews who had met and married in prestate Palestine. She was born on September 1, 1939, the day the Nazis invaded Poland. Built on the shifting sands of those turbulent years, her parents' marriage did not survive the war. Zipora was placed in an orphanage as an infant and was eventually sent to England to be raised by an adoptive family. Years later, she reestablished contact with her parents. We would visit my grandfather Julius Speier in Haifa when I was a child. He and I would go for walks in the hills overlooking the port. I remember the stale pretense of his dress shirt and jacket, so conspicuously out of place in the hot Carmel afternoons. He was European. He had never become an Israeli. Even a six-year-old could sympathize with his bitter and hopeless embrace of exile. He had no close friends. He had come to Israel with a degree in engineering, but he lost his job years before I knew him. He was estranged from his neighbors. His relationships with his own family were animated by resentment and hostility. In my clearest memories of him, he is shouting at my mother in German. He died still only haltingly conversant in Hebrew.

Forty years later, I found a box of old photographs that my mother must have collected. My resemblance to young Julius is unmistakable. He is smiling in those pictures, relaxed and carefree, even a bit goofy. In many of the photographs, he is hiking in what I assume is a forest near his native Guxhagen, in Germany, or swimming in the Fulda River, which ran through the village. In some, Julius is joined by three blond friends. The four pose for the photographer against different backgrounds, in different seasons of the year, arms around one another's shoulders, smiling broadly or making faces at the camera. They appear inseparable as they grow from boys into young men over a dozen photographs. My grandfather never spoke to me about his life in Germany. I will never know who those friends were, or if he was in touch with them after the war. I do not believe they were Jewish. They were of fighting age when the war began. Had they survived? Had they joined the Nazi movement, as many young men of their generation did? Had they turned on their childhood friend? Or had they perhaps saved him, persuading him to leave while it was still possible? Julius abandoned his life and his family's property in 1936, before most German Jews understood that this was the only trade that would save their lives. It could not have been an easy decision. The Speier family had lived in Guxhagen for centuries.

Since her divorce, my maternal grandmother, Eta, had

worked in menial jobs. None of her relationships after the
war had materialized into a marriage. When I knew her, she
was living alone in the Tel Aviv apartment my mother had
purchased for her, subsisting on a government pension. She
rarely left the apartment. On the occasions my brother Ron
and I visited her, she would send us to the market to buy
imported coffee, chocolate, or other items she considered in-
dulgences. She kept the shades in the apartment drawn during the day. The only light I remember in that space is that of
the television, reflected on Eta's pale skin.

It was only when I discovered that box of photographs
that I began trying to see Eta as a real person. In them, she is
a pretty young woman. She has blond hair and wears coordinated outfits that appear perfectly ironed, even in the humid
Mediterranean summer. In one of the photographs, she is
sitting in the middle of a group of twelve men and women,
possibly on a kibbutz. The people around her are standing in
dungarees, their feet wide apart, arms crossed in front of
them, as though they are impatient to get back to the fields.
Two members of the group hold a sign bearing a hammer and
sickle. Eta is wearing a white blouse with a light, embroi-
dered vest, punctuated by a thin black necktie. Considering
the utilitarian sensibilities of those times, Eta's look seems
defiant, almost subversive. She sits with her back straight
and her hands folded in her lap. I never knew Eta to have
political interests or opinions. She appears distinctly out of
place with these radicals, whoever they were.

Also in the box is a professional portrait of Eta's brother,
my great-uncle, Shimon (Simon) Romm. Shimon is wearing
a suit and tie; his hair is perfectly combed. He smiles warmly

through elegant eyeglasses. An inscription on the back of the photograph, surprisingly written in Hebrew, reads, "To my dear sister, who is more precious to me than all things precious: I wish you a happy and blessed new year, 5698, from Mir." Mir was a yeshiva in Belarus, where Shimon had been sent to study when his younger sister left for Palestine. The Gregorian year is 1937. Two years later, the Soviets had occupied Belarus and were facing the German Wehrmacht, massed on the Polish border only a hundred miles to the west. Shimon fled east, first to Vilnius, then to Vladivostok, then to Kobe, Japan, then to occupied Shanghai. He survived the war and emigrated to America, eventually joining the faculty of Yeshiva University in New York as a professor of rabbinic studies. I visited him a number of times as a child. By then he was a respected elder rabbi, but his smile had the same warmth that I now see in the picture. I associate that smile with Eta, and with the tender words Shimon had shared with her. Somebody had appreciated her. There had been a place for her somewhere, just not among the Jews of Palestine.

When I knew Eta and Julius, I was too young to sympathize with the tragedy of their destroyed vitality. They could not have explained it to me, even as an adult. The bones of their broken identities had set wrong and hardened in place, leaving them permanently crippled. The prospect of resetting these old bones, or even recalling their correct alignment, was too painful for them to consider. Never having known them as full human beings, I remember them primarily as symbols of the unacknowledged fate of a generation of survivors, the lucky ones.

As a young adult, my mother wandered. Having tried to build a life in London, Milan, and, briefly, Tel Aviv, Zipora met LeRoy at a fund-raising event in Miami. They were married within months. LeRoy was smitten by Zipora's exotic beauty and her cosmopolitan sophistication, but his family looked down on her. They were established Americans. They had a floor underneath them. They resented this European reminder that the floor might not be so solid, or that there might be a glass ceiling above it. Their disdain extended to Ron and me. Since my father died in 2007, we have not spoken with his sister. I don't even know if she is still alive.

On the other hand, LeRoy's glass ceiling was too high for Zipora to even recognize. She could not hear it shatter when I was accepted to Exeter. As far as she was concerned, her son was just going to a good school. To her, my options had never been limited. Exeter would be lucky to have a student like me, Jew or Gentile, and surely must have known that. At the time, I shared Zipora's obliviousness to the limitations America might once have imposed on a Jewish boy. By my generation, those limitations existed mainly in the minds of America's Jews. My own ignorance of them liberated me to dare.

As far as Exeter was concerned, my mother was right. The school was no longer a white Protestant male bastion. It was just a good school. My classmates came from around the United States and the world, curious, ambitious, and diverse in their interests. I found context for introspection in Exeter's heterogeneity. Without a uniform standard to which I could conform, I discovered that I would have to define myself. There were student communities, societies, and athletic teams against which I could test my evolving identity. I joined a few clubs and became active in the student leadership of my dormitory. My father had had us running and swimming competitively from early childhood, and I tried out and joined the track team. But these were just activities. They would not help me define myself.

When I arrived, in 1986, there was a significant Jewish community at Exeter. The Jewish Student Association held a weekly Sabbath dinner, which I attended for the first time midway through my first semester. I felt welcome immediately. I liked the community that I met, but I was also drawn to the ritual. Shabbat represented a weekly milestone for me, providing an important opportunity for reflection during this formative period. Dinner was led by the Reverend Robert Thompson, Exeter's chaplain. Reverend Thompson brought enthusiasm to an event that for many of us was a first exposure to spirituality. His sermons, presented more as interactive discussions, introduced me to the concept of Shabbat as a mode shift, a day of rest from one type of industry but an energizing activation of another. Individual ambition, competition, and stress could fall away, leaving a sense of union with the others around the table. Community, during Shabbat, was not only the aggregation of its members but an organism unto itself. On Shabbat, I began to perceive a new relevance for myself as a member of a community, a cell in a bigger organism.

We were lucky to have Reverend Thompson, and happy for him to be one of us for a night, but the reverend also officiated at Exeter's Christian Fellowship Union and the academy's interfaith service. He was the spiritual leader for almost everybody who sought spiritual leadership at Exeter. He set a distinct and recognizable tone, respectful of all faiths and worldviews, socially conscious and socially responsible. Perhaps echoing its original Calvinist sensibilities, the Exeter religion I experienced sought to identify and highlight commonalities among people of diverse backgrounds. Faith itself seemed secondary, serving only as a conduit to a common spiritual canon. I attended one interfaith service and, recognizing Reverend Thompson's familiar meditative air, identified the similarity of its tone with that of Shabbat dinner. From my perch on the Protestant pews of Exeter Church, I was suddenly confronting the universality that had been informing my conception of Judaism. The spiritual exercise we conducted on Friday nights was generic. If it was at all distinct, it was distinct to Exeter—not to Judaism. It was still beautiful, but only incidentally Jewish, only insofar as the congregants happened to be Jews, and the blessings we recited were translated from a Jewish text.

I still enjoyed Shabbat. I liked Reverend Thompson and found value in his guidance. But I began to question whether being Jewish actually meant something more for me, something distinct from the Exeter Shabbat dinner. I had never been a believer, but God did not seem essential to my search. I was conscious of my link to a people, even though I did not know its story. I suddenly wanted to know it, and my interest gathered urgency over the next few months.

Starting in my second semester, I enrolled in every possible academic course that addressed Judaism. I read the Bible and studied modern Jewish history, including the history of Israel. As I came to know our story, I began to discover value in our legacy. We had laid much of the foundation on which modernity rests. We were the original codifiers of the key questions that still define the societies we live in. Our ancestors had authored monotheism and midwifed the emergence of Western civilization, contributing many of its seminal leaps—the foundations of justice, Christianity, socialism, psychoanalysis, relativity. Our contributions in medicine, literature, music, art, and the sciences are a defining weave in the fabric of world civilization, without which contemporary humanity would be unrecognizable.

The more I learned, the more ashamed I felt of my ignorance. It was a betrayal of a never-before-considered responsibility. Not only was I linked to this people, I actually was a link between its past and its future. Despite its minuscule membership, despite dramatic mutations in practice and in circumstance, the chain of peoplehood had remained unbroken for two hundred generations. I was suddenly overwhelmed by the ease with which I could break it. Until that point, I realized, I had unconsciously assumed that I *would* break it. Judaism had meant little to me before I met Reverend Thompson. I had never thought of continuity. Given my surroundings and my sensibilities, I was set to be the last link in my own family's chain, not because I had given this eventuality the consideration that a legacy of four millennia might have merited, but because it had just never occurred to me.

Of course, the betrayal was not mine alone. I had received no Jewish education. Like many American Jews of my age, I had not known Jewish community in any meaningful way. For successive generations of my recent ancestors, Jewishness had been inescapable. They had had little reason to question its value, or to debate opting out. For many, Judaism was just a hindrance that they would gladly have cast off in their struggle to become Americans.

At Exeter, I became aware of a tension that would come to guide the direction of my life. I was beginning to realize that membership in a tribe demands boundaries. As Jews, we were defined by particular codes, values, rules, and rituals that we did not share with others. At the same time, I was an individual and a Universalist. I saw sectarian borders as artificial and even dangerous. I cherished my freedom to associate as I wished, and I valued my objectivity. Even as I began discovering value in my Jewishness, I encountered repeated reminders of my belonging to a broader tribe. I remember track and field tryouts in the winter of 1986. I had just run a four-hundred-meter time trial in under fifty-three seconds, securing myself a position on the varsity track team. I was elated. University applications were looming, and competitive sports would provide a much-needed boost to my résumé. As I walked toward the locker room, I thought back to the conversation I had had with my roommate less than a week earlier. It was Spiro who had convinced me to try out. I knew I could run but had been cowed by the seriousness that Exeter seemed to ascribe to its sports programs. The sheer grandeur of the George H. Love athletic center's architecture, with its statuesque concrete facade and state-of-the-art facilities, suggested that an amateur from South Florida who had run only with a barely funded local team should keep his distance. Spiro's argument—that neither of us would be sitting here in a dorm room at Exeter had we limited our ambitions to the familiar and realistic—had won the day.

Walking back to my dormitory through the athletic center's high-ceilinged corridor, past squash courts, swimming pools, and hockey rinks, I paused to consider how my world had just become a little bit bigger, my options expanded. I felt I could digest more of this place than I might have the day before. Until now, I had avoided some of the grandness that had been too bright for me to look at directly. I stopped to read the plaques commemorating the teams of past decades. Some of their members' names were familiar. Exeter and Andover had produced American presidents, business leaders, academics, and artists for two hundred years. Plaques like these bore reference to family names such as Grant, Rockefeller, Eisenhower, Kennedy, Roosevelt, Heinz, and Bush. That morning, I took one of many small steps into a very specifically American world of privilege. Even then, I recognized the irony in the ivy-covered red-brick walls and white New England steeples feeling a bit more like home, just as I was becoming a Jew.

Affiliating with America was a different exercise from affiliating with Judaism. Most members of the American tribe could ignore any tension between the universal and the particular. America's existence had not been threatened in our lifetime. Its sheer size rendered any single member's affiliation inconsequential. American individuals were free to join other tribes if they chose, or to be tribeless, identifying exclusively as individuals without threatening the tribe's existence.

This is not the case for the Jews, a tiny community, ancient and enduring but never secure. I could already connect the dots to this community's extinction in high school. I recognized the tragic cycle of Jewish history. Societies rarely embraced the Jews. They tolerated us at best, and seldom for long. In some cases, tolerance might progress to limited integration, and even ascendancy, but grace had always been temporary. It was inevitably followed by tragedy, forfeiture of rights, expulsion, violence, and, periodically, the threat of total extermination. In that second semester at Exeter, I came across the iconic photograph of a boy, thought to be Zvi Nussbaum, taken in the Warsaw ghetto. The seven-year-old stands wide-eyed, hands up, surrounded by Nazi troops pointing rifles at him, as his community looks on in terrified submission. I understood the power of that image, but it sparked a different reaction in me than I suspect it provokes in most viewers. The obvious juxtaposition of fragile innocence with brute barbarism was not what captured my interest. The Nazis themselves were irrelevant, a generic malevolence, interchangeable with the mobs of the Iraqi Farhud, the Cossacks, the Inquisitors, the Crusaders, and dozens of hostile majorities within which the Jews had lived over the last nineteen centuries. They had all come and gone. It was the community in the background that was relevant. As its tormentors replaced one another over the centuries, that community had remained constant.

But despite its legendary intelligence and scholarship, my people seemed to suffer from an inexplicably chronic naïveté. Its complacency had shockingly steered it, over and over again, to this heartbreaking point, unable to protect its own child. Although the photograph was taken in 1943, almost four years into the war, it seems to capture the moment in which these people's Jewishness first dawned on them, the moment they discovered they were not Poles, not Spaniards, not Arabs, not Englishmen. They were Jews, and their time had run out again. These Jews would not have time to relearn their people's ancient and recurring lesson. Reality was descending too swiftly, exposing the suddenly glaring absence of a contingency plan. Stripped of agency, they now lived only as witnesses to their community's march to its inevitable death, children included. The child in the photograph was only one generation removed from me. He could have been me.

I soon realized, however, that I could just as easily have been a member of the community in the background. Here I was at Exeter, an American, oblivious to the burden of vigilance that ought to have been wired into my consciousness by two thousand years on perpetually borrowed time. Was I really any different from the Jews of 1943 Warsaw? If the tragic Jewish cycle had finally ended here in America, how would we know it? How would we distinguish the moment of arrival from the illusions of permanence that have lulled our ancestors into fatal complacency so many times over the centuries? Would there be a clear sign that we were now true Americans or true Europeans, permanent members, no less integral to our communities than any of our non-Jewish fellows?

I did not have an answer. I still don't. But conversations with other Jews, at Exeter and within my own family, made it clear that few Jews of my generation even grappled with the question. The question was clearly irrelevant to the Jewish *individual* in pursuit of the American dream. I understood, however, that it was a vital question for the Jewish *community*. If we did not ask it, repeatedly and publicly, we were living as precariously as Zvi Nussbaum's family and neighbors did in 1943. Virtually the entire ghetto perished within weeks of that photograph.

The conflict that I would recognize only later had become inevitable. I knew too much to escape the orbit of community but had grown up too detached from it to forfeit my individuality. I would spend decades seeking reconciliation of the tension between Particularism and Universalism, first in Israel, then in the remnants of Diaspora, and then back in America. But it was not to be found in any physical location. Conflict and reconciliation are both embedded in the complex code that governs Jewish nationhood everywhere. Jewish community is the medium through which that code runs. It is the evolving code that in turn defines the community. But as Jewish individuals have become safe, in America and in Israel, their communities have eroded. Modernity will end Jewish history and, with it, the distinctive contribution of the Jews to human history—unless the code, and the community that serves as its medium, can be revived.

America was my starting point. I had an idea of what made me American. I felt ownership in America. When I turned eighteen, I became a voter, formally empowered as an architect of America's future. This empowerment was a key to my loyalty to the enterprise, despite its imperfections. I could accommodate the imperfections, even as they had historically related to American Jews. I could accommodate the outright falsity in our founding charter. The Declaration of Independence was wrong. Not all men were created equal in its eyes. Black men were not equal. Women were not even addressed. But our founding generation had intentionally equipped us with the means to change that. Forming "a more perfect union" is a grammatical error, but one perhaps purposefully inserted in the Preamble to the Constitution. It establishes the concept of relative perfection, a goal that evolves and expands together with our sensibilities, always dependent on context. This admission, and the mechanism that equipped us to address it in perpetuity, has been key to America's reconciliation of its practical imperfections with its nobler ambitions. My family had believed in America. They had fought for America on the battlefields of the Europe they had fled, even though they were still among those *not* created equal at the time they fought. But, aware of their alternatives, they happily bought in to the American enterprise.

Of course, my own buy-in would not matter if it turned out that America was subject to the same cycle my ancestors had weathered so many times. In that case, the decision to buy in would eventually no longer be mine. If my American identity were forcibly revoked, as my grandfather's German nationality had been, *Jew* would remain my only national affiliation, the affiliation that history had never allowed us to shed. My need to understand what this meant in practical terms took shape at Exeter. I found my answer in Israel.

I enrolled in a teenagers' tour of the country in the summer of 1987. It felt like a suitable conclusion to my year of discovery. But witnessing Jewish self-determination was more than a summary. It was a revelation. I had spent the last six months questioning my generation's place in the cycle of Jewish history. Not having met other American Jews who shared my obsession with the question, I had come to consider my thinking original, even subversive. Still, it was strictly academic. In Israel, I encountered a people that was reclaiming control of its fate in practice. They were not passively questioning the cycle as I was. They were breaking it. There would be no more evictions. These Jews had come home. At Exeter, I had been haunted by a shameful impression of the Jews as sheep led repeatedly to slaughter. Israel was our redemption. In Israel I discovered dignity, whose absence, I now realized, is what had loomed so malevolently for me in that photograph.

By the time I returned to Exeter for my senior year, I knew I had reached a crossroads. Israel would feature in my life, but I would have to figure out exactly how. I began studying Hebrew intensively with a teacher provided by the academy. I immersed myself in the history and in the geopolitical complexities of Jewish sovereignty in the volatile Middle East. If Zionism was to thrive in the long run, it seemed Israel would have to find some peaceful, if not cooperative, modus vivendi with its neighbors. I bought a book on elementary Arabic and picked up a few sentences. I applied to the School of Foreign Service at Georgetown University, which had a Hebrew program and one of the best Arabic programs in the country. I spent the next two summers traveling through Israel, the West Bank, Gaza, and Egypt. I used a college year-abroad program to try living in Israel.

At the end of my first semester at Tel Aviv University, I made the decision to stay. I was pursuing a membership that

would become central to my identity. I sensed that my community was here. Tel Aviv was thrilling—culturally vibrant,
confident, and original. My Hebrew was improving quickly. I
was making friends. I had a girlfriend. I was drawing from an
exciting source of energy I had never encountered before.
Most important, I felt purpose. For the first time, I was in the
right place, on the right mission for me, the only mission I
could pursue after asking the questions I had asked. I was
lucky to recognize that discovering purpose at such a young
age was a rare privilege. Had I gone back to Georgetown, I
would have coasted along with my class, to law school or to
Wall Street, making incremental commitments to a different
life. The window of opportunity that was now open might be
closed next time I looked.

The one crack in my conviction was my father. Our agendas had coincided up to this point. I had been his willing
protégé, racing his baton toward the finish line of American
assimilation. My family had handed me a lead built over generations. If I just held it, the race would be ours. But I had a
different agenda. I turned my back on my father's American
dream to follow my own. I knew he would not understand
the trade. He never did.

I transferred my Georgetown academic credits to Tel Aviv
University. I graduated, after plodding through two more semesters in Hebrew, and applied for Israeli citizenship. I was
twenty years old. I received draft papers almost immediately.
I reported to the Israel Defense Forces induction center outside Tel Aviv on a rainy November morning, carrying a duffel
bag with a shaving kit and a week's worth of socks and under-
wear. As I stared at the giant concrete structure from the

adjacent bus stop, it occurred to me that once I passed through its doors, there would be no way back. Of course, there already was no way back. I had resolved to become an Israeli, and military service was the definitive Israeli rite of passage. Until my conscription, I would be a citizen only on paper. Service would be my ticket to true membership, and I was prepared to pay full fare. There was no other way.

The IDF induction center registration hall was a cavernous space. Hundreds of recruits stood in five or six lines, waiting to be processed. I had little idea what the next day or two might hold, whether this was just a way station, or if I would be tested and processed here. I watched people as they left the registration desk and continued through one of five doors. There was no sign that suggested what waited behind those doors. It was difficult to tell who was disappointed and who was satisfied.

A large poster hung over the main registration desk, bearing the slogan THE BEST WILL FLY. In the background, a fighter jet roared off a desert runway. It was an advertisement for the Israeli Air Force Academy, and a jab at everyone standing in that line. It implied that if we were not among the very few who would end up at the Air Force Academy, we were *not* the best. I could not look away. I was impulsive and naïve, I knew. I realized the ambition was absurd, but my sights were suddenly set.

I looked ahead in line, and then around the hall, wondering if anybody among the hundreds of young men I could see might end up at the Academy. Some appeared to be more likely candidates than others. I noticed a number of young men in small groups chatting casually in line, people who seemed to know one another. Perhaps they had gone to high school together. They seemed relaxed and confident, as though they were insiders who already knew where they were headed. I noticed other young men who had clearly arrived prepared. Heads already shaved, they would skip the hallmark ritual of the induction center barbershop. They looked to be in great physical shape, backs straight, already military in bearing. They did not chat with the others. It seemed they, too, knew exactly where they were headed, as though this entire process was little more than a procedural nuisance for them, delaying their arrival at units that already awaited them.

But most people just looked frightened. Despite my resolve, I was in their camp. We were numbered parts, inching forward on a conveyor belt toward an impassive processing apparatus. Until now, we had been individuals. When we came out the other end, we would be part of a machine. Our opinions, interests, and relationships would no longer define us. We would be categorized according to our utility to the machine. I reminded myself of my goal. I was here to become as Israeli as I could become, even if I did not know exactly what that might entail.

I was processed, issued uniforms, boots, socks, a new duffel bag, and a towel. I took a blood test and received a necklace with three dog tags. One was to remain on the necklace, the other two to be inserted into special slots in my boots. I asked the boy behind me in line if he knew why we put dog tags in our boots. He told me it was so that we could be identified even if our upper halves were missing. We entered a medical testing hall. After waiting for my results, I was informed that I had no special issues. I was directed out to a courtyard and told to stand among a growing cluster of recruits.

In the evening, we were assigned to cots arranged across a concrete pavilion, under large shading nets. I spent the night listening to the conversations around me until they died out and were replaced by the hum of a distant highway, occasionally drowned out by ambulance sirens. The next morning, we continued to written aptitude tests. I finagled an extra fifteen minutes by claiming weak Hebrew.

At the end of day two, I was relocated to a separate lot with several hundred recruits who had qualified for a week of Air Force Academy testing. The tests were conducted at YARPA, the Unit for Aviation Medicine. We had interviews with psychologists and sociologists, and more aptitude exams. I was subjected to sensory deprivation and spatial disorientation. I played on videogame-like simulators, solved mazes, took apart mechanical contraptions and put them back together. Sometimes I played alone, sometimes against opponents, and sometimes with teammates, always under observation by Air Force psychologists and sociologists taking notes on clipboards.

I was standing in line for another blood test on the first day at YARPA when the red-haired candidate in front of me noted my American accent and made a point of loudly informing me that my prospects were dismal. I did not belong here. This became a subject of conversation in the line. People behind me began offering advice on alternative paths that

I could pursue in the military. "Somebody like you could be in artillery. A guy in my class went there. Artillery is much less intense. Better fit for somebody like you." It was in that line that I learned the concept of the YARPA Guinea Pig, a recruit who does not qualify for the Air Force Academy but is admitted as part of a periodic assessment of the Academy's screening process. There are no YARPA Guinea Pigs in reality, but the consensus in line seemed to be that I might be one.

As I sat in the chair with my arm extended, the redhead leaned over the nurse taking my blood and whispered, "You stay out of my way. Understand? Look at me and tell me you understand what I am saying." I did not look up. The young nurse said nothing. I spoke to no one for the rest of the afternoon, hoping to avoid provoking more threats. The IDF might turn out to be a lonelier adventure than I had bargained for, but I would not be bullied out of the dream I was chasing: full membership. The question of whether I would meet the challenge on that poster or pursue the next best opportunity I was offered would be answered by the testing process.

At the end of the day, we stood in formation as a member of the testing staff read out the names of those who would be immediately reassigned to testing for other units. All others could report for testing again the next morning. Each night, after the list had been read, I reestimated my chances of surviving the week. As the odds improved, I began to entertain the audacious notion that the Air Force Academy might be a realistic ambition for me. The week wore on and the ranks continued to thin. On Sunday, the staff read out the final list of candidates who were excused. I was not on it. I had passed the YARPA process and would be staying on for a week of field testing.

The test began at night. Several hundred of us deposited our wristwatches and other personal items in storage lockers. We boarded buses and headed out of the Air Force testing center parking lot. Shades were drawn on the windows. We were warned not to speak, and not to sleep. After a safety briefing, we rode in darkness and nervous silence for about three hours. The last few minutes of the ride were on a bumpy dirt road. When our bus stopped, the doors opened to a clamor. We were hustled outside, into a frenzied scene. The night blazed with harsh electric light. Heavy helicopters passed low overhead, kicking up showers of desert sand. Electricity generators whirred loudly at the edges of a large encampment. Military trucks rumbled along the perimeter. A crew of uniformed men shouted at us through megaphones. We were ordered to arrange ourselves in formations, three deep. We were issued colored armbands and water canteens, had numbers stenciled on the backs of our fatigues, and were broken into groups. Stumbling around in confusion, we were forced down for push-ups whenever the pace of events seemed to slow.

My group's first mission was to erect a large military tent over a designated position within the camp. Most of us had never seen a tent like this. We could not tell a main pole from a crossbeam, and we did not know if we had enough of either. There were no instructions. Each time we failed to meet a construction milestone, we were ordered to take everything down and move the tent to a new location. We shouted over the surrounding din in near hysteria, struggling to cooperate with one another, trying to decipher messy arrangements of canvas, beams, and tethers. Often we thought we recognized progress only to realize we had made a mistake earlier on, forcing us to dismantle everything again.

By first light, we had started construction in several different locations and still did not have a standing tent. I noticed the people with the clipboards from the previous week hovering at the periphery of our activity, taking notes. Tent construction went on at the same frantic pace until the sun was at its zenith and the day had become hot. I estimated we had been at it for about twelve hours. My tent crew had developed some ability to work as a team by this point. A leader had emerged, a kibbutznik with a decent understanding of how large tents worked, at least more decent than the rest of ours. We had all learned and improved our understanding through successive construction attempts. The daylight was helping as well. As our effort began to take the general form of a standing tent, I saw that eleven other tents stood arrayed in a large semicircle, all close to completion. The helicopters had disappeared at some point during the night. The generators had been off since dawn.

We were arranged in formations of around fifty dusty, sweaty, heaving recruits, each group standing in front of its drooping tent. For the first time since arrival, we stood still in the dry, hot breeze. I looked around us. Almost nothing interrupted the flat desert that stretched between our camp and the horizon in every direction. I had no idea where I was. An

Air Force officer arrived at the focal point of the semicircle. He stood erect, his pressed, fitted uniform contrasting harshly with the dust-caked figures arrayed in front of him. He took his time, surveying us calmly. When his voice finally came over a public address system, it was soft, jarringly civilized after the chaos and panic that seemed to have become the rhythm of our lives.

"Welcome to the Gibush. We are excited to have you here. This will be a trying week. You will eat much less than you normally do. You will sleep much less than you have before. You will be tested under significant physical and mental pressure. The fact that you have made it this far means little. Few of you will survive to the end. Please bear that in mind. If you feel your prospects are low, you have the option of retiring to the bus parked behind me at any time. The bus is air-conditioned during the day, and heated at night. Once you board the bus and sign a form waiving your right to rejoin this program, you can enjoy a Coke, put your feet up, and read a magazine. Each time a bus fills up, it will depart for Tel Aviv. I can tell you from experience that the buses depart more frequently during the second half of the week than the first. So if you are not sure about this, I recommend you do yourself a favor and board the bus now. There is no point in putting yourself through the whole process if this is not for you. I wish you all luck."

Nobody moved. The officer departed in a jeep and was replaced by a thickset drill sergeant in battle fatigues. He leaned forward threateningly, his chin thrust out in incomprehensible rage, his voice almost hysterical. "From this point on, you zeros do not look at any staff member at eye level!

While they address you, you remain in position 2. If you do not maintain position 2 in adequate form, you will drop to position 1. If you do not maintain either position, you get your ass on the bus." Position 2 was the upper station of a push-up, arms extended. Position 1 was the lower push-up position, arms bent, chest lowered just above the ground. "Why are you zeros still standing? Position 2!" The thud of hundreds of bodies flung earthward announced the beginning of a new regime.

We spent the next hour receiving briefings on the exercises ahead, all of it in position 2, position 1, and new positions we were taught, such as the Dead Cockroach—the upper station of a sit-up. I was already shaking with muscle spasms in the first briefing and could not imagine how I would last the week. I told myself that I couldn't possibly be in the worst shape among hundreds of recruits, and that others were surely feeling the pain. I decided not to budget energy, or speculate on how hard it would become as the days wore on. I would just focus on getting through the moment. I reminded myself that I had actually wanted it to be difficult. This is what I had signed up for—the full-fare ticket. This was me becoming an Israeli. I resolved that if I did not make it, it would be because my body had stopped working. I would have to be dragged onto the bus.

The briefing over, we were hustled to areas behind our tents, where we found swollen sandbags, stretchers, and telephone poles arranged on the sand. We were given sixty seconds to have all of the equipment off the ground, above shoulder height. A company commander appeared in front of us, ordered us to follow him in silence, and set off at a brisk pace toward the northern horizon. We staggered off after him, equipment rattling and lurching, wooden splinters breaking off the poles, stretcher handles digging into our shoulders. The commander never looked back. He knew we were behind him, jostling, shifting weight from side to side, trying in vain to find a painless position under the load, all in silence, scrambling to keep up.

After about two hours, we stopped to fill our canteens at a water carrier. We were dripping with sweat. Dusk was falling. The desert temperature was dropping quickly. The clipboarders observed from a distance on jeeps. They had been following us all along. As the company commander set off again without warning, and we hastily hoisted the poles and sandbags back onto our shoulders, I was overcome with a feeling I remember clearly so many years later. I was in the right place, and this was the right mission. I had entered a zone, and I stayed there for the rest of the week. The outside world shrank to nothing. I was all here.

About half of us stood in the semicircle at the end of the week. Of those, about half received a passing score in the field test and were admitted to the Air Force Academy. Of those, two dozen stood for graduation two years later. Of those, a handful had earned the wings of an IAF fighter pilot, and I was among them. I was bound for an Operational Training Unit and from there to F-16 school. Several years later, I qualified as Flight Lead and began commanding formations in combat. That Air Force training exercise, meant to simulate life in enemy captivity, had been one of the many critical rites of passage through which I would ultimately become an Israeli. Entrusted with the lives of other pilots and weapons systems operators, hundreds of millions of dollars in hard-ware, and, most important, the critical missions of the IAF, I had become as Israeli as I could have dreamed of becoming. At least in my own mind, I had arrived.

For the first time, I was able to look around me and appreci-ate the club to which I had gained membership. Before my conscription, I had lacked the time and the maturity to assess the Israel that lay beyond my utopian conceptions. During my Air Force service, I interacted with only a thin cut of Is-raeli society, honing a very specific set of skills which de-manded all of my mental and emotional capacity. I had no relationship with the rest of Israel. The Israel I discovered as an adult was thrilling. As I found more time to engage with people outside the Air Force, I encountered a density of human intellect and emotion that I still consider unique. This density conspires with the diversity of Israeli society, and perhaps with the conditions of Israel's regional reality, to define the spirit of Israel, soulful, tribal, honest, blunt, so-phisticated, and confident. It lifts me as high today as it did then. The old energy from that dungeon still wells up every time my flight touches down at Ben Gurion Airport, and its light dims a little bit every time I take off. I remain as grateful as I ever was for my membership in the Israeli family.

But as I approached the end of my service and began prepar-ing for a life beyond the Air Force, I also began to consider

Israeli Judaism, the ideal I had been fighting for. Like America, Israel had brought the blessings of security, freedom, and prosperity to many individual Jews. Would the complacency that accompanied these individual blessings in America plague the Jewish nation in Israel as well? We had survived wars of extermination. We had made the desert bloom. We had built a thriving economy on innovation and grit. But now that all of this had been accomplished, what did we stand for? What was next for the nation-state of the Jews? Was there a unifying vision for Israel's future? Did we need one? As I came to know more of Israel, I began to understand that Jewish statehood carried different and contradictory meanings for different Jews. Israeli politics had come to reflect these contradictions, devolving into an array of competing partisan constituencies promoting short-term and fundamentally conflicting agendas. Each applied its resources and skills to scoring parochial victories at the others' expense, myopically admiring its brushstrokes as we collectively painted ourselves into a corner. Considering our people's historic susceptibility to tragedy, a fundamentally divided, visionless, and consequently rudderless Israel suddenly looked as vulnerable to me as the complacent American Judaism I had left behind eight years earlier.

As my discharge date approached, I began to concede that I had spent a decade of my young life ascending what had turned out to be a false peak. The conviction that had propelled me through the trials of becoming Israeli had been naïve, even hollow. There might still be a path upward, but I was no longer confident that my destination awaited at its summit. I suddenly did not have a next step.

I took a long weekend to get some distance from the intensity of daily operations at the squadron, traveling south to the Sinai desert. My squadron mates and I had spent holidays in the Sinai over the years. It was familiar enough that I could hike the desert alone. Setting out from the Bedouin fishing village of Nuweiba, on the Gulf of Aqaba, I climbed into the mountains to its west with a jerrican of water on my back, following an old Air Force map. As the coast receded behind me, I felt myself swallowed by the profound quiet that had once drawn a generation of Israeli travelers to this peninsula. The cues we unconsciously rely on to track the passage of time—the sight of pedestrians flowing through city streets, the undulating hum of automobile traffic, the rotation of diners at restaurant tables—are so decidedly absent in the Sinai. The desert's towering crests and jagged ridges stand resolutely still, as they have for eons. The entire human story barely registers against the desert's eternity. Moses and the Israelites might have crossed here three thousand years ago, but that could as well have been yesterday. Standing in the path of the Exodus, I saw the impasse I had reached against a panoramic continuum that dwarfed it. I might need a map and a compass to navigate my own individual track, but my people's path was so long, and so meandering, that following it required only a general sense of its direction.

The Exodus had taken three generations. All but two of the roughly six hundred thousand male Israelites who began the journey in Egypt would die in this lonely wilderness over the next forty years. It was their children and grandchildren who ultimately entered the Promised Land. The individual Israelite had no deliverance to celebrate. He died having known only the travails of the journey. The central and defining value that Judaism ascribes to the Exodus cannot be realized by any individual Jew. That value is attained only by the *nation*.

If the destination I was seeking did indeed lie ahead, my own narrow path might end before I reached it. Walking in the wide path of my ancestors, however, I was able to accept this prospect. A more precise route might materialize for me, but I could keep moving even without one, preserving momentum while I sought a precise direction.

I applied to business school and was admitted to Harvard. It would be an opportunity to zoom out of the narrow intensity of military life. I looked forward to being back, for a time, among the important segment of my people that I had abandoned in America, in unwarranted haste. My curiosities also extended beyond the Jewish People, and once my decision was made, I became excited to explore them.

But I would be back. As a practical matter, I committed to continue flying as a reserve pilot. I would return during business school vacations for training and operations at the squadron. I would study the Israeli economy, with which I was unfamiliar, in the hope of identifying a professional opportunity that would bring me home to Israel after school. I sealed this commitment with a final unintended blow to the Wiener family's assimilationist ambitions. Following a tradition begun by Israel's founding fathers, I traded my Diaspora name for a Hebrew one. My surname would no longer evoke the memory of transient centuries our family had spent in or near Vienna. It would become permanently linked to our origins here in the land of the Bible. Keinan is a dry riverbed that runs along a steep ridge, deep in the Negev desert. The entire length of the ridge, and of the gorge beneath it, is strikingly beautiful but rarely seen, as the area falls within the boundaries of an Air Force bombing range. The name Keinan would be my private badge of belonging to Israel.

I returned to the conscription center to receive my discharge papers. Walking through the induction hall for the second time in eight years, I thought back to the clamor of thousands of high school graduates lining up to serve. This time I was alone. My footsteps echoed as I walked toward the exit. Unadorned with the bright banners and posters of draft season, the walls looked neglected and forgotten, too impotent to have launched thousands of careers, spawned lifelong friendships, catapulted young people to greatness, and condemned others to premature deaths. But these were exactly the fates this hall had dispensed for fifty years, the fates it had bestowed on the young men in that line eight years earlier.

As I pulled out of the parking lot, I took a last look back at the chapter that had closed. I was on the road again, still seeking, but better outfitted for the quest than I had been the last time I had changed course. I was still an American, but I was also an Israeli now—not because other Israelis had become unable to sniff me out by accent or manner, but because I had earned my citizenship. I stood at an uncommon vantage point, an insider in two worlds who had achieved escape velocity from both. The fact that I could identify fully with either made me beholden to neither. But history had proved, many times, that there was one identity I could not escape. I was a Jew.

For the next seventeen years, the journey that began at Exeter would take me back and forth between Israel and the United States. I spent two years at Harvard and joined a private equity firm in Israel after graduation. I invested in Israeli technology companies for four years, then left to help launch the asset management firm that would become Clarity. I worked in Clarity's Tel Aviv and New York offices and traveled the world for the company. Amber, my wife of eighteen years, and I raised three daughters, first in Tel Aviv and then in New York. When we were living in the United States, I traveled home to Israel to fly and, occasionally, to fight. When we were living in Israel, we threw ourselves into social action in the causes of education, economic development, and Jewish identity. That was my external life, my résumé. What was brewing beneath the surface is this book.

THE END OF DIASPORA

My generation is witnessing a critical turning point in Jewish history. Until the first half of the twentieth century, the Jewish People was distributed across the world, in hundreds of distinct communities—the Diaspora. The Second World War marked the beginning of the most dramatic physical reorganization of the Jews since the beginning of Diaspora. European Jewry was decimated in the Holocaust. After the war, almost all of the nearly one million Jews of the Middle

East and North Africa departed their countries as refugees, mainly for Israel. The Soviet Jewish community had numbered three million people before the war. By the mid-1990s, it had also emptied almost completely, mainly into Israel. Ethiopian Jewry moved to Israel in its entirety at the same time. The remaining Jewish populations of Western Europe and Latin America are now in decline. Many members of the French Jewish community, now the world's third largest but already less than one tenth the size of either America's or Israel's, intend for their children to work and establish families outside France. As of 2016, almost 90 percent of the world's Jews resided in either North America or Israel, and the world Jewish population continues to concentrate in these two geographies. If the trend continues, we will soon be forced to recognize the practical end of nineteen hundred years of Jewish Diaspora. From this point forward, I will refer to the era that began with my generation as the post-Diaspora era.

The past two generations of Jewish life in both America and Israel have been thrillingly successful episodes in the context of Jewish history. In both countries, Jews have prospered, culturally and materially. The anti-Semitism that afflicted, but also united, their ancestors in Europe and the Middle East is almost completely foreign to them. With the dissolution of Diaspora, however, the Jews have lost the diversification and physical breadth that preserved them. Historically, Jews expelled from one nation found safe harbor within the Jewish community of another. When Jews were exterminated in one geography, they survived in others. Even though it is a result of prosperity, today's concentrated Jewish architecture is far less resilient than the Diaspora's. Like an animal species that undergoes an especially successful mutation, the Jewish bloodline has narrowed. The surviving members of the species are exquisitely adapted to their environment but vulnerable to sudden changes to it. We are witnessing such a change right now, and, barring a radical evolution, it will result in our extinction.

In America, Judaism is insufficiently compelling to the critical mass of Jews that is required to perpetuate the nation's survival. At current rates, intermarriage will end American Judaism, in any form we would find recognizable today, within three generations. In Israel, three separate models of Jewish sovereignty have found purchase within three separate segments of the Jewish population. These models conflict with one another to an unsustainable degree, and they have never been reconciled. If current trends persist, Secularist Jews, one of the three segments, will gradually see their model of Jewish sovereignty defeated. This segment will disengage from Israel and build lives in America. Like the rest of American Jewry, it will dissolve into greater America within two or three generations. Those Jews who remain in Israel, communities we will visit in the book, will be unable to sustain themselves economically or militarily. They will eventually succumb to the violent reality that befalls most minorities in the Middle East.

Of course, current trends almost never persist, at least not in linear form. They either accelerate or decelerate. The Jews could have even less time than we think. But there might also be a way to take control of the Jewish future. The Wisdom of the Crowd, the essential tool of Jewish governance in Diaspora, has survived Diaspora's decline, bruised but fundamentally intact. This tool can be resuscitated and adapted to the mission of Jewish self-governance in the post-Diaspora era. The Crowd, supported by technology, can reverse the above prognosis and empower the Jews to define their future. Before introducing the medicine, however, we must understand the diagnosis.

2

America: Dying in Our Sleep

WHO ARE WE AGAIN?

Picture a meteor barreling through the clear night, its fire illuminating the earth below. At its core is solid rock, cold and static. At its surface is the molten blaze itself, particles shorn away, oxidizing and combusting with brilliant intensity. The meteor's tail is dark, its explosive energy suddenly spent. Permanently detached, it blends peacefully into the night sky. The three layers constitute a single phenomenon. In one interpretation of Jewish history, Orthodox Particularism has served as Judaism's rock core, static and uninteresting to many observers. Universalist Judaism is the fire created through friction with the atmosphere. The meteor's dark tail represents the ensuing generations, permanently detached from the core.

If this metaphor applies, it has been most compelling

during those windows in history when Jews were able to interact freely with society at large, to thrive, create, and contribute within a broader sphere. These were periods that also accommodated apostasy. From Jesus Christ to Josephus Flavius to Juan de Valladolid, from Moses Mendelssohn to Sigmund Freud, few of the Jews' blazing lights bequeathed Judaism to their descendants in a form that lasted more than one or two generations. The unprecedented, and growing, concentration of world Jewry in the United States, together with the exceptionally low barriers to integration in American society, conspires to endow Jewish assimilation in America with a potency unique in Jewish history. We may be experiencing the brightest, but last, meteor shower in the history of Jewish Diaspora.

I grew up in a predominantly Jewish neighborhood in Miami, but like my neighbors, and like our contemporaries in most Jewish communities in the United States, I was able to wear my Jewishness lightly. My family attended synagogue (temple), but only on the High Holy Days. We fasted on Yom Kippur and we held Passover Seders, but we ate bread during the week of Passover. My brothers and I all performed some version of a bar mitzvah ceremony, some more rigorous than others. Our family behaved in accordance with the standards that most American Jews maintain. We were not wealthy but we were charitable, Jewishly and generally. Our dinners typically took the form of a loud debate on history or politics. We played word games and solved math riddles on long drives. We were pressured into achievement, mainly by our mothers, who accepted no compromises, especially in education. But the arena in which we aimed to register those achievements was a non-Jewish arena. We didn't go to Jewish schools. We did not aspire to be Talmudic scholars. We didn't know what that was. It had not been our parents' priority to educate us Jewishly. Their parents had neglected to educate them Jewishly. We would become doctors, lawyers, and engineers, and the firms that had rejected my father's generation would embrace ours. We mixed with everybody in the classrooms and on the playing fields of our youth, Jewish or not. Our parents and grandparents might have struggled in vain to become regular Americans, but for our generation, that ambition was within reach, and most of us achieved it.

When I was seven years old, I wanted to change my name to Scott. Despite having become an American, my mother had given me the Hebrew name Tal, which means "dew." My brothers all had American-sounding names. I was the only one who had to spell my name when I was introduced. Teachers would ask me to pronounce it several times, in front of the class, on the first day of school every year. My best friend, Eddie Willis, who was familiar with my problem, had suggested the name Scott. I trusted Eddie's judgment in this matter. I thought he understood that changing my name would do more for me than just ease introductions to new people. A better name would ease my initiation into the club in which we all seemed to want membership, Club America.

I occasionally spent Sundays with Eddie's family, beginning with morning church services. I would follow along in the hymnal as the congregation proclaimed its faith in Jesus Christ. I knew this was not my tradition, but I had no sense that our respective rituals might be incompatible. I did not know my own tradition well enough. I spent Christmas Eves at Eddie's house, and his mother always made sure I had presents to open with him on Christmas morning. I participated in his church's Easter egg hunt every year. I learned how to say grace at Sunday lunch. One or two other families from the congregation might join those meals, where the conversation usually involved boating or fishing stories from the preceding Saturday and gossip about other members of the congregation. Periodically, this gossip would disparage one of the members, accusing him of weak faith. I did not know exactly what faith was, but I understood intuitively that it was a currency. You needed to hold a certain amount of it in order to maintain membership in the community. Whether you had faith or not, it seemed to me, it would be wise to behave as though you did. It would be even better if you could convince yourself.

I lost touch with Eddie after leaving Miami for Cardigan Mountain, a boarding school in Canaan, New Hampshire, when I was ten. Zipora and LeRoy were newly divorced. Our half brother, Clifford, had left my father's house before I was born. Jeff had just gone off to college, and Doug was living with his mother. My younger brother, Ron, and I were the only complication standing between our parents and their fresh start. In their haste to remove this last obstacle to freedom, they failed to find a school that would accommodate both of us. Ron went to a school called Rumsey Hall, in Connecticut. Separated from each other, with no family left to anchor us in Miami, Ron and I were launched on divergent trajectories that year.

It was in the sixth grade at Cardigan that I first remember feeling Jewish. The school had very few Jewish students, and

I immediately felt something was missing for me. In retrospect, it was not the Jewish rituals, to which I had been exposed only lightly in Miami. It was more subtle, a new set of expectations I was required to meet, the old set suddenly irrelevant. The argumentative tone of my family's dinner conversations, to which we had all contributed, was almost never heard at Cardigan. Dress and demeanor, which had not been important before, suddenly were. I did not know how to tie a tie. My mother had equipped me with a clip-on tie, which I wore to class during my first month at Cardigan. That tie was the sort of shameful mistake that would keep me at the bottom of the social pecking order for a long time. My new classmates quickly clarified this lapse for me.

I might not have associated my ignorance of Cardigan's prevailing conventions with my Jewishness had I not looked different from the other kids—darker-complexioned—and had I not borne a name that required explaining. I never experienced anti-Semitism, but I understood, as most eleven-year-olds would, that my fortunes would be tied to successfully adapting to a new regime. So I learned how to tie a tie. Although Cardigan was a different world from Keystone Point in Miami, I could still gain acceptance there. My origins were not the obstacle they had been for my father's generation. Once I conformed, I was free to thrive, and I did.

My first murky notions of the general framework of Jewishness had been illuminated at Cardigan by its sudden absence. Most Jews in America can recognize that framework when they see it, but defining it in specific and differentiating terms eludes us. When surveyed on the value or meaning of Jewishness, most Jews cite the Holocaust, note an affinity for Israel, or list elements of religiosity. Some draw a blank, or allude to notions too weak to support real affiliation with the Jewish People, such as Jewish humor, or Jewish food. We do, however, tend to recognize Jewishness through its sudden absence.

When my brother Jeff came home from college on winter break and announced that he intended to marry his then girlfriend, who was not Jewish, the news did not surprise us. We knew Betsy well. She and Jeff had been together for a long time. Their relationship was serious enough that a proposal should have been forthcoming. Still, my father, who was rarely ever upset, went out to the pool after Jeff left and swam furious laps for hours. Had my brother crossed some invisible line of which only my father was aware?

During spring break, when Jeff, Doug, Ron, and I were in Miami, my father took us to Mario the Baker, a noisy Italian restaurant where we would not be overheard. He had been simmering for the past three months. Over dinner, he lectured us on the importance of Jewish tradition, and of preserving the legacy we had inherited. I am not sure what outcome he was hoping for. I do not believe he expected Jeff to break off his engagement. All he could possibly do was to impart some of his own ambivalence and confusion to Jeff, and maybe rescue the rest of us.

"This issue was very important to my parents. They are gone now, so they can't tell you themselves," he said. "It was also important to their parents."

But he had always encouraged us to rise above convention and to think for ourselves.

"Was it only important to your parents, or is it important to you, Dad?"

"Of course it's important to me. Why do you think we are talking about it?"

"How important? If it is so important, why is this the first time we are hearing about it? Why should it matter to us?"

"Maybe I should have been clear earlier, but I am being clear now."

"Are we not supposed to even date non-Jewish girls? What happens if we do and it gets serious? What about conversion? Do we get partial credit if she converts?"

"That's a different question. That's more complicated."

It was Passover, and we were eating pizza as we debated the value of Jewish tradition. The unintended irony was completely consistent with our upbringing, and comically incongruent with my father's admonitions. Where was the line between observing a kosher Passover and marrying out of the tribe? We were Jewish, but were we not American as well? Could the identities not coexist? Would we lose either identity if we married the wrong person? Did we have to choose? And if we did, was it not clear that we would be American?

As elementary schoolers, we had repeated the Pledge of Allegiance every morning. We celebrated Thanksgiving and the Fourth of July with family and friends, Jewish and Gentile. We were surrounded by the symbols of our American identity: flags, images of our Founding Fathers on coins and bills, the national anthem at our sports events. Our exposure to America was far more constant than our exposure to Judaism was. And it was not just symbolic. Members of our family have now been American for five generations. They have been educated in America's universities, and they have fought in America's wars. Uncle Gerry lost more than a third of his bomber group over Europe. Uncle Dave lost his leg below the knee to a German bullet at Monte Cassino. Much of my father's class at City College never came home from the Pacific war, which my father had played a role in ending. They were all fighting for America. None of us had ever risked his life for the Jews.

By my generation, we were taking ownership in America for granted. The sense of belonging we felt would have been completely alien to our Jewish forebears in Europe. My French Jewish in-laws still speak of "the French" as an identity distinct from their own, even after generations of living in France, steeped in French culture, speaking French as their first, and in some cases only, language. In France, they would always be Jews. But this was America. If our Jewishness mattered little to the Gentiles around us, why should it matter to us?

America represents a zenith in Jewish history, at which Jews have achieved numerical concentration unprecedented in the Diaspora, financial prosperity, and political power. They enjoy the option of overt, unapologetic Jewish identification that, in their neighbors' eyes, does not negate their Americanism. Unlike the nations of Europe and the Middle East, America formally welcomed its Jews as equal citizens from the start. The welcome was not always unanimous or warm, but the violent anti-Semitism that has existed almost anywhere there have been Jews has never found purchase in America.

Ralph Waldo Emerson's term "smelting pot" idealized the process of Americanization, juxtaposing American assimilation of immigrants with a European model of ethnically based nationalism. American society was meant to merge and subsume immigrant identities. These immigrant identities were not replaced in the immigrant's own generation, but his children, and certainly his grandchildren, would often be just American.

In his 1908 play *The Melting Pot,* Israel Zangwill celebrates the notion of a singular, universalist American identity that could transcend the racial tribalism that would ultimately doom Europe. David, the play's protagonist, proclaims in a monologue, "America is God's Crucible, the great Melting-Pot where all the races of Europe are melting and re-forming! . . . Germans and Frenchmen, Irishmen and Englishmen, Jews and Russians—into the Crucible with you all. God is making the American."

Zangwill's ideological foil was German-born Horace Kallen, ironically, the first Jewish professor at Princeton University. In a 1915 essay in *The Nation* entitled "Democracy Versus the Melting Pot," Kallen introduces the concept of cultural pluralism. He envisions a model of America not as a melting pot but as a "symphony of civilizations," each culture remaining distinct but contributing to a dynamic whole. Kallen's is the more Jewish model for America, for reasons I will describe later. Over the last century, however, it is clearly the melting pot that has emerged to define Americanism. America's assimilationist force has few successful contemporary

parallels, and it has been a key factor in America's global ascendancy. Of course, this means that America poses a long-
term threat to its many subidentities, particularly the smaller
ones. Thrown together in public school classrooms, on playing fields, and in workplaces, Americans are forced to accommodate one another socially and culturally. Fidelity to
immigrant roots weakens over successive generations, not by
coercion but through participation in and contribution to the
evolving American character. Large groups, such as Latino
Americans, may have the critical mass to survive the union
and remain intact over many generations. Small groups, like
the Jews, tend to have less staying power.

All three of my older brothers ultimately married non-
Jewish women. Intermarriage was not a goal, of course, but a
natural outcome of the social setting in which we were raised.
Most of the women, most of the people, we knew happened
not to be Jewish. However, had you asked any of us, we would
have responded that our Judaism was important to us. Judaism was the box we ticked for *religion*.

Although no specific religion or denomination is formally
representative of American institutions such as the presidency, the justice system, or the military, religiosity features
prominently in all. Our currency bears reference to God.
We take oaths on a holy book before testifying in court and
upon inauguration to political office. Tombstones at military
cemeteries carry religious symbols—crosses, stars of David,
and crescents. But despite the prevalence of religious symbolism in American life, the distinction among different religions is secondary. In politics, we have become accepting
of most religions for purposes of electability. We have had a

Catholic president, a Mormon presidential candidate, and an openly observant Jewish vice presidential candidate (for whom the majority of U.S. voters cast their ballots). Jews are represented heavily in the legislative and judicial branches of the United States government. All American war dead are eligible for burial in the same cemeteries. Military chaplains regularly provide spiritual services to soldiers of different religions—together. The "interfaith service" is an American concept, widely perceived as a religious rite despite the fundamental theological incompatibility of practically any two faiths. The religion these chaplains are really preaching is Americanism.

Most American Jews relate to their Judaism in this generic American manner. Judaism is less a distinguishing characteristic than an expression of commonality with fellow Americans. Hanukkah, for most American Jews, is not the celebration of a specific theme in Jewish history; it is the way Jews celebrate Christmas. Hanukkah's relationship to other Jewish holidays—Sukkoth, for example—is far less clear than its relationship to Christmas. Understanding the *particularities* of Judaism is a lower priority for most American Jews than establishing Judaism's *commonalities* with the majority, primarily Christian, American religious groups. In this sense, many, if not most, American Jews really see themselves as Jewish Americans. "American" is their dominant identification. "Jewish" is a modifier to the noun "American."

That noun can carry many other modifiers, like "Democrat," "lawyer," "activist," or "Yankees fan." In today's America, most of these other affiliations are open and welcoming of new members. Some recruit new members aggressively and professionally. Major League Baseball, for example, is not often thought of in the context of religious affiliation, but it competes with religion for the same scarce resources: its members' time, emotional investment, financial investment, and loyalty. Major League Baseball actively seeks new members (fans) and invests heavily in retaining existing members. Major League Baseball assumes an open and competitive marketplace for members. As an organization, it understands the need to deliver value to its members in order to win their loyalty. It also understands that it is competing not only with the National Basketball Association and the National Football League but with every other affiliation in its members' lives: hobbies, school, work—and religion.

The religion barrier removed, Jews' social opportunity set in North America is mainly non-Jewish. Most of the people with whom an American Jew interacts do not mind, or even note, that he is Jewish. He is American. (Secular Israelis are no different. The only reason most secular Israeli Jews marry other Jews is because that is who they meet. In fact, intermarriage rates among Israeli Jews living in America are even higher than the rates for American Jews.)

And why not just marry for love? Is that not really all that matters? I do not view my brothers' intermarriage as a failure or a disappointment on an individual level. Love and happiness are elusive. I fault nobody for seizing them, whether they come in the form of a Jewish mate or not. But as sound as this logic may be for the individual, it threatens the collective. The economist John Maynard Keynes popularized the phrase "Paradox of Thrift." In an economic recession, the individual's best interest is served by saving money. Since he does not know how long the financial downturn will last, it is reasonable for the individual to hoard as big a nest egg as possible to help weather the storm. But if everybody saves, nobody spends. As spending declines, manufacturers and service providers suffer and are forced to lay off workers. These workers, now unemployed, have even less money to spend. In a vicious cycle, the economic crisis deepens, hurting everyone. What is good for the individual can be very bad for the collective.

There is a critical mass of intermarriage beyond which the continuity of our people becomes impossible. Some level of Jewish attrition is inevitable given America's inclusiveness, but the current rate of attrition is absolutely unsustainable.

The prospective extinction of American Jewry cannot be seen as just an American phenomenon. Due to the massive proportion of world Jewry that resides in America, American attrition impacts global Jewry to an unprecedented extent. In the history of Diaspora, windows that accommodated assimilation opened to only a narrow segment of world Jewry at any given time. Even then, they remained open only briefly. Today a large window is open to half of the world's Jews and shows few signs of closing. Furthermore, Israeli Jewish immigration to the United States has become increasingly easy. According to the Israeli-American Council, there are more than one million Israelis living in the United States. The American assimilation threat will ultimately impact Israeli Jewry as well.

THE MATH

The math behind the extinction of American Jewry is straightforward. According to a 2013 Pew Research Center survey, of all American Jews who marry, 58 percent marry non-Jews,[*] which means that only 42 percent of Jews who marry marry other Jews. The average number of children in an American Jewish family is 1.9. If one assumes that all American Jews marry, the next generation of children born to two Jewish parents will be less than 40 percent the size of the current generation.

But not all American Jews marry. And those who do marry do so later in life than previous generations did. In the year 2000, 60 percent of American Jews were married; in 2013, only 51 percent were. Assuming that the current rate of intermarriage remains linear, and that Jews who marry other Jews continue to produce 1.9 offspring on average, and assuming that 90 percent of Jews will ultimately marry and produce their 1.9 offspring, the size of the next generation of American Jews who have two Jewish parents will be only 36 percent the size of today's. The generation after that will be 13 percent the size of today's—almost complete collapse in two generations.

Some have argued that these trends may be cyclical, or self-correcting. That is certainly possible, but they could also be exponential, or accelerating. Consider, for example, that as the American Jewish numerator shrinks, and spreads over a growing denominator of Americans in general, surviv-

* pewforum.org/files/2013/10/jewish-american-survey-full-report.pdf.

ing Jews will find it increasingly difficult to meet and marry Jewish spouses, raising the rate of intermarriage. Already today, outside Jewish centers like New York, California, Illinois, Florida, and to some extent Pennsylvania and Massachusetts, Jews find it difficult to meet other Jews frequently enough to sustain high rates of in-marriage. The list of Jewish centers with critical mass will contract with each generation, a phenomenon that could quicken Jewish numerical decline.

Some argue that the Ultra-Orthodox core of Judaism will always survive, no matter what happens to Conservative, Reform, and unaffiliated Jewry. Before speculating, however, it is worth noting that Ultra-Orthodoxy, and its relationship with non-Orthodox Jewry, have evolved considerably in the last hundred years. In most of the Diaspora, for most of Jewish history, only one theological denomination of Judaism prevailed in any region. Of course, there has always been a spectrum of devotion, but the option of joining another stream of Judaism was generally not available. The less devout simply engaged less intensely. They might attend synagogue less frequently, but the synagogue they did attend was the same synagogue their more devout contemporaries frequented.

This homogeneity of practice helped to keep the Jewish community fused. There was a constant flow of ideas between the most observant and the least observant. The continuum that existed in the Diaspora, in which Jews with different levels of religiosity interacted socially, commercially, and on occasion religiously, forced a reconciliation between

Universalism and Particularism. An evening scene in turn-of-the-twentieth-century Vilnius or Warsaw might have featured a young religious man praying intently at the family table while his secular brother sat across from him annotating a socialist pamphlet. Each would observe the Sabbath differently, but during the week, the two might work together as partners in the business that sustained their family.

This sort of contact barely exists today. The continuum has been broken. The vast majority of Ultra-Orthodox Jews, in the United States and in Israel, have little contact with secular Jews. We typically view each other as completely distinct communities with almost nothing in common. Most Ultra-Orthodox shun interaction with other Jews. Their Judaism is expressed only within their insular communities. Most non-Ultra-Orthodox Jews interact freely with other Jews, and with non-Jews, but not with Ultra-Orthodox Jews. The mechanism through which a religious core once transmitted its cultural DNA to future generations in the Diaspora is now broken. A surviving Ultra-Orthodox enclave does not ensure the survival of Judaism as a whole—at least not as Jews know it today.

If Ultra-Orthodoxy has indeed become an entity separate from Judaism as a whole, we have even less time left. The 2013 Pew survey puts intermarriage rates in the non-Orthodox Jewish community (Orthodox here includes both Ultra-Orthodox and Modern Orthodox) at 71 percent. By the same math used above, the next generation of Jews who have two non-Orthodox Jewish parents would be 24.8 percent the size of the current generation. The size of the generation after that would be only 6.2 percent the size of today's—tens of thousands of people, spread across a United States population on the order of 400 million. Fifty or sixty years from now, assuming that people meet randomly, an American Jew of marrying age would meet another Jew, of the same generation and the opposite sex, in only one in several thousand encounters. Outside of the remaining one or maybe two concentrations of non-Orthodox Jews in America, and of Jews so intent on having a Jewish spouse that they will seek one online and relocate in order to marry, the incidence of Jews even meeting potential Jewish spouses will be so rare as to render that generation the last of non-Orthodox Jews in the United States.

A NOTE ON SEPHARDIC JEWRY

Some have argued that Sephardic Jewry (Jews whose recent roots are in Spain and North Africa) and Oriental Jewry (Jews from the Middle East) have been more cohesive than Ashkenazi Jewry, their members less likely to marry out. Sephardic Jews have not split into formal streams—Orthodox, Conservative, and Reform. All adhere to a similar orthodoxy, albeit to varying degrees. Intermarriage data specific to Sephardic Jews in the United States is difficult to find, but even if this contention is correct, its impact on the trends discussed here is minimal. Sephardic Jews make up only about 5 percent of the American Jewish population. There is also little data available on intermarriage between Sephardic and Ashkenazic Jews, but the two mix freely today. Anecdotally, for example, the rabbi of New York's Shearith Israel (Spanish and Portuguese) synagogue is Meir Soloveichik. Rabbi Soloveichik is the descendant of a prominent Ashkenazic rabbinic dynasty. Shearith Israel, founded in 1654 by Sephardic Jews, is the oldest Sephardic Jewish institution in the United States. Already small in size, and mixing freely with Ashkenazic Jewry, America's Sephardic Jews are unlikely to alter the trajectory of Jewish decline in the United States.

In Israel, Sephardic and Oriental Jewry were originally disenfranchised minorities, underrepresented at the highest ranks of government and the military. Intermarriage between Ashkenazic, Sephardic, and Oriental Jews was relatively uncommon. That is no longer the case. Israelis increasingly identify along lines unrelated to geographic provenance.

THE BEST WAY TO DIE

American Jewry is dying in its sleep, but perhaps that is not so bad. All nations rise and fall. The fact that the Jewish run has lasted longer than most does not, in itself, mean it should never end. Dying peacefully in our sleep is certainly the best way to die. In the Spanish Inquisition, the Russian pogroms, or the Holocaust, Jewish extinction would have been the cumulative result of the violent deaths of millions of individual Jews. In America, it will have been the result of love. That is a tragedy only if you believe that, for some reason, there should be Jews in the world. For those who are absolutely certain that we are ready to go extinct, there is indeed no reason to alter our course. Those who harbor doubts, however, should remember that extinction is permanent. We will not be able to change our minds once we drop below the threshold of critical mass.

There are many theoretical arguments that attribute value to the survival of Judaism as an asset for individual Jews and even for humanity at large. But one *practical* argument speaks more objectively, and with greater urgency, than all of these. The option of treating the prospect of communal extinction as something other than a tragedy is a luxury available only to American Jewry. The scenario that would end Israeli Jewish existence is less subtle, and it will look much more familiar to students of the violent history of the Jews.

3

The Jewish State

American politics reaches deadlock, even crisis, over issues such as taxation, healthcare, and trade policy. While these issues, of course, figure in Israeli politics as well, they are overshadowed by far more existential issues. Israel struggles for consensus on questions as basic as the shape of the country on a map, or Israeli citizens' basic rights and obligations to society. Israel's defense challenges are immeasurably more intimidating than America's. America benefits from friendly relations on both of its borders, while the world's two largest oceans separate it from its enemies. Israel is a narrow sliver of land, smaller in area than New Jersey, at the center of the most violent region in the world. Hundreds of millions of Israel's neighbors call for the country's destruction and demand the annihilation of its people. To that end, these neighbors have launched three all-out wars in the short time since Israel's independence. Israel prevailed in all of these, but Israelis understand that the first time they lose will be the last.

Most fundamental among its existential challenges, Israel is the self-proclaimed nation-state of the Jewish People, but there is little consensus among Israelis as to what that means. Born in the nineteenth century, modern Zionism gathered much of its momentum in the 1920s. Palestine had just come under British jurisdiction after centuries of Ottoman rule. The notion of reestablishing Jewish sovereignty had focused world Jewry on Israel as the potential seat of Judaism. But this meant different things to different people.

Theodor Herzl, Zionism's founding father, had almost no religious education as a child in Budapest. His vision for Israel was a political solution to what he saw as the Jewish Problem. The Jews were stateless wanderers. A state would bring them dignity and safety. Israel would be just a nation among nations.

Asher Ginsberg, better known by his pseudonym, Ahad Ha'am (One of the People), was born farther east, in Kiev, and raised religiously, in the Hasidic tradition. Ahad Ha'am envisioned a state specifically Jewish in character, but secular. Israel would be a cultural hub of world Jewry, a nexus where diverse Jewish culture could renew itself and thrive.

Rabbi Abraham Isaac Kook, born in Latvia, became one of the most renowned Torah scholars of the twentieth century. Rabbi Kook saw great theological significance in the rebirth of the Jewish State as the fulfillment of a messianic prophecy. Kook was decidedly Zionist but also decidedly religious. He saw the two as inextricably connected.

Prestate Palestine was also home to a non-Zionist religious Jewish population whose original members had lived in Jerusalem and other Jewish centers in the Holy Land for generations. This community had no interest in Jewish self-determination. They would agree to live under any government, Turkish, British, or Jewish, until the Messiah himself delivered Jewish sovereignty.

In 1920, the British government installed Sir Herbert Samuel as the high commissioner for Palestine, responsible for the administration of what would become Israel, Jordan, and the Palestinian Authority. Samuel created an office that would serve as his interface with Palestinian Jews on religious matters and would help to draft the British policies that affected Jewish religious life in Palestine. It was called the Chief Rabbinate, and it would be managed by two chief rabbis, one Ashkenazi and the other Sephardic. (Rabbi Kook would become the Ashkenazi chief rabbi.)

In the months before independence in 1948, Israel's de facto prime minister David Ben Gurion's government in formation met with Israel's religious establishment. Their agenda was to work out the religious authorities' role in Israeli government as soon as the British Mandatory Government handed over control of the emerging state. Of course, religious affairs were just one area of governance that would have to be established. Ben Gurion was busy overseeing the construction of the many institutions that would be required to govern the embryonic nation. He was negotiating with the United Nations Special Committee on Palestine on the conditions of the nation's birth. He was preparing the nation for war. Within months, the still undeclared and unarmed Jewish State would be invaded by five Arab armies tasked with its immediate annihilation. Ben Gurion had little time to negotiate the precise role that religion would play in the Jewish State. He simply agreed to the status quo and, in effect, ceded many of the civil rights of Israel's future Jewish citizens to the authority of the Rabbinate. Critically, these included family law, recognition of marriage, the definition of Jewishness for purposes of civil rights in Israel, and the recognition (or rejection) of conversions to Judaism. The agreement also led to the establishment of separate education systems, religious and secular, with separate curricula and separate budgets. Ben Gurion's concession is aptly named the Status Quo Agreement. The moniker conveys the reality precisely. No strategy. No public debate regarding exactly what Israelis mean when they say "Jewish State." The agreement just extended the status quo that had been arbitrarily imposed by the British Mandatory authorities. In religious terms, for the first time since the Roman destruction of the Jewish Temple and its High Priesthood, Judaism was suddenly governed by a hierarchy.

Three minority factions have been locked in constant battle over the definition of Jewish statehood ever since. Each has fought to bend Israeli government and society to its own parochial vision for Israel's relationship with Judaism. We will refer to the three groups as the *Territorialists,* the *Theocrats,* and the *Secularists.* These groups have never reconciled their conflicting views on the definition of Jewish statehood, or on the very meaning of Judaism. They are separate societies. They are educated in separate school systems with different curricula. They are segregated geographically.

The Territorialists live mainly in the settlements of Judea and Samaria. The Theocrats live in Jerusalem, in Bnei Brak, and in scattered but homogenous communities like Ramat Beit Shemesh or Qiryat Sefer. The Secularists are concentrated in greater Tel Aviv. To understand the fundamental incompatibility of their current respective visions, we must spend some time with each of these communities.

THE TERRITORIALIST VISION

One could argue that religious Zionism is the oldest variant of Zionism. In different forms, it has existed since the Roman expulsion. Although Rabbi Kook is viewed by many as the father of modern religious Zionism, the movement was transformed dramatically by the Six-Day War of 1967. Until that war, Israelis' national ambitions amounted to little more than survival. Crammed into a narrow strip of land (nine miles across at its narrowest point), outnumbered and outgunned by neighbors committed to their annihilation, they were not in a position to hope for much more. Israel's quick and decisive victory came as a shock to most Israelis. Even in retrospect, it seems almost miraculous. For some, particularly some religious Zionists, divine providence was the most straightforward explanation for the triumph. The divine interpretation was especially compelling in light of the specific lands that had been conquered. I am not talking about the Golan Heights, captured from Syria, which had tremendous strategic value but were of little religious interest. The same is true of the Sinai Peninsula and the Gaza Strip, captured from Egypt. Sinai was a strategic buffer, three times the size of Israel proper. It had oil, and long coastlines on the Mediterranean and Red Seas. But aside from having been the backdrop for the Israelites' forty years of wandering under Moses, it also had limited religious significance.

The Jordanian front was different. Israel had done everything it could to keep the Jordanians out of the war, but Jordan attacked and, in the savage battle of Jerusalem, was defeated. Israel's victory yielded Judea and Samaria, the heartland of ancient Israel and the resting place of its patriarchs and matriarchs, Abraham, Isaac, and Jacob and Sarah, Rebecca, and Leah in Hebron, and Rachel in Bethlehem. It yielded the Old City of Jerusalem and the Temple Mount. Jews had been banished from these sites completely since the Jordanian army had conquered them in 1948. Before the war, the Israeli paratroopers who ultimately secured the Old City could only have dreamed of visiting them. Suddenly, they controlled them. For the first time since the Roman occupation, the site of the Great Temple was in Jewish hands.

Messianic associations were unavoidable. For many religious Zionists, political Zionism had served a merely earthly purpose. Israel was just a refuge for the Jews. Almost any swath of territory between Haifa and Eilat would have been suitable for that purpose. But this particular land was divine. After nineteen hundred years of exile, God had just granted it back to the Jews, and the generation of 1967 had been blessed to bear witness. This *was* Zionism's destination. Returning the divine gift was not a human prerogative.

Beginning soon after the war, a small community of religious Zionist activists began putting up makeshift outposts in Judea and Samaria in a bid to make the Jewish presence there permanent, in defiance of Israeli law. The government was seeking to negotiate peace with Jordan by returning the territory, and that original settler community was a thorn in its side. As it became clear, however, that the Jordanians would refuse to negotiate with Israel, government resolve against the settlers weakened. A small segment of the movement succeeded in evading the authorities and built the first Jewish settlements in Judea and Samaria. The Jewish population there has swelled to several hundred thousand people over the subsequent decades. But only a minority of these people would insist on remaining in place at all costs. This is the group I call the Territorialists. Of course, the Arab population that came under Jordanian rule in 1948, and under Israeli rule in 1967, also remains in Judea and Samaria today. This population has also swelled—to over two and a half million. It identifies as Palestinian.

My first intimate encounter with the Territorialists occurred in a roundabout way, when I was an instructor at the Air Force Academy. In 1994, an aeronautical engineer named Alice Miller applied for admission to the then all-male Academy. She was rejected on gender grounds and brought a legal suit against the Air Force. Her case reached the Israeli Supreme Court, where she prevailed. Although Miller did not make it past the early phases of flight school, she created a precedent that many young women would follow. The first two women made it through to the flying phase of the Academy when I was an instructor at the Combat Flight Instructors School. It became my responsibility to build a study unit at the school called Instructing Women Cadets. The U.S. Navy had recently introduced sweeping revisions to its policies regarding integrating women into combat roles following the Tailhook sexual assault scandal, and it was understood that there was more to this challenge than just treating women as though they were men. The culture of the Israeli Air Force was such that sexual assault was not at the top of our list of concerns; our focus was more on maximizing the professional skills of our crews. Were there special considerations, physical, academic, or social, that we should include in our pedagogy? What effects would the presence of women have on the male cadets, or on the instructors? I spent a good deal of time in the Primary Training Squadron when the two women were based there. I flew with both of them extensively and debriefed other instructors who flew with them. I observed their interactions with the other cadets and interviewed them.

Cadets slept six to a room during the Primary Flight Phase. Evenings in the rooms were devoted to long study sessions. The cadets had volumes of material to digest, and it made sense to study together and quiz one another regularly. It was also a chance to blow off steam together with an occasional prank, wrestling match, or contest of some sort. Dormitory life was an important bonding experience—for the men.

The two women were housed in a separate wing of the dormitory. They had a study pair, not a study group. One of them was dismissed from the Fighter Track after about a month, leaving the remaining female cadet to spend her evenings alone. This was not healthy. Speaking with some of the men about holding a coed study hall every evening, I encountered a spectrum of reactions. Some felt their study sessions would not have the same focus if a woman was included. Some, I suspect, would have been happy to see the remaining female cadet wash out, leaving less competition for one of the few coveted slots on the Academy graduation stage the next year. Among a few cadets, I detected a fundamental resentment of the new reality that women were even at the Academy. Becoming an IAF pilot was a mark of status in Israel, specifically masculine status. Women might dilute its potency.

On the extreme welcoming end of the male cadet spectrum was Uri. Uri (not his real name) was a religious Zionist. Like women, religious Zionists were a new community at the Academy. There had been religious cadets, and even air crew in the past, but their numbers were too small to influence Air Force culture in any significant way. Until the 1990s, the Air Force was dominated by Israel's then secular nobility, the kibbutzniks.

Uri actually came from a small settlement deep in Judea and Samaria. He was not one of the nominal settlers who lived right across the Green Line, the border between Judea and Samaria and Israel proper. He was the real deal, a Territorialist. At first, I assumed that his acceptance of the women cadets had to do with both groups being outsiders. I knew how lonely that was. But as I came to know him better, I began to appreciate that it went deeper. Uri had been raised with a specific vision for how his society should look. The land was inextricable from this vision. Uri was powerfully driven, but not by competition, as most of his classmates were. His ambition appeared to be simply to serve his people's vision as well as he could. He took instruction as if he had no ego. He was genuine. He dug deep into his in-flight errors during debriefings. He never reveled in his successes. He judged nobody. He was the first to volunteer for an unpopular chore, and he performed it with a smile and a sense of humor. He harbored no cynicism or pretense. He was all about service. He was also a good pilot. I admired Uri. I tracked his progress through the Academy, operational training, and F-16 school. I was disappointed to see him assigned to a different squadron. I would have been honored to serve with him.

Uri harbored no misgivings about the women in his class. He interacted with them as he did with the men. The women could sense his ease. They were more open around him, and around the one or two other National Religious cadets in their class. This surprised me. Had I given it much thought, I would have assumed the National Religious cadets would arrive indoctrinated in a rigid dogma that frowned on women serving in roles like these. The opposite was the case. These young men actually set a behavioral standard—in this and other areas.

As more National Religious pilots, including National Religious women, joined our ranks, I began to appreciate that Uri was not unique in his approach to service. Over the course of the 1990s, the National Religious movement came to form a sort of new guard within the IDF. They were the new kibbutzniks, overrepresented as a proportion of the general population. They took leadership positions, not only in the Air Force but throughout the frontline combat units of the IDF. Women have served in combat roles in the IAF for years now. They have become an integral part of the flight crew community. But the more profound shift in IAF culture in the 1990s was the changing of this guard. National Religious enlistment raised the standard in the IAF. It made us a more professional, more effective, and more humane organization.

I am not in touch with Uri anymore. He retired from active duty in the Air Force a few years ago and returned to his settlement, where I believe he works in farming. He still flies in the reserves. I found myself gravitating toward members of the National Religious community during my last years in reserve service. Some were Territorialists. I respect not only the professional and moral standards that the Territorialists represent, but the ethic that underlies them. I found that, contrary to popular conception among many Israel observers, few of these people harbored any antipathy toward their Palestinian neighbors. After many long debates with Territorialist friends on Israel's future and on peace prospects with the Palestinians, I fully accept their claim that Jews should have as much right to pray at the tombs of the Jewish patriarchs and matriarchs as Muslims do. I accept their argument that Israel upholds religious freedom in territories under its control, and that this tolerance will not be reciprocal. It never has been. All faiths have enjoyed free access to their holy sites in Jerusalem since 1967, when it became Israeli territory. Before 1967, when it was in Muslim hands, Jews were completely barred from Jewish holy sites. This would likely be the case in a Muslim-controlled Hebron or Bethlehem as well.

The Territorialist vision, however, clashes fundamentally with Israeli Secularism over the value of sovereignty in Judea and Samaria. There are only three possible endgames in Israel's conflict with the Palestinian Arabs. At this point, the choice among the three is in Israel's hands. (A Palestinian partner could improve the outcome of one of the options, but, notwithstanding familiar protestations from some specific quarters in the Israeli political establishment, Israel does not really need a partner.) The dividing line between Israel's relatively large religious Zionist population (including those who currently live in Judea and Samaria) and the small minority I call the Territorialists is in their prioritization of the three options. It is only the Territorialists who would choose Option 1 or 2.

Option 1. Israel could annex the West Bank and grant Israeli citizenship to its Arab residents. This would have two benefits. The first is that it would guarantee Jewish access to Jewish holy sites. The second benefit is that military control of the territory affords protection for the Israeli interior. A troubling precedent most Israelis point to is Israel's withdrawal from the Gaza Strip in 2005, which resulted not in constructive state building, but in Gazan Palestinians' destroying the economic infrastructure that Israel left behind for them, and turning Gaza into a Hamas rocket base that launches frequent attacks on Israeli civilians. This base is sponsored, like the Hezbollah base in Lebanon, by the Islamic Republic of Iran. Of course, Gaza is much closer to Israel's vulnerable population centers than Lebanon is. Judea and Samaria are even closer than Gaza.

This first option would also impose extremely high costs. Israel would be importing the deepening social crises plaguing most of the Middle East. Through annexation, the death cult that inspires the suicide bomber, the juvenile knife attacker, and the pedestrian-ramming truck-driver terrorist would be woven into the fabric of Israeli society permanently.

Israel would also be opening itself to the prospect of demographic suicide. Many argue the precise statistics, but even the most optimistic of demographers must concede that Muslim Arabs would immediately become a majority, or at least a very large minority, within Israel if Judea and Samaria were annexed. Democracy and demography would reduce the Jews of Israel to another minority in the Middle East. Recognizing the fate of most minorities in the Middle East (consider Christians, Yazidis, and Baha'i), this scenario warrants a sober and open debate on the price Israelis should be willing to collectively pay for sovereignty in Judea and Samaria.

Option 2. A second option is for Israel to annex the territory but withhold citizenship from its residents. The benefits here include those associated with the first option but also include Israel's remaining a Jewish-majority state.

Of course, Israel would also be claiming permanent sovereignty over people who have no representation in Israeli government. Democracy is a basic tenet of Israel's foundation, and a principle still demanded by the vast majority of Israel's citizens, including my religious Zionist friends. Most Israelis that I know would find their very loyalty to the state undermined if Israel ceased to be a democracy. Many would immediately seek to establish lives elsewhere. As Israel's best and brightest departed in frustration, the Israeli economy would falter. Israel could also become internationally isolated to an economically unsustainable degree. Of course, as in Option 1, Israel would not be freeing itself from the crises plaguing the rest of the Middle East. It would be embracing them permanently. Like the first, this option is likely to represent the end of Israel as we know it. It is difficult to imagine benefits that would justify this cost.

Option 3. The third option (I have sought a fourth and never found it) is to withdraw from most of the territory, with or without an agreement with the Palestinians. If the Palestinians collectively choose to build a state, there will be a Palestinian state. If not, the West Bank will likely become another rocket base. As in Gaza and in Lebanon, the rockets will be nestled among civilians. Israel's self-defense will be difficult, and fraught with Palestinian civilian casualties.

I acknowledge how bitter this outcome would be to most Israelis, myself included, but it must be seen in light of the real alternatives. After a withdrawal, the step-up in Israel's security challenges would be significant but incremental, not quantum. Israelis already live under rocket threat. Even without a West Bank rocket base, Israel is facing an ever-growing rocket challenge on multiple fronts: Gaza in the south, Sinai farther south, the failed state of Syria in the northeast, and the failed state of Lebanon in the north. Palestine would be one more front. Rocket exposure would certainly be increased, but there are measures Israel could take to mitigate it. The technological solutions that Israel currently fields could be fielded in far greater numbers. Israel's fleet of Iron Dome batteries could and should be expanded by a full order of magnitude, alongside other technology solutions. Budgets currently tied to maintaining and protecting the settlement network could be freed, and applied to building these necessary defenses.

Israel's defensive posture could also improve in some ways. Facing a sovereign country instead of an occupied territory, Israel could be far more aggressive in defending itself than it currently is. From a soldier's perspective, the nature of interaction with a neighboring state, even if it is an enemy state, is far more straightforward than service within an occupied population. Intimate daily contact with enemy civilians is morally and emotionally debilitating for the average eighteen-year-old recruit. This is an important point, and I will address it in more detail later.

Many argue that the loss of Jewish access to holy sites is unfair. I agree. It is an egregious injustice. Some argue that it is unfair to yield concessions to a Palestinian leadership not willing to end violence or even to recognize the Jewish State's right to exist. I agree with that as well. But fairness is not the most compelling objective here. For many Israelis, most I hope, Israel's survival is the most compelling objective. Israel is not likely to survive if the Jews become a minority. It is not likely to survive as an undemocratic state. This leaves only one option.

Israeli political framing of this conflict typically offers perfect peace, perfect justice, or perfect security as benchmarks for policy, but this is dangerously misleading. Perfection is not on the menu. The only relevant benchmark for any of these options is the other two options. There is nothing else. Obfuscation and denial will eventually take decisions out of the hands of Israelis. If this happens, those decisions will be made by people who do not have Israel's interests at heart. The Israeli government has already begun to shirk responsibility for the fate of its citizens. Instead of ending the current deadlock, unilaterally if necessary, the Israeli government hides behind the professed need for a Palestinian "partner," allowing the Palestinians' refusal to behave as a partner to dictate the viability and timing of Israel's own strategic decisions.

The segment of Israeli society represented by the Territorialist vision is the smallest of the three, but its impact is the most immediate. The Territorialist vision, and its associated trade-offs, must be debated and decided upon now, by all of Israel. Indecision will not make the territorial issue disappear; it will only transfer its solution into somebody else's hands. That will likely end in tragedy. When that point of no return is crossed, and Israel finds it is left with only Options 1 and 2, Israeli Secularists will be forced to decide if a nondemocratic state or life as a minority in the Middle East is a value worth fighting for. I will examine that decision later in the chapter.

THE THEOCRATIC VISION

In the winter of 2008, I attended the funeral of a relative of one of my Clarity colleagues at a cemetery in central Israel. I had arrived early and mistakenly parked at a different lot from the other Clarity employees. After the ceremony, I walked to my car alone, on a gravel trail winding through a small pine forest. I noticed a narrow track branching away from the trail, to my left. About ten meters down that track, a sign read ALTERNATIVE CEMETERY. Curious, I followed the path as it wound downward around the south side of the wooded hill atop which the main cemetery stood. I continued downhill for a few minutes, finally entering a clearing populated with a few dozen graves. The first headstones I encountered were adorned with Russian Orthodox crosses. They marked the graves of recent immigrants from the former Soviet Union, presumably either married to Russian Jews or otherwise non-Jewish but eligible for Israeli citizenship. Israel's Law of Return grants citizenship to anyone with at least one Jewish grandparent. The threshold of one-quarter Jewish stems directly from the Nuremberg Laws under the Third Reich. People who were Jewish enough for the Nazis would be Jewish enough to be guaranteed safe harbor in the Jewish State. Indeed, all other routes of escape had been closed to those Jews in the late 1930s. Israel's role as the Jewish refuge has enjoyed widespread consensus among Israel's Jews from the beginning.

But details of the nature of Israel's Jewish character had been left ambiguous by the Status Quo Agreement, secular and religious camps each harboring their own conflicting interpretations. With the Theocratic camp in control of meaningful aspects of Jewish life in Israel, these incompatible forces were bound to clash with unpredictable results. One of these is that safe harbor in Israel does not guarantee all of the rights of full citizenship.

Curiosity drew me past the first Russian Orthodox graves, and I came to a headstone bearing the Star of David and a Russian name. The man had been born in 1987, presumably in the former Soviet Union. He had died in July 2006, when Israel was engaged in a ground war in Lebanon. He was nineteen years old when he died, an age at which most Israeli men are in military service. Had he died in battle? Had he been one of the young men and women defending Israel's northern towns and cities from Hezbollah rocket attacks in the Second Lebanon War? Based on the star on his tombstone, it seemed he had considered himself Jewish, or at least his family had. Would he have chosen to be buried among his comrades in the Jewish military cemetery, or in this "alternative cemetery"?

Back at the office in Tel Aviv that evening, I went online and found these stories: Nikolai Rappaport, born in Krasnodar, had been killed in Lebanon. He was refused burial in a Jewish cemetery because he was not recognized as Jewish by the Rabbinate and was taken by his mother back to Krasnodar, where he is buried today.

Lev Peisakhov, born in Azerbaijan, died in battle at age twenty. His mother, Svetlana, was not Jewish. He was not buried with his comrades, as he would have wanted to be, and as they would have had it, but beyond the fence of the Beit Shean Military Cemetery, an area reserved in Jewish tradition for suicides and people convicted of capital sins.

In a recent Memorial Day service, the IDF chief of staff honored each of the past year's war dead at the military cemetery at Mount Herzl in Jerusalem and inadvertently walked past the grave of Staff Sergeant Yevgeny Tolotzky without stopping to pay his respects. Yevgeny was not Jewish enough for his burial plot to lie among those of his comrades. It was out of the chief of staff's field of view.

These are examples of the real-world manifestations of Israel's failure to reconcile its competing visions. Aside from

the Theocrats, most Israeli Jews find these manifestations
outrageous. If those soldiers had considered themselves Jewish enough to have fought and died in defense of the Jewish
State, most say, we should certainly consider them Jewish
enough to be buried with their comrades, in the Jewish tradition. Svetlana Peisakhov reflected this view in an interview
she gave months after her son's death. "My son deserves what
every other hero killed in the Israeli army gets," she said.
"How can it be any different? I want to look those rabbis in
the eye, those who decided to put my son in a corner, and
talk with them. They don't even send their sons to the army."

The Rabbinate's authority extends beyond burial rites to
many areas that impact the lives of non-Ultra-Orthodox Israelis. For example, it rules on accreditation for hotels and
restaurants in Israel as compliant or noncompliant with Jewish dietary laws. These rulings, of course, bear real-world
business consequences. The Status Quo Agreement left public transportation on the Sabbath fully functioning in Haifa,
restricted in Tel Aviv, and completely halted in Jerusalem.
The Rabbinate qualifies prospective citizens' Jewish creden-
tials for purposes of full citizenship and the rights thereof. It
certifies conversions to Judaism. A naturalized Israeli, having
been converted by a rabbi in the United States, may find his
conversion retroactively disqualified by the Rabbinate when
he applies for an Israeli marriage license.

Marriage, even outside Israel, between a citizen born
Jewish and a citizen born non-Jewish whose conversion to
Judaism is not recognized by the Rabbinate is not recognized

in Israel. This has an impact on the couple's lives, whether they care about the Rabbinate's opinion or not. Marital status carries tax implications. It affects the legal status of a couple's children. It affects a couple's freedom to divorce. A Jewish woman whose divorce is not recognized by the Rabbinate may not legally remarry. There is no civil divorce in Israel. A woman may not divorce her husband unilaterally. She needs his permission. This can be a mere technicality among secular couples, but Ultra-Orthodox rabbinic courts may, and often do, withhold permission from women in Israel's Haredi community who seek divorce without their husbands' approval. These women have no recourse in civil courts.

A handful of social organizations* have been established to bridge the gap between religious and secular Israel. Despite these important, and often effective, efforts, many secular Israelis still consider themselves antireligious, and most of Israel's Ultra-Orthodox religious establishment regards secular Israel as its political and cultural enemy. As Israel's Theocratic population grows, it has begun imposing its standards on other Israeli citizens through nonlegal means. The public bus system, for example, has become a battleground between the Ultra-Orthodox and other communities. In certain Israeli neighborhoods, public buses have become segregated; men sit in the front, and women sit in the back. This is a contravention of Israeli law, but it is enforced by vigilante Haredi passengers when they constitute the majority on a bus. Women who try to resist the segregation have been verbally accosted, spat on, and even forcibly removed from

---

* See Gesher (gesherusa.org/about/) and Tzohar (tzohar.org.il/English).

buses. Women whose clothing has been deemed immodest have been physically blocked from boarding buses. This has included female soldiers riding home on leave.

El Al airlines is Israel's flag carrier. The company was government-owned until 2003 and is still heavily regulated. Many who have flown on El Al will be familiar with scenes like this one: In 2016, Renee Rabinowitz, an eighty-one-year-old resident of Jerusalem, boarded an El Al flight from New York to Tel Aviv and was already in her business-class seat when a much younger Ultra-Orthodox man arrived holding a boarding card that assigned him the seat next to hers. This man adhered to a practice within Ultra-Orthodoxy that calls for physical separation between men and women. He asked that Mrs. Rabinowitz be moved from her seat. A flight attendant politely offered Mrs. Rabinowitz another seat in business class, and the eighty-one-year-old agreed to move. She made two trips, with the aid of her cane, to transfer her hand baggage to the new seat.* This sort of demand has become frequent on El Al flights. When the women being asked to move are less compliant, awkward standoffs occasionally ensue, leading to costly flight delays. The Theocrats' demands occasionally go beyond seating arrangements. On a 2015 El Al flight from Moscow to Tel Aviv, the captain was compelled to halt the PG-13-rated in-flight movie in deference to Ultra-Orthodox travelers. One Ultra-Orthodox passenger on a 2016 El Al flight from Warsaw to Tel Aviv, objecting to the immodest in-flight movie, went on a rampage in the cabin, damag-

---

* In June 2017, an Israeli district court ruled that El Al may no longer request that women change seats in order to accommodate other passengers' religious preferences.

ing equipment and frightening other passengers until he was restrained.

El Al has been one of the most visible fronts in the war between Secularists and Theocrats for decades. Even though the company loses money in most years, it may not conduct passenger operations on the Sabbath and on Jewish holidays. This has been a demand of Theocratic parties since the first Ben Gurion government. An airliner loses money every hour it is on the ground. Financing costs alone can be $15,000 to $20,000 per aircraft per day. Being grounded for one day out of every seven reduces revenues by a highly significant 14 percent. Who made up the shortfall for all of the years that El Al was government-owned? The Israeli taxpayers, a population largely devoid of Theocrat members. Who was deprived of the right to travel on Saturday? The same Israeli taxpayers.

The alienation of Ultra-Orthodoxy from other constituencies in Israel transcends most other issues, dividing communities and even families. When I was studying at Tel Aviv University, my great-uncle Rabbi Shimon Romm's Israel-based family invited me to a wedding. There was an Orthodox women's section and an Orthodox men's section, with a tall divider in between. A third section, at the back, was reserved for people who, I took it, fell into neither category. I was seated there. Rabbi Romm had taken an interest in me as a child, even though we came from different worlds. He was an Ultra-Orthodox scholar, a professor at Yeshiva University, and I was a kid from Miami, tanned dark, with dirt under my fingernails. His children and grandchildren spent their weekends deepening their understanding of Torah and Talmud. I spent mine trying to increase the number of laps I could swim underwater. We had little in common, but we were family. I felt Rabbi Romm's warmth when we visited his family in New York.

I felt no special warmth from the family in Jerusalem. I attended one or two more family functions, but once my intention to take Israeli citizenship and enlist became clear, I found I was no longer invited. I had unknowingly taken a position on the wrong side of the divide, and they made it clear I was not one of them. I was not insulted. The real affront had taken place earlier, at that first wedding. Seated with me at the neither-nor table was Shimon Romm's son, Samuel, who had moved to Israel years earlier. While still upholding the strictures of Orthodoxy, Samuel had integrated into broader Israeli society. He was a religious Zionist. He and his son had served in the army, making them black sheep in their family. Practicing the wrong kind of Orthodoxy, Samuel was pushed as far away as I, religiously illiterate and only a distant family member, had been.

In retrospect, I did not see the Israeli Romms as family either. Tragically, from my current vantage point, I could barely recognize them as members of the same people. In the United States, Shimon Romm's family worked and paid taxes like everybody else. In Israel, they did not. In the United States, they did not impose their values on other Jews. In Israel, they did. Their contempt for those members of their own people whose taxes paid their living expenses and study stipends, and who fought and died in their defense, made me angry to an extent that prevented me from trying to understand them. The scorn between Secularist and Theocratic

Israel is mutual, and I joined the fray almost immediately after arriving. Secularists reject not only the idea of establishing common cause with their Theocratic neighbors; many see religion itself as their enemy. Jewish sovereignty has had the perverse effect of turning a very large swath of Jewry against Judaism.

Amber and I discovered in 1999 that we would be forced to fight the religious establishment in order to be married in the way we intended. Marriage by a Rabbinate-approved rabbi is a long and often onerous process. The engaged couple is required to make representations regarding their religious observance and sex life. This may require that a secular couple lie about their past and make false commitments regarding their future. Amber has always been the practical problem solver in our relationship. She saw the Rabbinate as little more than an unpleasant obstacle we would have to overcome in order to be married. Perhaps more sentimental in my attachment to Israel, I was angry at the prospect of consecrating our marriage through this fraudulent and intrusive process. We found our compromise in a loophole that demanded some administrative complexity but preserved the integrity of our marriage ceremony. This loophole highlights the absurdity of Jewish governance today and the threat it poses to Jewish survival.

We were married in a perfunctory civil service at the office of the city clerk in New York City in April 1999. Amber's sister and a friend joined us, our friend as the New York State–mandated witness. We brought the marriage license we had purchased the day before, waited our turn, presented our identification, presented our witness's identification, paid

$25, and received our Certificate of Marriage Registration. We paid an additional $35 for a Marriage Certificate for Foreign Use. We were now married as far as the Israeli government was concerned (the Israeli Interior Ministry recognizes foreign weddings between two citizens who were born Jewish), but not as far as Amber and I were concerned. We called this our administrative wedding.

In June, we married again. It was sunset in the old amphitheater on Mount Scopus. We had chosen this short window, exactly when Jerusalem's harsh summer afternoon light yields to the warm red of the desert sunset. Jerusalem's pace slows with the light, and for about thirty minutes, the city is timeless. The glowing hills of Judea offered no hint as to our particular placement in history. The light reflected in the faces of our witnesses could have reflected in the faces of our ancestors, who might have stood in the same place two thousand years earlier. Jerusalem rests on the ridge that forms the western rim of the Jordan Valley. Judea rolls downward to the Dead Sea in the east, the deepest place on earth. The caves of Qumran in the valley below had, for more than two thousand years, silently sheltered scrolls bearing the ancient text of the Bible. Across the valley floor, the mountains of Moab rise up solemnly, their purple faces standing out against the shaded canyons behind them. At this hour, they look close enough to touch.

In a Jewish wedding, the groom traditionally places a ring on the bride's finger and vows, "Behold, you are consecrated to me with this ring according to the laws of Moses and Israel." Moses himself had stood on Mount Nebo, directly across the valley from us, gazing into the Promised Land where our ceremony was being held.

Amber's witnesses came from around the world. Mine were members of the 144th Squadron. Nobody could have understood this moment as they did. They knew my strange bond with the Jewish People, both voluntary and ambivalent. They had known me in my struggle to conform and were privy to its secretly indecisive outcome. They accepted it, and I was still one of them. They had embraced Amber since the first days of our courtship, on the shores of the Red Sea. They were our family.

We were married by Rabbi Gary Tishkoff from Hebrew Union College, a Reform Jewish institution. Rabbi Tishkoff had not asked us to lie about our life together. He had not asked us to justify our decision to marry. He would not withhold his approval of that decision, or condition it on our satisfaction of alienating requirements. This was *our* marriage. He worked with us to create a ceremony that would articulate, to each other and to our community, a genuine commitment to this union, to a future family, and to our Jewish tradition. We did not bother to apply for approval from the Israeli Rabbinate. The self-proclaimed nation-state of all Jews would under no conditions accept a marriage consecrated by a representative of the Reform movement, the largest Jewish movement in America. Yet this was the marriage that held all of the meaning for Amber and me and that binds us to this day. For purely legal purposes, we are married in Israel by virtue of our New York State Marriage Certificate for Foreign Use, issued after a perfunctory ceremony performed by a clerk who happened to be of the Protestant faith. Amber and I had just added our link to the Jews' thirty-nine-hundred-year-long chain, right in the cradle of Jewish civilization, despite Israel's marriage laws, not because of them.

My concern as an Israeli citizen and taxpayer is that my interests are not served by Israel's current administration of its citizens' transportation, marriage, divorce, burial, and other services. My concern as a Jew is more fundamental: The meaning of Jewish statehood, as expressed in Israeli governance and policy, has not been defined in a manner that applies to most Jews. All Jews, including the Theocrats, must have a voice in forming this definition. Any other arrangement compromises the validity of Jewish statehood and, in the long term, makes it unsustainable.

THE SECULARIST VISION

For the purposes of this book, I define a Secularist as an advocate of separation between religion and government. This group includes both secular and religious members. Jewish statehood, for the Secularist, is defined as Herzl or Ahad Ha'am would have defined it: a democratic refuge for the Jewish People. Individual Jewish citizens of Israel would be free to practice Judaism as each saw fit, or not to practice at all. Over the last century of Jewish settlement in the Land of Israel, various Secularist factions have emerged, each cultivating its own relationship with Jewish religion. Today, many of us associate Secularism with progressive, high-tech Tel Aviv. This was not always the case. Israel's first Secularists were socialists. Their vision for Jewish statehood was not only secular, it was antireligious. It was the Secularists, in fact, who may have fired the first shots in Israel's war of competing visions.

In the summer of 2001, Amber and I traveled the Silk Road from Uzbekistan to Mongolia, moving overland wherever possible in the hope of meeting local people and tasting life off the tourist track. Anton, the guide we found in Bishkek, the capital city of Kyrgyzstan, at the beginning of a two-week trek through that country, happened to be of Russian origin. He agreed to take us on a tour that would end at the Chinese border crossing at the Torugart Pass, in the Tian Shan mountain range.

Unlike Uzbekistan, which joined the Soviet Union in the 1920s, Kyrgyzstan was incorporated into the Russian Empire in the 1870s. One of the notable contrasts between the two countries is in ethnic assimilation. While Uzbekistan is generally integrated, ethnic communities in Kyrgyzstan tend to be segregated. As Anton was a Russian speaker, we spent most nights as guests in small ethnically Russian agricultural settlements called *kolkhozi*. Our first night in a *kolkhoz* was on the northern shore of Issyk-Kul, the largest lake in Kyrgyzstan. It was sunset when we came up the winding drive into the heart of the settlement. Our entire trek, to this point, had been a deep immersion in the foreign and the exotic, but here I suddenly experienced an unsettling sense of familiarity. I recognized this place. It took me a few moments to put my finger on it. It had to do with the utilitarian architecture, the landscaping, apparently designed for low maintenance, the loose arrangement of structures in concentric circles around large communal buildings at the center, which was also the highest point. Starting down the path to the cement bunker that would be our guesthouse, I caught the reflection of the sun on Lake Issy-Kul below, lighting the undersides of the leaves on the trees around us. Suddenly transported to the mountains overlooking the Sea of Galilee, I realized that a *kolkhoz* was a kibbutz.

We stayed up late speaking to our hosts in the broken Russian I had acquired at Exeter. I had rarely encountered people so isolated from modernity. Kyrgyzstan is not well traveled. Our hosts had met few foreigners before us. They were uninformed on world events and had never heard the names of the world leaders of the time. Their lives, in 2001, were not meaningfully different from what I imagined their grandparents' or great-grandparents' to have been fifty or a hundred years earlier. It was as though we had stepped through a hole in time. Still, our interaction flowed easily. I had spent many weekends on kibbutzim where friends from the Air Force were members. I knew my friends' parents and grandparents. I had an intuitive sense of the cues to which these Russian *kolkhozniks* might respond in conversation. I felt comfortable with them. I felt I knew them.

That night, I sat up thinking about the early days of European Jewish settlement in Palestine. Central European Jewish intellectuals, like Herzl and Ahad Ha'am, or Max Nordau, the Hungarian writer and physician, had been among Zionism's architects; but the builders who came later, the *practical* Zionists, had come from the East—from Russia. They began arriving in the late nineteenth century, in a trickle that grew to a stream in the early twentieth century. Having suffered social alienation, economic hardship, and violence under the Romanov czars, many Russian Jews had been drawn to the revolutionary movements of the late nineteenth and early twentieth centuries. Jewish representation among the Bolsheviks was high. But anti-Semitism did not die out with the czars. It ran so deep in Russian tradition that it infected even the postreligionist Socialists. Initially well represented in the revolutionary leadership, Jews ultimately found themselves estranged from the new Communist Party. It was these Jews who picked up in practice where Herzl had left off in theory. Even though they had been spurned in Russia, their Zionism came colored with a deep socialist zeal.

Unable to sleep, I tried to imagine the vision that had guided these Israeli *halutzim* (pioneers), who would emerge as Israel's political and military elite. Was it closer to Ahad Ha'am's prophecy of the ingathering of the exiles, reinvigorating Jewish culture and civilization within the protective structure of national sovereignty; or to the un-Jewish dream of replicating Bolshevism, but in a country that would accept people who had been born as Jews? The Air Force had already given me the hint of an answer.

As a student at Georgetown making final preparations for my college year abroad in Tel Aviv, I took special care to pack Jewish paraphernalia. I brought a set of phylacteries and a tallith (prayer scarf) I had received as a bar mitzvah gift, though I was not familiar with the proper use of either. I had a *kippah* (yarmulke) I had forgotten to take off after a wedding, and a Hebrew-English Bible I had bought secondhand for a college paper and had kept in my Washington, D.C., basement apartment for some future use. As it turns out, I do not remember seeing any of these after my arrival in Israel.

My initial experience of actually living in Israel was decidedly irreligious. Religious practice had never featured significantly enough in my life for me to notice its absence in Israel—until Yom Kippur in the Israeli Air Force.

I had fasted and attended synagogue on Yom Kippur since the age of thirteen, in Florida, in New Hampshire, and in Washington, D.C. Yom Kippur was a significant event, almost the *only* event in my Jewish calendar until those Shabbat dinners began at Exeter. Every year, I would take a two-day leave from school and catch a bus to the town of Lenox, in western Massachusetts, where I would stay with family friends, Ann and Sid Rachlin. We would drive to the Reform synagogue together on the eve of Yom Kippur after a light, unsalted meal at home and a last drink of water. I did not know many of the congregation's members, but I might as well have been in any progressive synagogue in America. There were academics, writers, artists, and professionals who kept weekend homes in the area, drawn by Tanglewood, the summer base of the Boston Philharmonic Orchestra. Most men wore khaki, tweed, and running shoes, observing the custom of shunning leather on Yom Kippur. The Kol Nidre service featured many of the traditional prayers and rituals of Yom Kippur, but it centered on the rabbi's sermon, which usually involved linking the Yom Kippur themes of atonement and forgiveness with contemporary, real-world issues. The earnest listeners sat in the first two or three rows. The rest of the congregation chatted on the back benches, quietly enough not to disturb. A large contingent rotated between the back benches and the lawn outside, where louder conversations on matters typically unrelated to Yom Kippur ensued.

Although I spent little time in Lenox other than on Yom Kippur, I was always conscious of the sense of community I experienced there. My stress at having left school just as the academic calendar was getting into gear dissipated during the service, as I became reminded of the newly discovered importance of my membership in a tribe. Ann, Sid, and I would drive home from synagogue and spend the next day walking around the neighborhood, visiting their friends. At the end of the day, we would break the fast festively at home with their neighbors, and I would board a bus back to school.

I did not know what to expect at Hatzerim Air Force Base in the Negev desert for Yom Kippur 1991. I was so engrossed in the Academy curriculum, I don't remember having had time to contemplate it. I vaguely assumed that here in the Jewish homeland, the highest of the High Holy Days must be held in special reverence. In the days leading up to Yom Kippur, I overheard odd exchanges between my Academy classmates regarding our plans for the holiday. It sounded as though we were going to borrow a bunch of kids' bikes and go on a tour, first to the nearby IAF Museum to hang out with the female tour guides, and then down the highway that leads to the city of Beersheba. I didn't pay much attention to that chatter. I was very focused on keeping my head above water at the Academy and didn't have time for the Israelis' jokes, which I still didn't get.

When the eve of Yom Kippur finally arrived, a rare calm descended on the base, something I remember never having experienced in the United States. All vehicular traffic stopped by late afternoon. People were out and about, strolling in small groups, suddenly out of step with the brisk tempo that was normally so constant it almost seemed a feature of Hatzerim's topography. It occurred to me that it was time to prepare for a spiritual milestone in my Jewish journey. I assumed we would walk to the synagogue, which I had never seen, that evening, and become immersed in the spirituality of the High Holy Days. I stopped at our mess tent for a last meal and began preparing for services. I came out of the showers as the sun was setting. Walking back to my tent, I was surprised to notice the tangy smell of cheese wafting through the evening air. I entered to find some of the kibbutzniks, then the majority of my class, working around a set of waffle irons arrayed on the floor, plugged into extension cords running out the back of the tent. They were making grilled cheese sandwiches. My first instinct was to look around for the one detail I was missing that would allow me to make sense of this, the wrinkle in Hebrew calendar keeping that explained why Yom Kippur would start one day late this year, or the *Candid Camera* crew lurking in the corner. Everyone enjoyed an occasional joke at the gullible American's expense. But this was real. I made my way to my cot as casually as I could, struggling to avoid betraying my confusion and a welling bout of panic. I had just committed years of my life to Israel, an enterprise it sometimes seemed I barely understood. There was no emergency exit.

When I was offered a sandwich, I took it without hesitation. Just like that, the single annual anchor of my Jewish identity melted in the heat of the Negev. We did not attend synagogue services, and I indeed spent the next day with my

Academy class riding children's bicycles, borrowed and otherwise procured from some of the observant families who lived on base. It had turned into a day of almost anything but atonement. But as the afternoon wore on, and the motley squadron of young men on children's bikes—my squadron now—cruised back toward the base, I realized I was passing a milestone. For the first time, I grasped a practical difference between being a modern Jew in America and being a modern Jew in Israel. In America, I had had to make an active effort to disengage from school and bond with the Lenox Jewish community over the fast and the Kol Nidre service. The ritual had been the confirmation of my membership in the tribe. In Israel, the ritual was unnecessary. I was riding down a public highway, vehicular traffic halted, not by decree but by consensus. The highway had likely once been a caravan path walked by my ancestors. Abraham, who had named the nearby city of Beersheba, may have been among them. My Judaism could be entirely passive here. My heritage was baked into the nation's calendar, and into the society that maintained it. It was baked into the path winding through the desert hills surrounding us. Whether I fasted on Yom Kippur or not (most Israeli Jews do), membership in the tribe was automatic, inescapable. It required no effort or knowledge. It could be taken for granted.

Or could it? There was another point, but it would not sink in for years. Grilled cheese sandwiches were not normally part of our lives. The Academy menu was quite Spartan, and we did not have time to prepare food for ourselves. The kibbutzniks had brought in waffle irons for this special occasion, a festive occasion. We were making a point of celebrating, with food, at a time when observant Jews were atoning and fasting. Though the original kibbutzniks may have hoped to sever the ties to their ancestors' religion and build a socialist utopia, Judaism was clearly still their descendants' focal point. Violating the fast so festively, of course, had nothing to do with socialism and everything to do with Judaism. These Secularist Israeli Jews were disdainful of the attributes they associated with European Jewry, but, perversely, it was their studied contempt for their grandparents' religion that kept Judaism alive in them.

Jewish religiosity was not the only feature of European Jewry that leaders of the kibbutz movement sought to eradicate. Israel's original political and military elite had drafted the blueprint for a new Judaism, a new Jew. The new Jew would not be dispossessed, huddling meekly in the Pale of Settlement to which the czar had banished him. He would live on his own terms, on his own land. He would not be locked in the *heder* studying Jewish texts, or even in the open libraries and universities of Central Europe reading secular texts. He would spend his life outdoors, working his land manually. Muscular and armed, he would defend this land. His heroes would not be learned rabbis or even secular scholars, writers, and scientists. They would be farmers and fighters.

The first year at the Academy was called the Foundations Phase. There was no flying during this stage, aside from a three-week period of initial screening flights in light aircraft. The training syllabus alternated between field programs, such as Basic Training, Jump School, and Infantry Line Service, and condensed semesters of mathematics, physics, aerodynamics, jet propulsion, meteorology, and regional geography. Cadets lived in temporary quarters, usually tents, and moved around the country frequently, spending about half of their time off campus. Actual flying started in the second year, the Air Phase, in which days were divided between training flights and classroom work.

The Air Phase began with Check-9, a high-intensity screening program in which those of us who had passed the Foundations Phase flew nine trial flights in light jet trainers. We knew, up front, that Check-9 would result in more than half of us being dismissed from the Academy, the survivors being assigned to one of six tracks for the remainder of flight school and of their Air Force careers: flight engineers, heavy transport pilots, transport helicopter pilots, attack helicopters pilots, fighter weapon systems operators, and fighter pilots. Like everyone else, I had thrown everything I had into Check-9. It had been the greatest challenge of my life. Immediately after our assignment to tracks, we moved into permanent housing at "the Hilton," a four-story concrete dormitory on the Academy campus. Fighter Track slept six to a room, with adjoining showers. After a year in the field, moving into a real room with a proper floor and ceiling was a rebirth. We had been admitted back into civilization. Instead of muddy infantry uniforms smelling of rifle grease, we wore clean clothes—a pressed uniform in class and flight overalls at the training squadron. We knew that the demands of the program would only increase at this stage, but it was difficult to resist briefly reveling in our new conditions. We had our own desks. I wrote letters to high school and college friends who had not heard from me in more than a year. I arranged a subscription to *Newsweek*. I spent a long weekend with my father, who had come for a visit from the United States.

A few weeks into the Air Phase, we had our first quarters-inspection at the Hilton. Inspection was a less formal ritual than it had been during the Foundations Phase. The Academy was beginning to impose discipline on the cadets more lightly, while raising its expectations for self-discipline. The emphasis had shifted from cultivating the trappings of good soldiering to delivering bottom-line performance. Over 90 percent of our class had been weeded out already. Those who remained were no longer in danger of being expelled for failing to meet preset standards in classroom performance or physical fitness. It was now a flat-out competition among cadets for one of the few slots on the graduation podium, and we would win or lose that competition in the sky. I was consequently surprised to be summoned to the Fighter Track commander's office after the inspection.

He opened the conversation by assuring me that this was not about poorly shined shoes or slack bedsheets. I knew that. He had often repeated his contempt for those formalities, and for anything that might dilute his cadets' focus on flight training. This was about his having noticed "non-Academy" literature on my bookshelf. It was Tolstoy's *Anna Karenina*. I had bought it secondhand at a bookstore in Tel Aviv during the weekend leave I spent with my father after Check-9. "Get rid of it," he said flatly. "You have no time for entertainment. As it is, you are hanging by a thread. Don't forget that half of your cohort will be gone before graduation. You are lucky to have come this far, and if you have any shot at going all the way, it is only if your head is one hundred percent in the program. Nothing exists for you outside the Academy." I thought anxiously of several reasonable objections to the commander's admonition, but I said nothing. I knew that I would take his advice, as I did almost any guidance I received from my superiors at the time.

I spent the remainder of the Air Phase completely focused on flight performance and course work. My commander's warning probably saved me from washing out. I had studied in competitive academic environments before, but the competition at the Academy was fiercer, the pressure far more constant, than any I had ever experienced. We were rated and graded every day, our scores on display for our rivals to assess. The surviving members of my class were smart, confident, and aggressive. They knew their make-or-break moment was now, and their focus was absolute. The more successful cadets typically came with an ambition honed over years, starting even before high school. They were exquisitely attuned to the Academy's standards and acutely cognizant of their standing relative to those standards—and to their peers. Their focus came from self-regulation. Both as a cadet and later as an instructor, I admired this group's ability to absorb volumes of material and apply it to complex missions under high-stress conditions. They respected one another, and although they competed aggressively, they played within the bounds of the Academy's rules. Their word meant everything to them—and to the organization. They lived up to their commitments. And when the time came, any one of them would trade his life for that of a comrade without hesitation.

As the Air Phase got under way, a number of leaders emerged among the contenders for one of those coveted graduation slots. I was not one of them. I struggled just to keep up. Although many of us would still wash out by graduation, our cohort had become small enough that the Academy began investing heavily in our success. I was assigned a tutor named Karnit. Her primary mandate was to improve my Hebrew, but Karnit really helped push me through the entire academic syllabus. She also worked patiently on my Hebrew accent, which we both understood to be a problem. For me, the social pressure was almost as intense as the pressure to perform. I was still grappling with the nuances of conforming to a new culture, and I cringed at the idea that every time I spoke, I reminded the others that I was an outsider. I became obsessive about perfecting my Hebrew. Today, most Israelis have trouble detecting any accent when I speak Hebrew, but for almost twenty years, when I was parodied in skits at end-of-year squadron parties, it was always with a thick American accent. In the early years, I would self-consciously suppress the instinctive wince that might betray my discomfort. As time passed, however, the gag became a welcome marker of the distance I had covered since clearing that early hurdle, and I owed much of the credit to Karnit.

The echoes of my conversation with the Fighter Track commander lingered for years. It was one of many incidents that periodically, sometimes ungently, corrected my trajectory. I felt, at the time, that I was the only cadet who had required that particular sort of correction, and I often wondered why.

The others had clearly arrived preequipped with the appropriate level of focus, and with the ability to switch off their non-Academy lives at will. After years in the Air Force, and a two-year stint at the Academy as an air combat instructor, I came to appreciate this group's self-awareness and control. I also came to understand that another phenomenon was at work here as well.

For all of their rigor, most of my classmates seemed uninterested in what I took to be a broader questioning of the wider world. I missed my interaction with that world at the Academy. My classmates seemed not to. I read my *Newsweek* issues cover to cover on Saturday mornings, even though they arrived three weeks late. That became a bit of a joke to some of my cohort, many of whom had trouble understanding my interest in matters that were so far out of the realm of our concern. I was a mystery to many of them, a naïve tourist who had taken a wrong turn two years earlier and, by some strange trick of fate, was still around. Every few months, we filled out 360-degree peer evaluations. In closed-door sessions, our instructors read our scores to us, along with our classmates' anonymous comments. Typical remarks for me would be "Thinks he joined a civilian flying club," or "Has no understanding that he is going to war after graduation," or, most injurious, "Is occupying the position of someone who deserves to be here." To many of my peers, I was still an outsider.

My reaction to this feedback was to try to conform outwardly, to emulate the bearing and demeanor of the Israeli fighter pilot. But the more granular my appreciation of that archetype became, the clearer it was that I did not fit into it, not genuinely. I questioned whether this was a commentary on my personality or a real clash of cultures. My peers had been cast in a precise and rigid mold, forged by the brutality of Israel's history—robust, focused, Spartan, almost two-dimensional. This stood in sharp contrast to the liberal arts mold in which I, like most American Jews, had been shaped. Among its kibbutznik elite, Israel's military culture not only discouraged intellectual breadth, it was suspicious of it. Following the world economy or reading Tolstoy was perceived by many of my peers as indulgent and pretentious. I was wasting time that was not mine to waste. I was prying into matters beyond our scope. Literature, history, and politics were not our business.

This worldview was more than just a necessity for surviving the Academy. I would eventually recognize it as a key to understanding the broader Israeli identity to which I was trying to conform. If you were a member of this particular elite in Israel, you adopted the single-mindedness of a warrior. I do not think this was Ahad Ha'am's ideal, or even Herzl's. It was the Russians', and without it, we might not have survived our first hundred years. But if it had been the whole story, we would not have survived Jewishly.

Of course, I could not see all of this as a cadet. As foreign as my new culture felt to me, as desperately as I suddenly longed for the Athens of American Judaism, I understood how essential it was that I renounce it and embrace this Israeli Sparta. It could not be an intermittent role for me to play, one of several hats I might wear. It would have to become my identity. As I reapplied myself, I turned my back on some of the old relationships I had just begun to rekindle, and on new relationships that had begun to develop outside this life. I stopped reading *Newsweek*. I pursued no hobbies. My briefly serious girlfriend left me. I had enjoyed writing short stories, studying Arabic, and playing guitar in college. I dropped all of these at the Academy and never picked them up again. I understood the archetype to which I was conforming, and I committed to a genuine transformation.

The transformation worked for me, as it has worked for many other individual Secularists. But it has left deep scars on Israeli society. Secularist Israel is a society of specialists. There are no liberal arts degrees offered at Israeli universities. At age eighteen, almost all Secularist Jewish Israelis specialize in acquiring a skill that will be applied not to progress but to defense. For a historically diverse Jewish society devoted to learning, this represents an unfamiliar, unnatural communal structure. Its implications are unpredictable. They were certainly not considered by Israel's Secularist founders.

In *The Garrison State*, the political scientist Harold Lasswell writes of the corrosive social process that takes root under conditions of leadership by what he calls "specialists in violence" in a democratic society. Secularist Israel is, of necessity, the Garrison State, composed of and led by specialists in violence. This specialization narrows our frame of reference, insulating and isolating us from much of the world—critically, even from those members of our own tribe who happen to live outside Israel. It blinds us to trends, the same global trends to which Jews have historically been so sensitively attuned. Insularity on this scale (45 percent of global Jewry lives in Israel) is a new phenomenon in Jewish history.

The burden that Secularist Israel's once necessary, perhaps still necessary, militarism places on the society's Jewish soul became clear to me through Amber's and my involvement in the founding of a high school named Hevruta, dedicated to providing the opportunity for ambitious Israeli students from disadvantaged socioeconomic backgrounds to receive an academically outstanding education. Assume that Secularist Israelis and American Jews enjoy similar educational experiences up to the age of fifteen or sixteen. At that age, their experiences begin to diverge sharply. The sixteen-year-old American Jew, motivated by looming college admissions, is buckling down academically. She has probably been studying hard for a few years already. Her extracurricular activities are structured and curated. She knows she must be well read and well rounded. She is aware of her strengths and weaknesses, and of the gaps in her knowledge and skills— such as writing, or languages. She addresses them methodically.

The sixteen-year-old Israeli Jew looks two years ahead and sees his impending conscription. He has already received his first round of draft papers. He will soon be summoned for predraft evaluations. He may be enrolled in military preparatory courses or battle fitness programs. His focus is shifting *away* from academics. If he is ambitious, he is busy getting in physical and mental shape for his evaluations. If he is less motivated, he is likely making plans to enjoy his remaining months of freedom, understanding that his entire life will soon be commandeered by the state.

The American eighteen-year-old is a freshman in college. If she had been accustomed to ranking near the top of her high school class, she now finds herself among students who were all at or near the top of their class. She is challenged to raise the level of her academic game. The new material she encounters represents a pronounced acceleration of her high school studies, but not a departure from them. The university as an institution is designed to support her individual development and self-discovery. In the coming years, she will begin to concentrate on one or two academic fields, channeling her energies and further accelerating her development in these areas.

Her Israeli counterpart veers abruptly away from academics at age eighteen. His energies are diverted to a stark and abrupt resocialization process. He finds himself in a melting pot of contemporaries with varied backgrounds, motivations, and ambitions. His first months in the institution are designed specifically to break any connection with his past and his individuality. The only academic material he encounters is martial, in no way a continuation of the history and biology he studied in high school. Once he is "soldiered" (a loose Hebrew translation), his focus shifts to the professional and brutalizing emotional challenges of combat. (This applies to women as well, though fewer women than men serve in combat roles.)

When the American is twenty-two, she enters the workforce or graduate school. She now has some responsibilities to others but is still able to focus on her own personal development. She can select the direction of her professional development. She may or may not be in her first choice of job or graduate program, but she is essentially the captain of her own career, which will begin gathering real momentum over the next few years as she develops practical expertise and starts to build a valuable network of professional contacts. She manages her own time, and she may develop extracurricular interests, cultural, social, or political.

Her Israeli counterpart has just completed his military service, assuming he has not signed on for additional time as required in certain units, or for officers. (There is a high correlation between participation in the Officer Corps and outsized social and economic contributions later in life.) Officers will go on to serve an additional one to nine full-time years (or even a whole career) in the military beyond their initial three. Having undergone a long and intense experience, the Israeli is likely to join the throngs of his contemporaries setting off for a six-to-twelve-month decompression trip to some far corner of the world. Trekking the Andes or the Himalayas, he may gain exposure to new cultural experiences, but his main interactions will be with other Israeli backpackers, often the same people with whom he served. By the time he returns from his travels, he is at least twenty-two years old. He has been absent from any academic framework for four highly formative years. He may not have been fully engaged in academics for five or six years. He now begins preparing for university. He might enroll in a preparatory course to retake his university matriculation exams in a bid to improve his scores after his long hiatus from exposure to the material. He will also need to prepare for his Psychometric Exam (SAT equivalent). When he does finally enroll in university, typically at age twenty-three or later, it is far from the immersive, nurturing experience his American counterpart enjoyed. He is typically working, part-time or at night. At this age and experience level, very few of his cohort are moving back in with their parents. He has rent and tuition to pay. His calendar is interrupted by periodic summonses to military reserve duty, which may completely remove him from university life for up to a month each year (up to two months for officers) and will often expose him to difficult experiences that create fresh emotional challenges upon reintegration with society and university life. This very part-time university experience, with the pressures of a job and the disruption of reserve service, leaves no room for a campus life or for academic experimentation. The student is focused on charting the straightest and narrowest path to a degree that will lead to a job. He will graduate from university at age twenty-six or older, with a very narrow set of intellectual exposures. His subsequent professional life will typically continue to be interrupted by reserve service until the age of forty.

Challenged to calculate the cost of Israel's defense burden, most analysts reference Israel's sizable military budget, the seventh largest in the world, and 5.2 percent of Israeli GDP. More thorough researchers add the sum of workdays lost to military service, active and reserve, multiplied by GDP per capita per day. Few attempt to calculate the qualitative impact on Israeli society's human resources. The intellectual and emotional effects of this ten-year divergence in academic and professional trajectories are an underappreciated force. They impede economic productivity and long-term societal development in Israel.

It is true that for some, military service offers a fast track to professional specialization and experience, particularly in the technology field. This is the case made in Dan Senor and Saul Singer's *Start-up Nation*. Some IDF units recruit eighteen-year-old prodigies, provide them with high-intensity immersion training in specialized fields such as computer science, mathematics, or languages, and then assign them to teams composed of multiple classes of prodigies, typically focused on a specific mission with deliverables that will impact national security directly. These recruits are groomed at a young age to function in intense intellectual environments, to perform in teams, and to take responsibility for outcomes. Graduates of this unique community indeed form much of the foundation of Israel's technology industry. But they represent a small fraction of the Israeli population. For most, military service is a costly detour from the life-broadening benefits of a serious education.

This detour is a cost borne by a narrowing majority of Israelis. Israel's Muslim Arab population (with the exception of Bedouins) and all but a few members of its growing Theocratic population are exempt from military service. Fifty percent of Israeli first graders are now either Muslim Arabs or Ultra-Orthodox Jews. The rest of Israel's first-grade population, the minority that will receive draft papers in ten or eleven years, is composed of the Secularists, the religious Zionists, a small community of Druze, Christians, and Bedouins, Israel's small Circassian community, and the Fourth Israel, whom I will soon introduce.

Israel's Secularists are no longer affiliated with the kibbutz. They now live mainly in Tel Aviv. The founders' socialist vision collapsed long ago and was replaced mainly by a Universalist capitalist vision, which holds democracy, free trade, and open engagement with the wider world as central values. Nor are today's Secularists all secular. It bears repeating that many observant Jewish Israelis agree that government should not dictate religiosity and that the burden of sustaining Israel, militarily and economically, should be shared broadly. As the Secularists' relative representation in the Israeli population declines, its vision is losing ground to the Territorialist and Theocratic visions.

Aside from their military service, the Secularists are the minority that contribute the most, by far, to Israel's export-driven economy. Of course, without a robust, developed national economy, Israel could not sustain its first-rate military. Some will cite that Israel receives almost $3 billion in U.S. military aid. Note that the Israeli defense budget is almost $20 billion. U.S. aid dollars must be spent in the United States, in accordance with very specific guidelines, making them less efficient than the other 85 percent of the budget. U.S. aid has contributed dramatically to Israel's security, but it covers only a small portion of Israeli defense spending. The rest is covered mainly by Israeli Secularists. Israel's shrinking Secularist community bears the bulk of both the defense burden and the economic burdens that underpin Israel's survival. In light of the looming defeat of their vision, it is be-

coming difficult for Israel's Secularists to justify shouldering
this growing burden.

THE BETTER DEAL FOR A SECULARIST

Writing from Israel in 2017, I find it increasingly difficult
to ignore the vast and widening gulf between two realities.
One lucky segment of humanity, its capital in America, is
engaged in progress and in improving the human condition. A less lucky segment, its capitals in Syria, Iraq, Yemen,
Lebanon, and much of the Islamic Middle East, is mired in
a crueler era and strains to pull all of humanity down with
it. Human talent in Silicon Valley networks the planet, reduces human dependence on fossil fuels, and cures disease,
while human talent in the Middle East is applied to orches-
trating suicide bombings and televising beheadings. Thank-
fully, Silicon Valley, and with it American Jewry, lives behind
robust defensive walls, unexposed to the world's harshest
realities. Its engineers innovate in the most benign environment in the world. The world's most powerful military fights
America's wars very far from their California homes.

Secularist Israel also belongs to that productive segment
of humanity. Its citizens innovate on a par with Silicon Valley's. They do not, however, enjoy the benefit of America's
protective shell. Their basic security must be defended constantly from threats immediately across their border, an
hour's drive from their homes. Their enemy's ideology is
genocidal. Its tactics impose paralyzing ethical dilemmas on
Israel's citizen soldiers. Israel's cancer therapies and diabetes
drugs, water technologies, network processors, and mobile

apps are created without the benefit of Silicon Valley's safe environment, making their success astonishing but forming the basis of a radical difference in the two Jewish communities' realities. Israeli Secularists can see their American cousins' reality clearly and compare it with their own. An American life is readily attainable for most Israeli Secularists who want it. Is America not the better deal? Most Israeli Secularists still choose Israel, but their sacrifice is becoming ever more difficult to ignore. When Clarity's portfolio managers and traders are called up for reserve service in Lebanon or in Gaza, their families, and the company, lose them not only for the days they are physically absent. The leap between war and work demands a radical emotional accommodation that takes time. One reality is a normal professional and family life that any Silicon Valley entrepreneur, Wall Street investor, or American Jew would recognize. The other is a world fraught with terror, loss, irreversible consequences, and unavoidable guilt.

Throughout the 1990s, the deadly standoff on Israel's border with Lebanon was constant. It often flared into open warfare. Unlike the Hamas-launched suicide terror attacks emanating from Gaza in the early 2000s, Lebanon's Hezbollah militia's principal mode of operation was rocket fire on northern Israeli towns. (Hamas adopted the Hezbollah rocket doctrine after Israel's departure from Gaza in 2005.) Contending with the rocket fire was primarily an Air Force challenge, and the Air Force struggled to draft and implement effective tactics. Israeli Air Force (IAF) battle doctrine, which traditionally relied on preemptive action against enemy air forces and armies massing on Israel's borders, was not suited to this scenario. We often had good intelligence on the locations of Hezbollah rocket stores, but these were almost always located in Shiite villages in southern Lebanon, in the basements and garages of civilian homes and schools. IAF rules of engagement categorically precluded targeting these weapons stores from the air. The rules at the time were blunt and inflexible, and that was clear to Hezbollah planners. We watched, powerless, as Hezbollah weapons stockpiles swelled in preparation for recurrent rounds of open hostilities with Israel. In the interim periods, we could only do our best to deter and prevent sporadic rocket fire. This typically meant trying to identify rocket crews in the act of deploying or launching, and targeting them on the spot, or as soon as possible after launch, provided we could catch them at a safe distance from Lebanese civilians and United Nations observers. This required fighter jets, which could get on station quickly, versus attack helicopters, which moved more slowly. Unfortunately, at the time, fighter jets were armed only with large-diameter munitions, with a wide kill radius. They were not as suited to surgical strikes as helicopters, which carried high-precision weapons with small warheads and were better equipped to attack moving targets.

Technology and doctrine to contend with this type of challenge evolved extensively over the 1990s, but for much of the decade we had few options. Due to our rules of engagement, the smallest available precision-guided munitions, five-hundred-pound bombs, were of limited tactical use in built-up areas. We would often have reconnaissance teams on the ground in Lebanon observing rocket crews as they deployed. We could usually get a laser mark on the rocket crews, either from the reconnaissance teams themselves or from drones flying overhead. Although this could reduce the time required for fighter aircraft crews to establish visual contact with their targets, we usually could not deploy laser-guided bombs. Hezbollah rocket launch sites were typically positioned too close to homes (often the homes where rockets were stored), and the risk to civilian lives was high. Laser-guided bombs (LGBs) were more accurate than standard iron bombs but suffered from inconsistent reliability. When they missed, they often missed by a large margin, striking far from their intended targets. This is acceptable on an open battlefield, where a far miss bears limited consequences, but LGBs were generally off-limits for use in or close to Lebanese villages. They were also relatively ineffective against moving targets like rocket crews making a getaway after launch. GPS-guided bombs were much more reliable but were less effective in dynamic situations or against moving targets.

With the exception of some specialized tactics, largely experimental and very expensive at the time, we were forced to operate in a primitive fashion, identifying our targets visually and attacking within a very tight set of constraints dictated by the threat environment, the target's distance from civilians or UN observers, and the weather. We used iron bombs (dumb bombs).

In the late 1990s, I led a mission in the Jezzine area, near Lake Qaraoun in eastern Lebanon. The IAF had begun dedicating resources to targeting Hezbollah matériel in transit between warehouses in Syria and their ultimate storage facilities or launch sites in Shiite villages across the Lebanese border. These were complex missions requiring good advance intelligence. Their dynamic nature posed demands on crews making decisions in real time. Weapons release windows were often brief. Weapons used to target moving vehicles typically had a longer time of flight. The tactical situation on the ground could change meaningfully between the time of weapons release and impact. It was far from a controlled environment. Oncoming civilian foot traffic or vehicles could emerge unexpectedly. Target vehicles could make surprise turns and stops. Hezbollah drivers and commanders knew to minimize their exposure on open roads and parked only in proximity to civilian cover. There was no way to conduct these operations without risk. The policy challenge to planners in Jerusalem and Tel Aviv was addressed in part by pushing decision making down the chain of command to formation leaders. This required a high degree of trust in a common set of values across an organization, balancing conflicting imperatives such as mission success, rules of engagement, crew safety, and personal moral frameworks in real time, typically with imperfect information.

We were sleeping in the ready room when the siren went off just before first light. My wingman (I will call him Dan) was an older reservist, a documentary filmmaker in his day job. Dan and I had flown together for years and knew what to expect from each other, but he was going through a demanding time professionally and had not flown much in the preceding weeks. We both knew he might be rusty, one of many considerations to keep in mind. The scramble code called for us to get directly to the aircraft and launch immediately. There was no time for a target briefing. We did not know where we were headed, but we carried heavy satchels of intelligence data, including satellite photo books, to be used as aids for in-flight briefing.

We slept in overalls, G suits, and flight boots. It took just a few seconds to strap into torso harnesses and helmets, grab the intelligence satchels, and step out of the ready room into a waiting transporter. The weather was as bad as it gets in Israel's coastal plain, driving rain and hail and a low cloud ceiling. Visibility across the airfield was limited. We drove down a dedicated lane to the alert hangar, hail pellets hammering the van's roof. We pulled into the brightly lit underground cavern, each of us jumping out as the transporter passed his aircraft. The hangar was buzzing with the choreographed hustle of the scramble, blue-suited mechanics and green-suited weapons technicians darting economically around the machines, finalizing preparation for launch. We were configured for endurance ground attack: a two-thousand-pound centerline fuel tank, two six-hundred-gallon wing tanks, Mk-84 two-thousand-pound general-purpose (dumb) bombs, laser targeting pods, and air-to-air missiles for self-defense. With an additional seven thousand pounds of internal fuel, we would be able to stay airborne for a long time and bring significant firepower to bear. We were also very heavy, which necessitated a long takeoff roll and high rotation and liftoff speeds. At our takeoff weight, the aircraft would accelerate gradually, eating up most of the runway before liftoff. With the surface slick and wet, we would be hydroplaning early. At that point, heavily loaded, it would be impossible to abort takeoff safely.

I thrust my satchel into the hands of a waiting ground technician and started up the cockpit ladder, a cockpit technician at my heels. As I straddled the cockpit rails, the technician yanked me down into the ejection seat by the G-suit hose, plugging it into a cockpit socket. As he connected my shoulder straps, I attached myself to survival harnesses, closed my lap belt, and plugged in my oxygen mask. I engaged Main Electric Power, initiated Inertial Navigation System calibration, and pulled the Jet Fuel Starter knob. The starter turbine burst loudly to life. The cockpit technician wedged the intelligence satchel into the cockpit beside me, removed ejection seat pins and canopy pins, and disappeared down the ladder handrail. The jet starter's now deafening howl echoed in the hangar. Further communication with the ground crew would be through hand signals.

I initiated the main engine start sequence. The cockpit technician detached the ladder and pulled away from the aircraft as the F-16's massive engine groaned, then began spooling up eagerly, first purring, then thundering. The canopy came down, seals locked, and the roar cut out abruptly, replaced by a familiar cockpit song. The Radar Warning Receiver chirped as it came up and initiated a self-test sequence. Weapons seekers growled and beeped. Dan's voice came in over the red radio, along with that of the squadron's tactical manager. The control tower came in over the green radio. We received clearance and departure instructions before the engine start sequence was complete. I engaged parking brakes and signaled the ground technicians to remove wheel chocks and back away from the aircraft. With systems still initializing, I applied power and rolled out of the hangar into the darkness, up a short taxi ramp and onto the runway. Dan lined up to my left. I could make out his helmet's silhouette in the pale green glow of his cockpit.

The yellow runway lights stretched out in front of us, dissolving into the storm hundreds of meters ahead. I finished my takeoff checklist, armed the ejection seat, locked shoulder harnesses, and activated the anti-ice system. I opened full throttle, and the aircraft lunged forward. Afterburner engaged, the rainy night lit up around me, the surge of acceleration pressing me back into my seat. Beads of rainwater that had covered the canopy streaked backward as the runway lights running along either side of me blended into a blurry line. Rotation, liftoff, wheels-up. The runway lights receded below, then abruptly disappeared as low clouds swallowed me. Eyes on instruments. It was five minutes since the siren had sounded in the ready room.

We received a target sector during climb-out and banked north through the storm. We understood that we would be operating within the Syrian missile umbrella, and conducted a test of onboard electronic warfare systems. At around 20,000 feet, still climbing through clouds and heavy turbulence, we made contact with two other combat formations, heading north from a different base. Our missions were coordinated. Dan and I began drawing intelligence material from the satchels. At about 25,000 feet we broke out of the murk into smooth clear air and a brilliant dawn. White light bathed the cockpit. We began establishing landmarks and anchors on the satellite photos and coordinating tactical vocabulary between us. We switched to encrypted radio channels early, and began getting a detailed intelligence stream. Our controller relayed that this was a high-value target, a designation meant to inform the attack formation leaders' decision making. My bias would be to take on greater risk in the face of obstacles to mission success.

As it stood, my own formation's target would be a bridge-like section of winding road just below a mountain pass. The other two formations, carrying precision-guided munitions, would be striking after us. We knew that our aim point could change, depending on a number of factors. There was heavy cloud cover over most of the region. We would need a big hole in the clouds to acquire our target visually, as laser designation would be ineffective in this weather. While we waited for a clear view of the target, we would be maneuvering around the towering cumulonimbus cells blowing east off the Mediterranean. I checked wind velocity at 30,000 feet. It was well over 100 knots from the west, which made for a dynamic situation. A hole in the clouds, even a large hole, would slide past quickly. If we did get a clear view of the target, it would be brief. We would have to hit it quickly.

The wind also limited our attack angle. Our target was on the east face of a ridge. Because of the steep terrain, our bombs would have to come in at an oblique angle, ideally with an east-to-west component. But headwinds this strong would steepen the bombs' ballistic trajectory significantly, lowering the aim dot on a CCIP (Continuously Computed Impact Point) bombsight. This could lead to a delayed release, jeopardizing accuracy. Attacking from north to south would throw the sights far to the left, also compromising accuracy. The best alternative that the high winds would accommodate was a west-to-east bombing run in a very steep dive.

I would not have liked this solution if the target had been farther south. The steep dive, in our "dirty" configuration (heavily loaded with munitions and fuel tanks), would take us to low altitude on pullout, expanding our window of vulnerability to ground fire. But this particular region had a lower concentration of Shiite towns and villages than the southern region. The weather also played in our favor in that we might quickly be obscured by the clouds after pullout. We would also be the first formation going in. We would be the ones waking people up. The second and third formations would be at greater risk. On the other hand, a west-to-east bombing run would take us deeper into the Syrian missile umbrella. In this configuration, we would be slower and more vulnerable to a long-range missile shot during pullout and ascent. As long as we remained in Lebanese airspace, there was little chance the Syrians would fire on us. They had not in a long time. Still, it was an uncomfortable place to loiter. We were plainly visible on radar to multiple Syrian missile battery operators, all having watched us for several long minutes before the attack, one trigger pull away from SAM (surface-to-air-missile) launch. If we were hit and forced to eject, the strong westerly winds would blow our parachutes into Syrian territory. In Lebanon, we had a chance of evasion and extraction, especially if we were far from population centers, or if we fell into Christian hands. Syria was more complicated, and rescue would be less likely. I considered jettisoning external fuel tanks, which would make the aircraft lighter, but we were already flying over populated areas. We were stuck in a dirty configuration for now.

The target area was almost completely covered in cloud as we came over it. We began circling at around 20,000 feet, waiting for a break to get a look at the terrain below. Occasionally, peering through small gaps, I thought I could make out some of our landmarks, but it was difficult to confirm identification with certainty. After a few minutes, our Radar Warning Receivers began chirping, indicating we were being tracked from the east. We held a defensive formation, scanning visually for SAM launches, still trying to gain a clear view of the target area. I was conscious of being gradually dragged eastward with the storm as we circled. We were in a confined operating space and might easily drift into Syrian airspace inadvertently if we lost track of our position. That would provoke a volley of SAMs.

We spotted a gap in the clouds about ten miles west of us. At the prevailing wind speed, the gap, if it held its form, would be over our target area in about five minutes. There would not be much time to identify the target, coordinate with Dan, and attack before the hole blew past, but this looked as if it might be our best shot. I was concerned that if we missed this opportunity, we might end up compromising the missions of the formations behind us, or aborting altogether. I took the formation west from the target area. My intention was to circle over the cloud gap and start identifying landmarks west of our target. It was better than circling over the obscured target area. This way, we might have some of our westernmost landmarks already identified by the time the gap blew over the target, possibly shortening the process of getting our bearings, confirming target identification, and attacking. It was also more comfortable to hold beyond the fringes of the Syrian missile umbrella. We dug out satellite map sheets of the western area and coordinated major landmarks between cockpits.

We both identified a distinctive bend in a deep river gorge as the most prominent feature on the pages. Once we could identify that bend visually, we might be able to jump to a smaller landmark farther east, and from that landmark to another, hopefully connecting the dots all the way to our target as the cloud gap blew toward it. But the sun was still low in the east. Most of the terrain beneath the hole was still shrouded in the darkness of the stormy dawn. Only its westernmost segment was getting sunlight. I realized this would complicate my plan of attacking west to east. We would have an even shorter window than I had hoped for. I was also disappointed to find a layer of icy mist below the hole. We could see through the mist from the east looking west, but as soon as we passed overhead and turned back east, the low sun, reflected on the ice crystals, made the layer nearly opaque to us. We were more than twenty minutes into the mission. Other formations were in holding patterns off the Lebanese coast, waiting for us to engage our target and vacate the operating area. Time was running out.

Still, we would need a solution to the visibility problem. I decided to make a brief pass beneath the clouds and mist to try to establish solid bearings. Until now, we were only imagining the dark world underneath. A low pass would give us a sense of the altitudes and dive angles at which we could expect the target to become visible enough to provide a clear aim point. I would also try to get that bend in the gorge into the center of my head-up display (HUD) and execute a corrective position fix of the aircraft's Inertial Navigation System (INS). Due to the rush of the scramble, we had not conducted a full alignment of our INSs. Significant drift might have set in by now, making INS positioning less dependable. I entered the coordinates of a specific point on that bend in the gorge and maneuvered to a position in which my dive would have me more or less pointed at it. I instructed Dan to stay above the clouds and track me by radar. I planned for him to make his own pass separately.

Positioned at the western rim of the hole, I rolled into a shallow dive to the east. My Radar Warning Receiver chirped reassuringly as Dan locked on me. The terrain became discernible at about 10,000 feet. Colors and features were always a bit different from what one imagined from above the clouds. In the seconds it took to orient myself, I was conscious of the silhouette I was casting down to hostile observers on the ground, a black dart streaking earthward against the backdrop of an overcast sky. My instinct was to get back above the protective cloud base immediately, but I needed to continue lower. I spotted the bend in the gorge, farther north than I had expected to find it. At this point, I must have been at around 8,000 feet above sea level. Rugged wet terrain slid by just beneath me. I banked left, brought a prechosen rocky ledge on the rim of the gorge to the center of my HUD, and took the fix. As feared, my INS had drifted. It was now centered, but it would continue to drift in the coming minutes. I looked east to see if I could identify any of the secondary anchor points on the way to the target. I could not. It was too dark under the clouds, and the viewing angle was too acute at this low altitude. I pulled up sharply at full dry throttle and allowed the clouds to swallow me. In a few seconds, I was back in the morning sunlight, about two miles north of Dan. We turned and repeated the maneuver, I now trailing him.

As hoped, within a few minutes the high winds had carried the gap in the clouds over the target area. It seemed the mist layer had also dissipated somewhat. We still had not made out the local anchor points, but we happened to be pointing at the target zone as we approached from the west. I took the opportunity to briefly aim my nose at the target marker in my HUD and was surprised to spot the snaking strip of road. I recognized the crescent-shaped bend, whose center point was our target. Luck has to be on your side sometimes, I thought. Pulling my nose wide to the left, I turned back to enter a shallow right bank, my eyes glued to the spot. I trusted Dan was scanning eastward as our Radar Warning Receivers began to tweet again. I flew a pattern that allowed me to keep the target in sight through occasional cloud shreds.

This was not best practice. Ideally, we would have insisted on first identifying our local anchors visually, methodically working our way from landmark to landmark, corroborating our observations until we could confirm that we were both looking at the same target and that it was indeed our intended target. But time was short and it looked as though this might be our only shot. I had just a few seconds to make a decision.

The Radar Warning Receivers whined insistently. Multiple SAM sites were tracking us. My cockpit was strewn with papers and satellite photos. My clockwise arc had now taken me west of the target, and I was finding it increasingly difficult to keep my eyes fixed on it through the haze and the cloud shreds. I briefly lost sight of it for a moment but managed to pick it up again. I had descended in a spiral to about 11,000 feet, a good altitude for commencing an attack. I was positioned appropriately for the steep dive I had planned. If we performed another 360, I might lose sight of the target for good. I made my decision. I would attack now, and alone, with Dan scanning for launches.

Master and weapons switches were already armed. I ran a final check of release intervals and fusing, then rolled onto my back, pulling down sharply. The earth quickly consumed my field of view and began to rise toward me. I initiated a flare sequence as a decoy against heat-seeking missiles, advanced the throttle to full dry thrust, and rolled 180 degrees to wings-level in a steep dive. I would need to accelerate to about 0.9 Mach for release. Other than very short glances at altitude and airspeed in the HUD, my vision was now tunnel-focused on the bend in the road. The CCIP sight line was straight and short, as planned. I began leading the aim dot up toward the target. My dive angle was close to 60 degrees, altitude 8,000 feet and descending fast, speed 0.87 Mach and rising.

Conditions in place, I entered a familiar zone. Time slowed abruptly. I disengaged from the chain of events that had led me here and lost any sense of a future beyond this moment. If there were missile launches or ground fire coming up at me, I would not see them. If my wingman shouted a break warning, I would not hear it. It would be stored somewhere in my head for replay as soon as this moment passed—in about a second. The left-right jolt of Mk-84s breaking off from my wings shook me back to the present. The aim dot was on target, wings level, 1.0 G, good launch conditions. I kept my thumb pressed down on the weapons release button. My throttle was already in idle, the engine cooling. I was low but had to pull out of the dive gradually. The external tanks were not yet empty, which imposed tighter than normal G limits. My nose crossed the horizon at low altitude but good speed. I gradually advanced the throttle to full dry thrust and continued pulling into a steep climb, looking over my shoulder at the target, waiting for impact.

What I saw startled me. There was a cluster of small structures about five hundred meters north of the bend in the road. I had not noticed them until now. They had not appeared on the satellite photo sheets. Something was wrong. The road extending north from the aim point also looked straighter than it should have been. The awful reality struck suddenly and unequivocally. This was the wrong bend. Maybe even the wrong road. Overcome with nausea, I held my breath waiting for the inevitable flash of my bombs' impact between the flares streaming out the back of the aircraft. It came without mercy. I went to full afterburner on instinct, now accelerating almost vertically. I could not see any launches, and I began to scan the road I had just hit for civilian vehicles. Our intended target was far from any village, calculated to be lightly trafficked at this hour. But this was a more populated strip of road. I saw vehicles farther south. I tried to scan the impact zone but could not get a clear view. Much of it was now obscured in a thick mushroom of smoke, debris, and flying earth. I desperately wanted to know the damage but could not indulge the impulse. The clouds swallowed me.

Back in the sunlight above the storm, I took a moment to push down a welling fantasy of replaying the last thirty seconds. I would confront my failure and its consequences later. At this point, there was nothing I could do for anyone on the ground below me. We had not closed our target, and we still had four thousand pounds of munitions on the aircraft. The mission was not over.

I reported our situation to the controller and told him we would be remaining on station for another ten to fifteen minutes. The formations off the coast would have to continue to hold. I took our formation west again, reordered my cockpit, and swung back around, intent on working by the book this time and hoping the weather would cooperate. It did. The cloud gap had expanded, and the mist continued to dissipate. We were able to make out our ground anchors and eventually identified the target. It indeed looked similar to the now smoldering section of road I had hit, but it lay almost a mile east. I should have noted their similarities and their proximity on contiguous satellite photos as we were studying, especially as we were approaching from the west, and both would be in the same field of view. Dan attacked and closed the target.

It was a long flight home. Dan sat about two miles off my right wing, suspended in silence. We had switched from combat channels to a traffic control frequency flying down the Israeli coast. It was still early in the day. We were alone on the network and I was grateful for the silence. There was nothing to say. The damage would not be known for a long time. It might never be. I would not have the privilege of demanding that knowledge. The doubt would be mine to keep.

The debriefing was long and painful, conducted first alone with Dan and then with the entire squadron. I summarized our findings and submitted them to be published for review by the entire flight crew community. This had been a personal failure for me, and a professional blow. More critically, my hands were now dirty. For the first time, I had caused injury to people we had intended not to harm.

I was not alone. Sitting around the table in the squadron dining hall, we spent a lot of time debating the moral implications of fighting a war in civilian areas. Under the prevailing conditions, it seemed we had no choice but to continue contending with the moral dilemmas and the ambiguity. We could not stand idle as rockets were fired at the Israeli civilians we were charged with protecting. We could only prosecute this war as humanely as circumstances permitted, and accept that unintended tragedies would inevitably occur considering the sheer volume of missions we were flying. This was just the reality. We already knew that future action in the more densely populated Gaza Strip was a possibility. I dreaded that. Some, at the time, said they would refuse orders to attack in these areas if it ever came to that. I understood this position; it resonated with me as well. But a looming break in the hierarchy was a frightening prospect. We would be put to that test before long.

Early on the morning of June 18, 2002, eleven-year-old Galila Bugala boarded her bus to school in Jerusalem. Galila was the Israeli-born daughter of Ethiopian Christian immigrants to Israel. She went to the Paula Ben Gurion School in Jerusalem, where she had just been given responsibility for planning her class's upcoming end-of-year party. Bus 32, headed for downtown Jerusalem, carried mainly schoolchildren and commuters at this early hour. Several stops after Galila's, twenty-two-year-old Muhammad al-Ghoul boarded the bus. Al-Ghoul, a student at an-Najah University in Nablus, was a Hamas operative. He was wearing an explosive belt wrapped in a layer of nails and ball bearings. The suicide mission was complex, and it had been planned and managed meticulously, from the recruitment of al-Ghoul, to target selection, to timing. As planned, the bus was indeed packed with children and commuters when al-Ghoul detonated his belt. The explosion tore its roof off and sent seats and body parts flying through its shattered windows and perforated walls into the street. Shrapnel and nails tore through Galila's young body, killing her, together with eighteen other Israeli civilians. Seventy-four were wounded, many losing limbs, most crippled for life.

The al-Ghoul attack was one of many at the time, part of the al-Aqsa Intifada, Yasser Arafat's reaction to the failure of Israeli-Palestinian peace talks in 2000. The Palestinian leadership, emboldened by Ehud Barak's withdrawal from the Israeli Security Zone in southern Lebanon in 2000, launched a wave of terror in Israeli cities. Suicide bombers like al-Ghoul killed hundreds in cafés and restaurants in Tel Aviv and on public buses around the country. Gaza was already semiautonomous at the time, most areas not policed by Israeli security forces. Israel's defense establishment scrambled to provide security. Although intelligence was generally good, targeting suicide bombers and those who dispatched them was difficult. They operated deep in hostile zones, mainly in Gaza. When timely intelligence surfaced, air power was often the only way to act on it, but the operatives intentionally maneuvered from within dense civilian areas. By this time, the IAF had developed a set of tactics that employed specialized precision weaponry, enabling highly surgical strikes, but there were still inevitable collateral casualties, and by 2002, it was only a matter of time before we would incur a serious mishap.

Gaza was more intimate than Lebanon. These were people we had once known well. In 1991, during the first Intifada, I was stationed in the Gaza Strip as a cadet in flight school. Cadets did two tours of line duty during their time at the Academy. We were stationed in a town called Deir el-Balah, in the old Ottoman police station at the town center. I had visited a Gaza Strip beach in 1987, on that tour of Israel for American high school students, and I remember meeting local leaders and being hosted for a traditional tea ceremony. I understood even then that there was political controversy around Israel's presence in Gaza, but in the street there was the sense of a stable status quo. If there was tension, it was not serious enough to disrupt social and commercial ties between people. There even seemed to be genuine friendship between our Israeli guides and their Gazan hosts. The Gaza

I found in 1991 was nothing like that. It was a war, and we were no longer guests. We were the enemy.

We worked in eight-hour shifts, posted at guard positions around the station itself, in support of border guard units conducting operations in the area. Over time, I became acquainted with some of the people in the neighborhood. We never spoke to one another, but I watched them as they walked through their daily lives. There was a group of young religious men, observant Muslims, who would make their way to and from the nearby Abu Salim mosque once or twice during a shift. There was a young man in a dirty Mercedes who would pull up to a small slaughterhouse near the station, pop the trunk, unload two or three bleating sheep that had been stuffed inside, and then take off. He would be back a few hours later to pick up sheep carcasses, load them back in the trunk, and drive away. I watched the young man's interactions with the proprietor. He kept his visits brief. He did not stand around chatting as other people did. He seemed intent on looking busy. I imagined that he was the son of a butcher and that, having joined the family business, he was now struggling to be taken seriously. Getting responsibility for that car would have been a milestone for him.

There was a local kid I took a liking to. I was still an outsider among my peers. We were a large group, and I had not yet become close with anyone. My Hebrew was choppy and accented. My nickname was the Spy, which I did not find funny. The boy also seemed to be an outsider. He must have been fourteen or fifteen, but he was smaller than the other kids in his cohort. They would sometimes gather after school to throw rocks and bottles at the soldiers. In these confrontations, there were leaders, and there were posers. The leaders put themselves out in front. They knew the soldiers were not allowed to shoot, but you never knew what might happen after you hit a border guard, himself just a teenager, in the face with a large rock. You could get hit or kicked if you came too close. Unintimidated, the leaders looked straight ahead, never turning to assure themselves that their friends were still behind them. If things got out of hand, and somebody got hurt, it was the leaders. The posers threw rocks only when they knew the others could see them, and they were the first to run when they sensed danger.

This boy was neither. He hung out at the back. He probably hated us as much as any of them did, but he seemed not to have figured out his role yet. He just stood there watching. I imagine he wondered why he needed to show up at all. I sympathized with him and found myself rooting for him, wishing he would pick up a rock and throw it at me. I would make a show of being hit, maybe win him some points with his friends and give him something to brag about at school. But he never did.

Sometimes I would see him in the morning, walking to school alone. One day, I was standing on the police station's perimeter wall as he made his way up the street below. There was nobody else around. We made eye contact. I was only two or three meters above him. I stopped myself from instinctively smiling and saying hello. He must have recognized me by now, though we had never spoken. I had an Egozi, an Israeli candy bar, in the top pocket of my combat vest, and I dropped it in front of him as he passed below. He picked it up and kept walking, without looking around or looking up at me. He wanted the candy bar but also knew how much his dignity would bear. He was very smooth about the whole transaction. I was impressed.

But the boy was not special in this sense. Nobody engaged me personally, even after some time had passed and I felt I knew the neighborhood. There were people I liked and people I disliked. I enjoyed watching their daily dramas. I thought they noticed us as well. I believed their show of indifference was intentional. We were close enough that they must have recognized our faces individually. I imagined they had epithets for us. The tall guy. The one who won't stop talking his entire shift. The weird guy who seems to shine his boots three times a day. Where does he think he is? They did not want to give us the satisfaction of humanizing us, but they must be curious, I thought.

On our last day in Gaza, we were loading the trucks that would carry our equipment back to Israel when a small car pulled to a stop just outside the police station entrance. There did not seem to be a good reason for the driver to be parked there, and he was not getting out of the car. I thought I recognized the car, but its position was odd, so I approached from behind to check it out. As I came close, I noticed the driver busying himself with something in his lap. His casual movements told me this was harmless, but I did want to see what was going on. When I came parallel with the rear window, I leaned down to get a closer look. The middle-aged driver was peering intently at his hair roots in the rearview mirror, comparing the color of his hair to that of a sample on the label of a bottle of hair dye he was holding in his hand.

He suddenly noticed me in the side-view mirror. I was caught off guard, leaning in awkwardly, clearly spying on him. Our eyes met in the mirror. Startled, he stuffed the bottle into a paper bag and put it aside angrily. He took one more look at me in the mirror, started the engine, and sped off.

I stood there processing our strange encounter and suddenly noted the elation welling up in me. For a moment, I realized, the man's fear that I might see him as vain or frivolous had been significant. In my clumsiness, I had not only surprised him, I had embarrassed him, turning us into something other than enemies. For a moment, we were both just human beings. It is this sort of accidental intimacy that made Gaza more complex than Lebanon.

One month after the 2002 bombing that took Galila Bugala's young life, we got a shot at the suicide mission's chief planner, the leader of Izz a-Din al Qassam, the military wing of Hamas. His name was Salah Shchadeh, and he had successfully planned and led dozens of deadly attacks on Israeli civilians. Shchadeh was a key player in the assembly of Gaza's terrorist infrastructure. He had been targeted on a number of occasions already, but all missions to date had been aborted, as Shchadeh had managed to place himself among Palestinian civilians before action could be taken. In the meantime, he continued to execute attacks on Israeli civilians, and we watched helplessly as the death toll mounted.

The mission launched from our base in a late-night scramble, catching its crew at the end of its rotation in the ready room. Shchadeh had been tracked entering a structure on the outskirts of Gaza City, and we had the building's coordinates. We did not know how long he would be inside, but we did not need much time. The target was hit successfully with a special-purpose thousand-pound Mk-83 with precision guidance, and the aircraft returned to base before first light. But there had been an intelligence failure. We would not know about it until hours later, but the house had been occupied by two families—Shchadeh's and another. The controller had been unaware of this. The result was catastrophic. Thirteen people were killed in addition to Shchadeh, nine of them civilians. Dozens were wounded. We did not have details, but word of the failure spread quickly, and an eerie, laden quiet descended on the base, announcing unmistakably that our lives were about to change permanently.

As the story hit the evening papers, the country erupted in outrage. The air crew community bore the brunt of the public anger. Citizens demonstrated at the entrance to the Defense Ministry. We were attacked by pundits on television and radio. Dan Halutz, IAF commander in chief, granted a number of interviews, trying to put the accident into perspective, explaining that Shchadeh's elimination would save countless innocent lives and that the resulting tragedy had been unintentional, an operational failure. Halutz was a great leader and a skilled combat pilot. But he was not a public relations professional. His interviews went badly and provided an angry press with more fodder. One ill-considered remark quickly became the rallying cry of our public detractors. In a retrospectively obvious attempt to provoke a sensationalist response, Halutz had been asked what the pilot felt at the instant of weapons release. He had intended to make the point that weapons release is a moment of intense professional focus, not of moral equivocation. Moral considerations need to be raised and resolved in advance, on the ground. But the terse, sometimes morbid conversational tone that played in our organization did not play with the public. Halutz's response—"a slight bump under the wing"—was interpreted as callousness at the taking of human life. That interpretation reflected neither Halutz's nor the organization's position, but the comment sparked a fresh round of recriminations and public debate. Government commissions of inquiry were established. Two Israeli civil rights groups filed class action lawsuits against the Israeli Air Force.

The indignation was not limited to the public at large. The attack and its result also split the air crew community. Our moral standing had been compromised in the eyes of the public that we served and to which we belonged. It had been compromised in our own eyes. We resented the missions we were flying and all of the implications they bore. We had undergone some of the most rigorous training in the world, had invested years sharpening our skills drilling against one another, preparing to fight and win a war against an enemy who outnumbered us and outmatched us in equipment. We would meet him in the skies over Damascus, or pounding through the Iranian air defense network. The enemy would be ready for us, conscious of all potential outcomes and reconciled with the worst of them, as we were. The enemy was not a child asleep in bed, unaware of the complexities of this conflict. Civilian lives were precious. All human life was precious, even that of the enemy combatant. This value was enshrined in the Israel Defense Forces' Code of Ethics, itself derived from the Jewish values on which we were raised—in Israel as much as in America. And yet here we were. We had desecrated it. There was no pride in that mission's result. Only remorse.

Halutz's response to what was becoming a morale crisis rested on the foundations of one of the most deeply ingrained institutions in the Israeli Air Force—the debriefing. IAF debriefings are conducted after every training flight and any important operation or exercise. Mission participants gather with their colleagues, present key decisions, review their execution, and share results, focusing primarily on mistakes. Superiors, peers, and subordinates all engage actively in the debriefing and are expected to question the operators' decisions and execution, offering direct, rank-blind criticism. The output of a debriefing is typically three actionable points for improvement. In the case of a major mishap, these findings are published for the wider air crew community to review, as the lessons from my mission in Lebanon had been. The process is thorough, uncompromising, and often harsh. It has been cultivated as an art form, not just a means for personal and organizational improvement, but almost as an end in itself. Air crew members are graded on their debriefing skills. In my time, some squadrons held debriefings of their debriefings. The Halutz debriefing was impactful and yielded much more than insight on the Shchadeh operation. It offered evidence of the embers of Judaism still burning within Secularist Israel. I will enter that closed-door session when I discuss the vital role those embers will play in revitalizing world Judaism.

• • •

First, however, let's look more closely at the sacrifice made by Israel's Secularists. I have discussed the professional and personal challenges of fighting and funding Israel's wars. I have discussed the shrinking benefit associated with bearing those burdens. Even if they overcome these hurdles, Secularists contend with another crippling reality: Their sacrifice is ignored or taken for granted by many of its main beneficiaries—in Israel and in the United States. Unable to understand the moral complexity of Israel's defense challenge, many of these beneficiaries even harbor contempt for their own defenders.

The Talmudic exercise of endless debate around a moral framework has been a Jewish staple throughout the history of the Diaspora. Moral perfection is the implied goal. But without sovereign power and its attendant responsibilities, Diaspora Jews have never been forced to contend with the practical messiness of actually governing. Moral *perfection* is a theoretical ideal. Real life can offer only a moral *optimum,* a compromise between the ideal of perfection and the limitations of human ability. This distinction has been used to explain differences in approach between "hawkish Israelis" and "liberal American Jews" who are critical of Israeli policy. The division is false. As is usually the case with Jews, there is a broad plurality of views in both communities. Some Jews, Israeli and American, implicitly reject the moral compromise demanded by sovereignty, holding themselves to a Diaspora standard that imposes often impossible expectations on the operators who must execute policy in practice. Living within a Jewish society, raised on the same Jewish values as their detractors, these operators bear an especially heavy moral burden.

I flew with United States Air Force and United States Navy fighter squadrons in joint exercises from the late 1990s until my release from reserve service. I formed friendships with U.S. pilots. Having now fought in Iraq and Afghanistan, many are perplexed by the level of Israeli public hand-wringing over what the Americans term "collateral damage." The issue for the American public seems more straightforward. You make meaningful efforts to avoid harming civilians, understanding that some number of civilian casualties is inevitable, especially in today's wars, when both countries' enemies employ their own civilians as shields. Civilian deaths are not a failure. They are part of the inevitable cost of war. Of course, individual American operators experience a much sharper reality than the public does, but this practical reconciliation represents the prevailing public ethic. This is not the case among Israelis, a population living much closer to the front lines, in a war whose tragedies stimulate much more attention than those of America's wars do.

There is a behavioral science game called the Trolley Problem, in which the subject is presented with a theoretical situation: A trolley car is heading for a fork in the tracks and is currently set to turn right. If it does turn right, it is guaranteed to hit five people who are standing on the right track, killing them. If it turns left, it is guaranteed to hit one person standing on the left track, killing him. The subject is told he is standing in the operator's station and can pull a relay lever that will reroute the trolley onto the left track. On average, about 90 percent of subjects elect to route the trolley to the left, saving the five but killing the one. Six people face death on the tracks. You have saved five of them, but you have killed one. Is your decision morally justified? Most respondents say yes—even morally imperative.

The experiment can be made more complicated by replacing the mechanism through which the subject acts—the lever. In the messier scenario, the subject is standing not in the operator's station but on a bridge over the tracks. The trolley is again bearing down on five people, but there is no lever to pull. There is a bystander standing at the edge of the bridge looking down on the tracks. Pushing this person over the edge, onto the tracks and into the path of the oncoming train, is guaranteed to kill him, but also guaranteed to save the lives of the five people on the tracks. The modification reverses the test's results. Only a small minority elect to push the person onto the tracks. Even though the result is identical in both scenarios, most people view the second scenario in a dramatically different light.

Most of us believe that the value of five lives is higher than the value of one. Our actions tend to be consistent with our beliefs when the mechanism we employ is indirect, giving us distance from its result. The visceral experience of direct action can be powerful enough to override moral beliefs, but subjects in the messier version of experiments like the Trolley Problem do not describe their decisions in terms of instincts overriding morality. They tend to describe their decision not to push the bystander onto the track as a moral decision.

Tested twice, some subjects change their minds, perhaps recognizing the conflict between reason and instinct highlighted by the game. We operators could never change our minds. When we took action, the results were permanent. Reconciling our experiences with a Jewish ideal is never as simple as measuring the value of one life against the value of five on the theoretical trolley track.

I remember the report of a civilian casualty of one of the operations, an aging Palestinian man who had worked at an Israeli cannery in Ashkelon before labor ties between Israel and the Gaza Strip were severed. An Israeli newspaper story mentioned that he had once been recognized as Employee of the Year at the cannery, and that the Hebrew-language certificate attesting to this achievement had somehow been found, framed, in the ruins of his Gaza home. I could picture a man I might have passed in the street. He might have smiled. The man I pictured was uninterested in conflict, proud of his affiliation with his co-workers at the cannery, who happened to be Jews. I imagined he would wish my family and me no harm, that he was not a willing participant in this war. I found it difficult to get the news story out of my mind. As much as I tried to rationalize the man's fate, counting it among the tragedies that befall many thousands of people around the world every day, this was a human life linked too closely to my own. I was not in Silicon Valley, and he was not in Afghanistan. We were both right here, I on the bridge, he on the trolley tracks below.

Twenty-seven pilots resigned in the wake of the Shchadeh operation, publishing an open letter of resignation from flight duty in the press. One, Yiftach Spector, had been my instructor after he retired from combat service years earlier. Yiftach was among the most admired pilots in IAF history, a personal hero to me. He had commanded a storied F-4 Phantom squadron during the Yom Kippur War in 1973, when the Air Force lost 102 aircraft and crews in the opening days. He was a multiple ace with twelve jet kills, one of them in a famous dogfight against sixteen Soviet-piloted MIGs over the Suez Canal in which five MIGs were shot down. He was one of the eight pilots who flew a 1981 raid on the Iraqi nuclear reactor at Osirak, a team to which not only Israelis are indebted. The world would look very different today if not for that mission. But after decades of service and sacrifice, Spector had decided he could no longer stand behind his mission. It was not about accepting or rejecting a specific assignment. We could not pick and choose our flights. It was a package deal, and he was returning the package. You could do that only once, of course.

I wondered if Yiftach would have signed the letter if he had had more than twenty-six cosignatories. What if the entire air crew community had quit in protest, leaving nobody to protect Israel? I chose to interpret my old instructor's signature as a decision to endow his approaching retirement with purpose. He was sending a message to his government, not neglecting his duty. And he was not asking the rest of us to neglect ours.

But his difficult decision highlights the burden that Israeli society, and by extension world Jewry, places on young Israeli Secularists. The entire Jewish world indeed benefits from their sacrifice. They are the last buffer between Jewish self-determination and a return to the helplessness of Diaspora. But they pay a personal price, and large segments of the Israeli and world Jewish populations fail to acknowledge it. A smaller but growing segment even view their defenders with scorn. This attitude is not sustainable.

When missions we flew were condemned in global forums, I found I could accommodate the most unrestrained hypocrisy with equanimity. I did not care much about the uninformed opinions of commentators and institutions that had not been moved to action when Jews were being exterminated. We were no longer relying on these people to protect us, and we would not seek their approval when we protected ourselves.

It was the Israeli press, and the occasional global opinion piece by a European or American Jew, that upset me. It was a betrayal when a Jewish writer ignorantly portrayed us as cavalier in the face of Arab civilian casualties, as if we were not doing everything in our power to prevent them, as if they did not haunt us personally, as if it had never occurred to us that they harmed Israel. When I read a Jewish writer casually throwing around nonsensical terms like "disproportionate response," as though this war was a business transaction in which we would readily exchange the life of an Israeli civilian for that of a Palestinian civilian, as though defense by whatever means necessary was a privilege to which only Americans or Europeans were entitled, I felt undermined by the very people I was serving.

The voices of these people rise again with every large military operation in Israel, but I have come to see them in a more benign light. During the Gaza War of 2014, *Haaretz* columnist Gideon Levy evoked the memory of Shchadeh in an editorial piece entitled "The Worst [the Most Evil] Will Fly," a Hebrew-language play on the poster I saw at the IDF induction center many years ago. Levy's assertion, that Israeli Air Force pilots were cold killers, wantonly—or worse, purposely—raining death on innocents below, was so wildly removed from reality and, as was often the case among media critics, so irresponsibly devoid of suggestions for a better alternative, that a number of pilots were moved to respond publicly, but we did so within the framework of reasoned civil discourse, in a television debate. Levy spoke from ignorance. He had no basis for his conclusions. Worse, they undermined the people who were putting their lives at risk to protect him and his family. They granted succor to enemies who intentionally orchestrated death among the civilians they represented and would readily murder Levy himself if ever presented with the opportunity.

When I was a younger man, I had little understanding of the wire that articles like "The Worst Will Fly" might trip in me. I was unknowingly jealous of the moral clarity that only critics can afford. It could never be so black-and-white for me. When I entered the fray, it was not with the emotional detachment afforded by the commentator's distance. I was there in my entirety, my fear, my anger, my aggression, and my compassion, all my angels and all my demons together. However righteous the cause, however humane the army's battle doctrine, the soldier's task is inherently violent. The demons he summons to fulfill it are unwelcome in the life of the citizen. His family demands that he leave them at the front when he completes his service. Society, especially a Jewish society, demands the same every time he returns from reserve duty. But the demons are a part of him. They surface necessarily when his mission demands them, and the best he can do is to suppress them when that mission is complete, an exercise that comes more easily to some than to others. It came easily to me until our first child was born, and I began to realize that my dreams for her future featured the image of a person very distant from the one I had become. As Ella grew, I noticed how closely she watched me, staring while I made her breakfast or pushed her stroller through the park. When I read to her, she would barely look at the pictures in her book, preferring to gaze up from my lap, as if sensing that the tenderness I hoped to convey through my reading voice was not the whole story. Despite my instinctive efforts to obscure it, I feared she perceived something in me that she could never square with that gentle voice.

In a recurring dream, I hurtled through a dark sky, only barely safe, and only by virtue of a proficiency in the ruthless vocation I had allowed to define me. Miles below, the innocent man from the Ashkelon cannery slept, unaware and unequipped, as we all would be in the critic's kinder universe, his room arbitrarily located too close to the intended target. I was conditioned to savor the familiar spring in the weapons release button surrendering under the weight of my thumb, and I did savor it. The satisfying kick under my left wing would signal success. The projectile would be independent of me now, sailing down an invisible beam through the darkness. The fates below me now out of my hands, I would begin a gentle turn toward base. My thoughts would skip to other matters, merging air traffic, landing conditions, debriefing, and the drive home. I would be at home by daybreak, cradling this newborn girl, still wearing overalls smelling of jet fuel. I would be at work later in the day, abruptly detached from all of this, immersed in the noises of another reality, voices from London and New York demanding their due attention over videoconference lines. The man would be gone, whatever family he had, ruined. My family would be oblivious, innocent of the deed. It would have been my thumb on the button. And behind the irrefutable logic of the Trolley Problem, behind my genuine revulsion at the tragic trade, would hide the shameful gratification of a soldier having completed his mission.

Most Jews today, Israeli and American, are inadequately equipped to appreciate the conundrum we implicitly impose on those who serve in combat. Many ignore it completely. A few, unconscious of the short-circuit in human cognition exposed by the Trolley Problem, condemn their own protectors outright and categorically. I fear the moment when the burden that we Jews, American and Israeli, impose on our Secularist defenders becomes too high to justify the benefits that accrue to them. Even as I value the spirit of dissent that animates much of the criticism I once found so injurious, I fear the long-term effects of ad hominem attacks like Gideon Levy's on the shrinking minority that defends us.

Years have passed, and Ella herself is now preparing to enlist. For whom will she be bearing the burden of service? For the Territorialists, whose vision could destroy the nation she is fighting to protect? For the Theocrats, who ignore her sacrifice and view her relationship with Israel and Judaism with contempt? For sanctimonious critics from both Israeli and American Jewish communities, who will vilify her for her service? While all of these voices legitimately contribute to Jewish democracy, we should note that Secularist Israel has an easier, less lonely option: America.

THE BASTARD CHILD

Fouad managed the fruit and vegetable store near our apartment in Tel Aviv. Amber and I had an account at the store. We lived close enough that we would rarely stock our kitchen with more than a day or two's worth of fresh fruit, as it took only a minute to walk over to Fouad's when we needed something. Once we were in the store, we would often spend half an hour talking to him. Fouad had emigrated from Iraq as a young man in the early 1950s. He told colorful stories of Jewish Baghdad in the 1930s and 1940s. Fouad's family had been educated in the English system. His father had served in a government position during the British Mandatory period in Iraq. Fouad could evoke the open-air markets he had explored as a child as if he had visited them just yesterday. His eyes would widen when he described the exotic vegetables—lubia, kohlrabi, okra—whose quality he claimed could not be matched outside Iraq. His childhood friends were not all Jewish. He grew up with Sunnis, Shiites, and Kurds as well. It sounded like a happy time.

Fouad also remembered the Farhud, the 1941 pogrom against Baghdadi Jews. He remembered being locked in his home for days as violence raged outside, finally emerging to a new reality in which hundreds of Jewish children had become orphans and an ancient community's ambitions were suddenly reduced to survival and immediate emigration. Fouad had not had the privilege of his parents' education. During his teenage years, his family's resources were channeled to the mission of escape. He arrived in Israel as part of Operation Ezra and Nechemia, the clandestine airlift of Iraq's Jews to Israel. His first years in Israel were spent in an absorption center, a glorified refugee camp somewhere near Israel's northeastern frontier. By the time he was resettled in a moshav north of Tel Aviv, Fouad was too old for school. He parlayed his love of food into a career as a vegetable distributor. It took him more than twenty years to save enough money to open his own store in Tel Aviv.

Fouad took pride in his produce. His relationships with some farmers went all the way back to his years in the absorption center. He would get the pick of their crops. Despite his high prices, customers would travel from across the city to shop at Fouad's. But most of them missed the point. The vegetables were not the story. Fouad was. He was a horticultural expert and an uncompromising professional. This was more art than business for him. He could spend as much time as you had discussing the optimum time to pick a white peach. He could forecast the onset of asparagus season weeks in advance. He would put a deposit down on his orders at the Cherkesky Farm before anybody else. He bought fresh eggs only from Kibbutz Givat HaShlosha, on his way in to Tel Aviv early every morning. Even in his late seventies, in poor health, he would dart around the shop with the energy of a child, perfecting arrangements of cherries or grapes every time a customer moved them. He would have me sample any fruit or vegetable he felt was particularly good when I came in, even if it was his last one. "I'm boiling an artichoke in the back. Come with me. You have to try this," he would wheeze out between breaths drawn through lungs choked with emphysema. The disease was advancing but seemed impotent in the face of Fouad's vigor. After ten minutes in the store, you were so full, you forgot what you had come to buy.

When we placed a big order, Fouad would send one of his sons to help us carry it home. His older boy, Avi, had dropped out of high school early to help Fouad with the business. Avi had served as an infantryman in the Givati Brigade, coming home to work whenever he had leave. He continued to serve in the reserves. His absence must have hurt the business, but Fouad believed in IDF service. He owed his life and his family to Israel. I can clearly remember him beaming, his eyes glistening, whenever I came into the store in uniform.

Fouad passed away years ago, but his vegetable store is still in business. Avi, himself now past middle age, manages it together with his brothers. Fouad bequeathed a trade to his children and left them a successful enterprise. They are lucky in this respect. But they still live on the old moshav and commute to Tel Aviv every morning. They cannot afford to live in the city their customers inhabit. They still work from before dawn until after dusk, six days a week. They have little free time. They cannot afford to indulge in art, culture, or politics. They have not developed positions on issues like territorialism, theocracy, or democracy. They do not have university degrees. They do not speak English. In economic terms, this is the best life to which they can aspire. They have no choice but to succeed in the produce business, which may prove to be the best option for Fouad's grandchildren as well.

Each of the three constituencies I have discussed, the Territorialists, the Theocrats, and the Secularists, has taken pains to solidify its own position within Israeli society. Unbound by a constitution, each is free to exercise maximalist claims on Israel's resources without taking responsibility for these claims' effect on society at large.

The Secularists controlled Israeli politics until 1977, anointing select institutions and individuals as power brokers within Israeli society and the Israeli economy. These individuals' descendants grew up in neighborhoods with good schools. They went on to successful military service and graduated from university into a world rich in economic opportunity.

The Theocrats, who initially shunned Zionist politics, eventually became coalition kingmakers, extracting economic rents from successive Israeli governments in the form of study stipends, welfare grants, and exemptions from civic duties.

The Territorialists, who began as an illegal underground movement but now enjoy powerful representation within Israel's governing coalition, demand massive economic resources to provide security and infrastructure to the settlement enterprise.

The three constituencies are served by three separate education systems, each tailored to its partisan needs, each requiring its own funding, governance, and infrastructure.

Much of Israel does not fall into any of these three constituencies and is not represented by their respective visions. The Fourth Israel is composed of the many Israeli Jews who are forced to struggle with the challenge of economic survival and have little time for ideology, and of Israeli Arabs, most of whom buy into none of the three visions. The Fourth Israel lives in areas that Israelis call "the periphery": Dimona, Beit Shean, Qiryat Gat, Afula, Acre, Eilat, Umm al-Fahem, Rahat, Jisr az-Zarka, Majd al-Krum. Its Jewish members send their children to serve in the Israel Defense Forces, where their representation in frontline combat units is high. They serve in the Golani and Givati brigades, in the Border Patrol Units. They make up the bulk of the IDF's combat support strength. They are mechanics, quartermasters, drivers, cooks, sentries, and maintenance personnel. Their representation in the elite intelligence units that feed into Israeli technology firms is far lower than the Secularists'. Compared to the Secularists and the Territorialists, they are underrepresented at the Air Force Academy, in the Naval Academy, and in the prestigious Special Operations Units. The resources consumed by the Secularists, the Territorialists, and the Theocrats come at the Fourth Israel's expense. This group's needs, the most important of which is education, will never be addressed without a master vision for the Jewish State.

THE FOURTH ISRAEL'S EDUCATION

By Jewish historical standards, Israel's diversion of resources to parochial interest groups has produced an astonishing mediocrity in general educational achievement. Measured by test scores, Israeli Jews underperform their U.S. Jewish counterparts significantly. Israel's ranking in the Organisation for Economic Co-operation and Development's Program for International Student Assessment (PISA) will surprise many who remember the Israeli school system of the 1960s and 1970s, which ranked at the top of the world in mathematics and science achievement. As of 2012, Israeli students rank only forty-first in mathematics, between Croatia and Greece, and forty-first in science, between Slovakia and Greece.

Many studies point to the high correlation between educational outcomes and economic development. Until it is fundamentally overhauled, Israel's education system will continue to condemn the Fourth Israel to permanent economic hardship. The question of whether Israelis are willing to challenge this mediocrity is rarely asked, because Israelis are largely unaware of it. The same PISA exams include a self-efficacy survey, measuring students' self-confidence in mathematics. Israeli students score near the top of that survey despite their middling test results. As a group, they are painfully ignorant of the realities that exist beyond Israel's borders.

The generic weaknesses of Israeli education have been debated publicly for years. They include overcrowded classrooms, overworked and undertrained teachers, and disruptive behavioral norms among students. All are real issues, but Israel also faces a curriculum crisis. The current school curriculum is underequipping a new generation for the challenges of contending with a globalized world. As global playing fields level, the world will increasingly polarize into winning and losing camps. One must question to which camp Israeli society is gravitating. Israel's youth need uninhibited access to the global discourse. Their most important tool is the English language.

The revival of the ancient language of the Hebrews is attributed primarily to Eliezer Ben Yehuda. Hebrew played a critical role in forging a functioning national identity for new Israelis. Twentieth-century exiles from Germany, Poland, Hungary, Yemen, Iran, Iraq, Egypt, and Morocco shared little cultural commonality, at least on a superficial, day-to-day level. They practiced different customs and approached their Judaism in different ways. These communities would somehow have to come together if they were to function as a society and an economy. They would have to fight shoulder to shoulder against invading Arab armies, the orphaned Polish-speaking Holocaust survivor fresh off a ship from British internment camps in Cyprus and the dispossessed Arabic-speaking survivor of the Farhud.

The revived Hebrew language would become their glue. Without it, they might not have established the unity so critical to their survival. Today, a rich and vibrant Israeli culture flourishes in Hebrew. Hebrew is also a direct link between Jews and the early chapters of their ancient culture. But too many Israelis today are fluent *only* in Hebrew, and this carries a cost. It disconnects most of Israel, particularly the Fourth Israel, from the rest of the world and, critically, from its American cousins. Only Secularist Israel, rigorously educated and oriented westward, largely speaks English.

THE FOURTH ISRAEL'S ECONOMY

Israel's is an island economy. It enjoys almost no trade ties with its neighbors. As a Saudi acquaintance once told me deflatingly, "You are not part of the Middle East." This state of affairs, which has existed since Israel's independence, has led to an increasingly evident bifurcation in the Israeli economy, reflected in society at large. Broadly, the two segments of the Israeli economy can be thought of as the Exporters and the Exploiters.

The Exporters, forced to compete globally, represent the most competitive and innovative segment of the Israeli economy. Israeli exports include telecommunications, semiconductors, software, Internet applications, medical devices, biotechnology, and defense systems. This is the economy that most non-Israelis, viewing Israel from the outside, are exposed to. This is Start-up Nation. It competes globally, and wins.

Israel's Exporters are almost exclusively Secularists. Fluency in the English language is pervasive in this population. A meeting between an Israeli start-up technology company and an Israeli venture capitalist might be conducted in spoken Hebrew, but the presentation materials will almost invariably be written in English, as will term sheets, contracts, and any other documentation. Emails within technology companies will typically be in English. Many technology workers are immigrants. Studies have cited the effects of Jewish immigration from the former Soviet Union in the early 1990s on the Israeli technology sector. This immigration, which has made up a significant percentage of the industry's total human resources pool, brought a wealth of technical talent, and a set of new perspectives. But it is also important to note the high representation of American, Canadian, English, French, South African, and Australian immigrant talent in the Israeli high technology sector. Large parts of these communities were originally transplants from Silicon Valley and other global technology centers. They arrived with diverse perspectives, insights, and relationships, developed through intimate interaction with global clients, partners, and competitors. The medium of this interaction, of course, is English.

The Exploiters make different use of the island economy. Just as Israel enjoys almost no regional exports, there are virtually no regional imports. This leaves large swaths of the Israeli economy immune to foreign competition. Israel's 2011 cost-of-living protest movement chose cottage cheese as its emblem because cottage cheese costs much more in Israel than it does in Europe. Dairy products, like other perishable items, are not suitable for long-distance shipping, so the Israeli economy's dairy needs cannot be met by imports from Europe. Regional cross-border trade is not possible, making dairy an exclusively domestic industry. As with many industries that require economies of scale, Israel's dairy industry has naturally evolved into a near duopoly. The market dynamics that develop around monopolies, which are not unique to Israel, have contributed massively to the cost-of-living increases that sparked the protest movement. Similar phenomena have plagued Israeli banking, asset management, communications, and credit card firms, along with the hospitality industry, airlines, retailers, and importers.

I chair a nonprofit organization called Koret Israel Economic Development Funds. We provide small business loans and microloans to entrepreneurs in Israel's economic periphery. Koret has issued over $400 million in loans to date. The default rate on Koret loans is below 2 percent. These small borrowers, mainly women, repay their debts. The smallest 10 percent of borrowers is far more creditworthy than the largest 10 percent. Why are the banks not working with these communities? Israeli banks lend to oligopolies. They have to. Monopolies and oligopolies represent the lion's share of Israel's corporate credit market. Israeli banks cannot afford to be left out of the few large deals on offer.

Like many of its borrowers, the Israeli banking sector is itself an oligopoly. Lack of competition *allows* the banks to neglect small borrowers. It is expensive to lend to small borrowers. Making many small loans requires more credit officers than making few large loans does. As a result, whole communities in the Fourth Israel are locked out of the credit cycle. This stifles economic development. It forces otherwise capable businesspeople into the welfare system, where hopelessness and low self-esteem often conspire to perpetuate their disempowerment. The island economy's impact on Israeli consumers is grave. Its effect on the Israeli labor force is tragic.

The clear division between the Exporter and Exploiter segments of the Israeli economy has created a large and growing income gap. Israel ranks second among OECD nations in income inequality. Less apparent, it has created an opportunity gap and a motivation gap. For most of those who lack the education necessary to enter the export sector in Israel, employment opportunities are relatively few and unattractive, certainly considering Israel's high cost of living. Transitioning to the export segment of the Israeli economy requires skills not cultivated in the Fourth Israel, among them fluency in English. There is very little middle ground in which people can make a competitive living in the domestic market. As the marginal difference between social security stipends and wages in the domestic employment market shrinks, increasingly large segments of the population opt for welfare support instead of working. Israel's welfare budget has been rising precipitously. In 2000, 331,000 Israeli households were receiving support from the Social Services Ministry. By 2014, 464,000 households (20 percent of Israeli households) were being served.[*]

Perhaps most grievous, the inequality within Israeli society breeds resentment. The inherent incompatibility between the four Israels is already unsustainable in the long term. This resentment, particularly between the most disenfranchised elements of the Fourth Israel and Israel's Secularist elites, threatens to turn Israel's evolving challenge of reconciling competing visions into a crisis.

Much of Secularist Israel is unfamiliar with the Fourth Israel's challenges. The Secularists live in one of the most thrilling cities in the world, Tel Aviv. Their orientation is global, not local. They are economically independent. They

---

[*] Taub Center (taubcenter.org.il/helping-hand-social-welfare-spending-in-israel/).

feel no pressing need to engage with the Fourth Israel's problems.

The Theocrats and the Territorialists effectively secure funding for the lives they aspire to through the political process, winning at the Fourth Israel's expense. Theocrats and Territorialists have a vested financial interest in ignoring the Fourth Israel's needs. Unrepresented, underfunded, undereducated, and trapped on an economic island, the Fourth Israel has been left to wither.

4

Schism

THE FIRST SCHISM: AMERICA AND ISRAEL

The fact that most American Jews have no idea how Israeli Jews commune on Yom Kippur, and vice versa, is a symptom of the separateness of the two communities, each evolving on its own path. In less than one hundred years, the eighteen-hundred-year-old model of Judaism as a multipolar, loosely linked diaspora has evolved into a distinct bipolarity. We are two largely self-contained, mutually unfamiliar structures. It was my generation that set the two communities on divergent courses. The distance between us is now growing rapidly.

This alienation is a recent development. When Israeli Judaism originally coalesced, it was intertwined with most of American Judaism. There are two fundamental approaches to sustaining Judaism in the United States today. One, espoused by most of Ultra-Orthodox Jewry, imposes insularity and ignorance on its members, limiting the risk of apostasy by restricting these members' exposure to the outside world and intentionally preventing them from acquiring the skills necessary to survive in that world. This is not a Zionist constituency. It cares little for an Israel created and sustained through mortal efforts. It does not and will not support Israel's survival.

A second approach, espoused by the Modern Orthodox, Conservative, and Reform streams of Judaism, is more consistent with the trend that has been in force for the past eighteen hundred years of Jewish history and has allowed Judaism to maintain its relevance. These groups struggle constantly to reinvent and revitalize Judaism. Over the past seventy years, a new force has emerged as central to the identity of this innovative Judaism: Israel. Israel has provided a wellspring of meaning for this segment of the American Jewish community. Jewish self-determination in Israel has endowed American Jewry with dignity. The image of Jews standing up to defend themselves, after centuries of disempowered victimhood, has fostered pride and confidence in three generations of American Jews, many of whom have also been thrilled by Israel's cultural vitality and its people's achievements in the arts, medicine, and science. The specific segment of American Jewry that sees Israel as a central component of its identity fuels massive efforts such as Birthright Israel, AIPAC, Israel Bonds, and a host of other institutions. It provides funding for Israeli museums, universities, schools, and nongovernmental organizations. This segment has become a minority among American Jews.

It is precisely this minority—most American Jews of my generation, and especially of my children's, have little interest in Judaism or in Israel—that finds its brand of Judaism increasingly unwelcome in Israel. When its members interact with Israel, the politicized Judaism they discover is unrecognizable to them. With the exception of Ultra-Orthodoxy, American Judaism exists along a fluid, generally mutually respectful spectrum of religiosity. Politics has little bearing on American Judaism. No Jewish group enjoys the legislative or executive power to gain political control over practical aspects of other Jewish groups' lives, so no group aspires to do so. Of course, this is not the case in Israel. The Israeli Orthodox religious establishment, having gained control over the center of world Judaism, exerts power over other Israeli Jews—and over American Jewry.

The Rabbinate's restrictions on Jewish women praying at Judaism's holiest sites extend, of course, to American Jewish women. This is an affront to people accustomed to gender equality in their home communities. The Rabbinate's refusal to recognize Reform, Conservative, and even many Orthodox conversions to Judaism in America undermines the authority of the vast majority of American rabbis and, by extension, alienates the majority of affiliated American Jews. A rejection by Israel's religious establishment carries the practical weight of Israeli law and cannot be ignored, even by non-Israeli Jews. Israel is the seat of Judaism, and the Israeli government is its official custodian.

Mere pronouncements from the Israeli religious establishment against Reform or Conservative American Jews carry the spiritual weight to alienate millions. In a 2015 radio interview, emblematic of the tone that has been adopted by Israel's religious establishment, Religious Affairs Minister David Azoulay said this: "The moment a Reform Jew stops following the religion of Israel . . . I cannot allow myself to call such a person a Jew."

The Israeli religious establishment has, by choice, begun to alienate an increasingly broad segment of American Jewry. As a blanket rule, Reform and Conservative conversions in America are disqualified in Israel under all circumstances. (Keep in mind that Reform Judaism is the largest organized Jewish movement in America.) This has been the case for some time. In recent years, even Orthodox conversions have been disqualified. These include conversions performed or approved by Rabbi Haskel Lookstein, who, for more than fifty years, led one of New York City's most prominent Ortho- dox Zionist congregations, Kehilath Jeshurun; Rabbi Gedalia Dov Schwartz, chair of the Beth Din of America for twenty- two years; and Rabbi Mordechai Willig, a dean at Yeshiva University, the educational institution most closely linked with Orthodox Judaism in America. Together with unaffili- ated Jews, the Modern Orthodox, Conservative, and Reform Movements represent well over 90 percent of American Jewry. Thus, more than 90 percent of American Jews have discovered that their Judaism does not merit recognition by the nation-state of the Jewish People. Can these people be expected to remain loyal to that state over time?

The religious establishment is only part of the problem. I recently spoke with an American Jewish friend—we will call her Sarah—whose son is in my daughter's class at a Jewish day school in New York City. Amber and I originally chose the school for its Israeli teachers, who would speak to our girls in Hebrew. It took us time to understand how much more value a Jewish day school could provide to an American Jewish family than a secular school might. Like most secular Israelis, we wore our Judaism lightly in Israel. The Dati (religious) establishment was so manifest that we found it easiest to define ourselves in opposition to it. Our wedding was an expression of our effort at self-definition. Judaism's constant presence, felt through the national holidays, which of course are Jewish holidays, the palpable peaceful descent of Shabbat, even in secular Herzlia, and our relationships with observant friends made Judaism inescapable. We took it for granted.

America, of course, is a different story. If an American Jew is not taking active measures to affiliate Jewishly, as I did on Yom Kippur growing up, he will most likely lose his Jewishness. My older brothers' Jewish experience is the rule, not the exception. Jewish day school provides an immersion in Jewish knowledge and tradition. Our school does this without a hint of proselytizing for any stream of Judaism. Jewish ritual and prayer are taught, but in an open format, which allows for broad interpretation. Our children are exposed to Jewish history, Israeli history, and Jewish and Israeli music and culture. Perhaps central to all of this is community. Children and parents gather frequently, at formal class events and in informal get-togethers. During our first few months at the school, we were invited to Shabbat dinner at the home of a different family almost every week. Had I been asked to picture this life from Israel before our move, I probably would have thought the cadence and intensity of such interaction excessive. Once we were in New York, however, it could not have felt more natural—and necessary.

Sarah and I spoke about a phenomenon we both had observed. Many Israelis who are transient in New York, as we were, treat the school as a way station where their children can maintain their Hebrew and get a good enough secular education that their transition back to school in Israel will be smooth. Many of us are uninterested in Jewish community, and unwilling to exert the effort required to maintain it. These families tend to avoid school gatherings. When they do attend, they cluster together with other Israeli families, often eschewing participation in the wider group's activity or discussion.

I understand their ambivalence. American Judaism's— even secular American Judaism's—heavy reliance on ritual feels foreign to secular Israelis. The efforts it devotes to community building seem forced, almost desperate. The American Jewish celebration of Israel, which necessarily takes a very wide view, seems ignorant and naïve in light of the granular reality that secular Israelis live. I agree with Sarah that there is a hint of scorn in these Israelis' approach to school gatherings. Although it is not backed by the force of Israeli law, this scorn can have as savage an effect as the Israeli government's formal rejection of most of American Judaism. It says, "We have little in common with you. We are uninterested in understanding your reality and see no use in helping you to understand ours." This sort of interaction reflects a growing rift that will threaten both Jewish communities. But it will threaten Israeli Jewry first, and far more tangibly.

American Jewry was once distributed across a continuum

of affiliation with Israel, from strongly supportive and heavily invested to generally uninterested. The uninterested end of the spectrum has grown broader. The thinning opposite end, Israel's strong supporters, is gradually being turned away, as key elements of its identity are rejected by the Israeli government and, increasingly, the Israeli people. Unless this changes, organized Judaism in America will gradually seek models for living a meaningful Jewish life that do not include Israel. Whether they fail or succeed, this represents an ideological failure of Zionism, and a direct threat to Israel's existence.

THE NARROW RUBICON

There was a honeymoon period of a year or two in which Israeli fighter pilots led a charmed life. It began with operational flight certification in your squadron. After four grueling, competitive years at the Academy, the Operational Training Units (OTUs), F-15 or F-16 school, and an in-squadron operational training period, you finally had tenure. When you were at the Academy, your friends were being dismissed regularly. In the OTU, you were competing to get into F-15 or F-16 tracks. After OTU and the type-schools (F-15, F-16, et cetera), you were split from your remaining friends into the various IAF fighter squadrons. Getting your operational certification signified your arrival. You were finally part of a permanent family. You were the low person on the totem pole, but if you were good, you would not remain there for long.

You also had an exciting new friend in the F-16. If other fighter planes had been designed around a big engine, or powerful radar, the F-16 was built around the pilot. You sat in a railless bubble canopy at the front of the aircraft, with 360-degree views. Operating weapons systems from the cockpit, what we called "switchology," was intuitive. Everything you needed was at your fingertips. The aircraft integrated and presented combat information simply, in one place. In a fight, you never had to take your hands off the stick and throttle or your eyes off your opponent. After a few flights, you were no longer riding in the airplane; you were wearing it, like a tailored suit, a rocket suit that would propel you from a standing start to a supersonic climb straight into the stratosphere. In a fight, you would turn so violently that no other fighter plane in the world could keep pace.

Your experience of reality was no longer limited to what your five senses could perceive. The aircraft's sensors were fused to your senses, the tactical picture they presented superimposed on the sky around you and the earth beneath you. I occasionally found it impossible to resist fixation on the incongruity between that darting ghostlike symbology and the static physicality of the earth onto which it was projected. Cruising into a high-altitude fight on a clear day, you could take in all of ancient Israel from a single point; Hebron, where Abraham had purchased his plot, the Valley of Ella, where David faced Goliath, and the caves near Ein Gedi, where he confronted Saul, all lay almost directly below. Mount Nebo, where Moses had stood for his only look into the Promised Land, would be easily visible to the east. Sinai, where he and the Israelites had crossed, was a quick traverse across Israel's narrow midsection to the west. The ruins of the Roman legions' camps at Masada, the Abbasid mosque of al-Aqsa, the Crusader fortress at Montfort, the Ottoman fortifications around Old Jerusalem, Napoleon's Hill at Acre, and the British army's base at Latrun, remnants of physical empires once thought permanent, nodded inertly to our own ethereal endurance and reminded me of the responsibility we had accepted to preserve it.

Grateful for the responsibility we had earned, confident in our aircraft, and safely established in squadrons, young pilots had a year or two to turn their attention to matters beyond the Air Force. After that, they would be assigned demanding leadership roles within the squadrons, at headquarters, or back at the Academy. At the time, Israeli society still harbored a romantic fascination with IAF pilots, especially fighter pilots. Whether or not we felt we deserved the attention, few of us were above making use of it. On Friday nights, our cohort was usually at a private party in some Tel Aviv apartment or nightclub. Those could go on right through to breakfast. On Saturday afternoons, we had beach parties. We could not afford Tel Aviv's great restaurants or its arts scene, but for those two years, I imagine none of us would have changed a thing in his life. We were young and vigorous. It felt as though anything of significance happening in the world must be happening right here, around us. Beyond the sense of purpose, we shared an intimacy, a trust, and a bond of loyalty I had never experienced before. Most Saturday nights, a group of fighter pilots would congregate at a small bar on LaSalle Street in Tel Aviv. All of us were recent Academy graduates, from two or three different classes. There were no girlfriends or outside acquaintances. It was just us and the stories of the past week in the squadrons. We celebrated milestones: successful operations, promotions, or nominations to serve as instructors at the Academy. We tormented one another over embarrassing publicized flight safety incidents, romantic flops, and humiliating defeats in training fights. Without the stress of squadron life, and the filters we put on for outside company, we were a different tribe on Saturday night. Having touched base and held on to it for a few hours, we would split up by midnight for another week at the squadrons.

For some of us, this honeymoon period extended into our stints as instructors at the Academy. Instructor candidates would undergo six months of instructor certification training at the Combat Flight Instructors School, housed on the Air Force Academy campus at Hatzerim. We would dedicate one day or night each week to our home squadrons and spend the rest of our days at Instructors School. The course load was interesting, and often fun. In order to refamiliarize instructor candidates with the cadet's experience of constant exposure to new stimuli, the helicopter pilots got to fly jets and the fighter pilots got to fly helicopters. We would pack food and fly out on off-road helicopter adventures through the desert, south of Hatzerim, stopping for lunch at scenic vistas that were inaccessible by road.

There was a morning ferry flight from Tel Aviv to Hatzerim every day and an evening flight back to Tel Aviv. My routine at the time was the same as that of most instructors or instructor candidates like me. I would leave my apartment early every morning on an old moped I had bought from a rental company. It was a short ride to the small airport on the outskirts of Tel Aviv, where I would catch the flight. Once I boarded the flight, I was usually asleep before the doors closed. We all were.

After the ferry arrived at Hatzerim, we normally had a few hours of classroom work at Instructors School and then flew three training flights. After the last debriefing of the day, we would scramble to put the training squadron in order and close up in time to make the ferry flight home. We would try to finish any homework or reading we had on the flight to Tel Aviv, freeing up another night in the city.

During those early years at the squadron and at Instructors School, a special project would come up every once in a while that required English language skills. I was the junior-most guy in the lineup and, conveniently, American, so these projects generally landed on me. They were usually tedious tasks, such as researching the malfunction history of some obscure aircraft subsystem in the technical manuals, or briefing foreign air force pilots on arrival procedures at an IAF base. I soon became informally established as the English project guy for the entire wing, which occasionally resulted in an interesting assignment. I once provided fighter escort to Jordan's King Hussein on an overflight of Israel. I participated in the IAF's first training deployment to Turkey and spent a week there on what felt like a vacation, speeding around that beautiful country at low altitude by day and exploring the city of Ankara by night.

One of my tasks was speaking to American Jewish groups on their missions to Israel. In the mid-1990s, when I was in Combat Flight Instructors School, I addressed a group from one of the United Jewish Appeal Federations on the IAF

Academy campus at Hatzerim. The UJA event was scheduled for late in the day, and I was hoping to get through it quickly enough to make the Tel Aviv ferry.

When I arrived at the auditorium, it was empty. I received word from the young soldier who served as its usher that the group was about ten minutes behind schedule on its tour of the base and that there might be further delays. I would be cutting it very close. I called the Instructors School squadron house to ask my friends to try to buy me a five-minute delay in the ferry's departure. Through the telephone receiver, I could hear the bustle of the squadron packing up for the day.

The auditorium was still empty. I walked outside to find the visitors standing in the parking lot. Outdoor refreshments were being served. Most of the visitors were chatting with their guides and politely eating dry Air Force cookies in the desert evening heat. Some had gone for a bathroom break. It would take time for them to come back. I was definitely going to miss my flight. I walked back into the auditorium and called the Bachelor Officers Quarters to book a room. I would have to settle for a lousy dinner on my bed at the BOQ, probably eat a lot of those Air Force cookies, and fall asleep watching TV.

The UJA group finally filed into the auditorium, faces glistening and red. The older members fanned themselves with hats and smiled enthusiastically as they noted the air-conditioning. There were a few teenagers wearing exasperated expressions. I could picture the arguments that had ensued when these kids' parents had announced that the family was going on a UJA summer mission to Israel. I sympathized. I wouldn't have wanted to be sitting here either, watching yet another Israeli walk me through a slide deck.

Eventually, everyone settled into their seats and I gave my standard IAF presentation, starting with the Air Force missions: defense of the nation's airspace, support of ground forces, et cetera. I went through a day in the life of a squadron, described the career path of an Air Force officer, and concluded with the strategic picture of the Middle East and its expected evolution.

I knew what to expect when I opened the floor to questions. Older people asked about the biggest threats facing Israel and my assessment of our readiness to confront them. Younger people, who normally became engaged at some point during the presentation after seeing some of the pictures calculated to achieve that effect, asked if I had ever been scared, or if anyone I knew from the Academy had died. I was prepared with rehearsed answers to these questions. The talk went as a dozen others had gone before it.

I usually left the auditorium after these talks, but I had nowhere to be that night, so I stayed and chatted with the group, who also appeared to be in no rush to leave. As I stepped down from the stage, people began to gather around me and introduce themselves. "I'm a cardiologist, recently retired," one said. "This is my twelfth trip to Israel," said another. "My son just graduated from Northwestern." Their openness reminded me of my childhood. These people could have been from Miami, or from Lenox, Massachusetts. I was surprised to find myself wishing they would stay longer. I had made a new home in the Israeli Air Force, but I suddenly realized that my old home was still standing where I had left it. I had never really shut that door, and now I had an urge to peek back inside.

I asked what the new Northwestern graduate was doing next year. Did he have a job lined up? What had he majored in? How was the job market today? But the group was more interested in my experiences. What did I think about the Peace Process? What is the flight time from here to Damascus in an F-16? What really happened with that American pilot who was shot down over Bosnia? I always imagined that people must be unsatisfied with the very general answers I could give to these kinds of questions, so I tried to connect personally. I told the gentleman who had brought up the downed U.S. pilot, Scott O'Grady, that I had read a good magazine article about the rescue. I asked how closely people followed the Peace Process. I asked whether they liked *The New York Times*'s coverage or *The Wall Street Journal*'s.

I was beginning to feel like one of the group when an older woman who had been standing just outside my immediate circle, listening quietly, leaned in and said, "I just want to tell you, young man: Your English is excellent. Almost good enough to be an American." I smiled and thought to make a joke about my steep university tuition having paid off but noticed that she was not smiling, just looking at me earnestly. She was complimenting me, admiring my mastery of what she took to be a foreign language. Other people nodded in agreement.

As I turned off the television in the BOQ late that night, I conceded that my feelings of nostalgia and kinship with these American Jews were not mutual. I was foreign to them. They could not get past the flight suit and the crew cut. It was as though they were meeting an actor backstage after a Broadway show and could see him only as the character he had just played. Lying in the dark, I was struck by the idea that I had inadvertently lost an important part of my Jewish identity by becoming an Israeli. At the same time, I wondered whether keeping that identity had ever been a real possibility. Looking back, the chasm between America and Israel seemed wider and deeper than it had been when I first crossed it. Could one person be at home in both of these Jewish worlds?

Many of Israel's American Jewish supporters identify with Israel because they believe it is the right thing to do. This is different from identifying on a visceral, personal level. Many do not know Israelis personally. Our common cause is based on a conceptual ideal rather than personal kinship. We are foreign to one another as human beings. This connection is more fragile than many of us tend to think. It is conditional, subject to differences in style and disagreements on policy. Other than programs such as Birthright, which sends young Jews who have never been to Israel on an intensive ten-day trip, we are doing little to strengthen our connection. If anything, we are sabotaging it.

Israel's viability will be deeply compromised if the country comes to represent nobody but its own inhabitants. Not only will it lose its moral raison d'être, it will struggle to sustain itself in practical terms. American Jewry has provided critical funding for Israel's social and economic development and has played an instrumental role in maintaining American diplomatic support for Israel. Can Israel afford to lose this partnership?

By the same token, Israel has endowed American Jewry with the confidence of a plan B and the dignity of self-determination for the past seventy years. For those with a sense of history, Israel is the safe refuge that Jews so tragically lacked during the Holocaust, when even America's doors were shut. How will the remaining generations of American Jewry be affected if their relationship with Israel is severed?

The interdependence of American and Israeli Jewry is as critical as it has ever been, but awareness of it is weakening quickly. There has been no defining event of separation between the world's two major Jewish communities, and relatively few on either side of the Atlantic have even noticed their drift apart. Like the frog in the proverbial pot of slowly heating water, we have failed to mark our incremental progress toward the boiling point.

THE SECOND SCHISM: THE SECULARISTS

Left unchecked, the split between American and Israeli Jewry will become terminal, but an even more dangerous rift is opening within Israel itself. Israel's small Secularist community fights Israel's wars. It sustains the export economy that funds the wars. As the self-proclaimed "beautiful face of Israel," Secularists serve as Israel's connection with the wider world. This is the only group that performs all three critical functions.

The Territorialists serve in the military, often with distinction, but contribute little to Israel's export-led economy and enjoy little engagement with the outside world. Considering the cost of maintaining and securing the settlement enterprise, this group is a net economic drain.

With very few exceptions, the Theocrats do not serve in the military, do not contribute to the economy, and seek no engagement with the outside world.

Jewish members of the Fourth Israel serve in the military and make up a large proportion of the workforce but are too embattled economically to embrace any social or political vision. They subsist from day to day, underfunded and undereducated. Their contribution to the Israeli economy is neutral to moderately positive. When Israeli Arabs are included, it is negative.

Few Israeli leaders even try to articulate a clear and compelling vision for *all* of Israel, certainly not a vision for Judaism in Israel. The Israeli electorate continues to demand little more from its leaders than the furthering of the immediate, parochial interests of the three conflicting minority groups. This has been the case since Independence. Today, sheer numbers are shifting increasing democratic power to Israel's Theocratic elements. With no comprehensive, inclusive vision for Israeli Judaism, the gravest danger facing Israel is the disenfranchisement of the Secularists. This process has already begun.

Israel loses many of its best and brightest when the children of Secularist Israeli families temporarily residing in the United States approach army age. Most of these families leave Israel planning to return. They may have gone abroad for a job, or for a degree. They may plan just to save enough money to afford a comfortable life in expensive Tel Aviv.

But the decision to enlist is different when considered from America than it is in Israel.

The behavioral economists Eric Johnson and Daniel Goldstein studied organ donation programs in Sweden and Denmark. Despite the two countries' cultural similarities, their citizens' willingness to donate organs is markedly different. At the time of the study, about 86 percent of Swedes donated, while only 4.25 percent of Danes did. Citizens in both countries make their organ donation decisions when applying for a driver's license. In the Danish application, the applicant is asked to check a box *if he wishes to join the organ donation program.* In the Swedish application, the applicant is asked to check the box *if he wishes* not *to join the organ donation program.* It would appear that most of us seek to avoid the effort of making serious decisions and that this avoidance instinct is strong enough to influence social trends decisively. We allow the status quo to guide us.

The Israeli eleventh grader living in Israel is surrounded by peers who plan to enlist. He will typically not think of service as an active decision; it is just what everyone does. But viewed from the distance of American shores, enlistment *is* a decision. Only from afar does it become clear that the benefits of service might no longer be worth the heavy personal costs.

Of course, we are not there yet. Most of today's best and brightest Secularists still choose to remain in Israel. The departure rate is a trickle and not a stream. But the progression from trickle to stream will be sudden, and once the dike bursts, there will be no way of halting the flood.

The experiment below was originally designed by two Swiss researchers in the field of behavioral economics, Ernst Fehr and Simon Gächter. Let's pretend that you and I are participants in a version of the experiment adapted for this book. We are among ten players sitting around a table. Each player is given ten $100 bills. They are ours to keep, as is any amount of money we earn playing the game. The game is played in rounds. In each round:

1. Each of the ten players must decide either to ante $100 into a pool at the center of the table, or not to ante. (You cannot ante any other amount; it is $100 or nothing.)

2. Once the size of the pool on the table is set ($1,000 if everyone antes), the organizer doubles it (in this case bringing the total pool to $2,000).

3. The pool is now distributed evenly among the ten players, irrespective of each player's contribution. That is, if everyone indeed contributed his or her $100 to the pool, generating a $1,000 initial pool, which was then doubled by the organizer to $2,000, each player would receive $200 back. Having invested $100, and having been paid back $200, each player will have netted $100. As a group, we will be $1,000 richer.

Let's begin:

Round 1: Off the bat, one player (me) chooses not to ante, even as all the other players (you among them) do ante. The initial pool is now $900 instead of $1,000. It gets doubled to

$1,800 instead of $2,000. Each player, including me, receives a payout of $180 instead of $200. Only $800 of value has been created by the group instead of $1,000. You have netted $80 instead of $100. But I, having ventured $0 and having been paid $180, have netted $180. I now have $100 more than you do.

You are confused. Do I not understand how this game works? Do I not realize that we can all get rich if we just cooperate?

You are also angry. You have contributed to making me $100 richer, while I made you $20 poorer than you could have been. You and your colleagues built value, making us all richer, while I destroyed value, making you all poorer.

On the other hand, nine players did act responsibly. The system may not be working perfectly, but it is still working. As long as the nine of you all remain loyal to one another, you are each still making $80, even if I withhold my ante again. That's better than nothing.

It turns out that in groups of ten people, there is often one who will withhold his participation in the first round. Everybody else, indeed most of humanity, is conditionally trusting. You, for example, recognized the value of cooperation, chose to participate in the first round, looked around to see how many others were participating with you, and then considered your strategy for the next round on that basis.

Round 2: Although torn, you decide to ante. You feel it is the right thing to do. We play the round, and you are again disappointed to see me withhold my ante but encouraged that the other eight players participated again.

A third and a fourth round yield the same results. Your eight kinsmen are still cooperating, but you are becoming nervous. It is true that the math has not changed, but you notice yourself getting angrier at me through successive rounds. You think about how satisfying it would be to teach me a lesson by withholding your own ante once, and demonstrating how fragile this game can be. You suddenly realize that the others are probably becoming angrier as well and might be thinking the same thing. Can you still trust them?

That question is answered in the fifth round. Eight of you ante, but a second player joins me in withholding his ante. There is now only $800 in the pool. The pool is doubled to $1,600, and $160 is distributed to each player. The new withholder and I each make $160. You make only $60.

As we prepare for the sixth round, you have become suspicious of everyone. If four more players defect, you realize, you will actually be losing money by participating in the next round. You can assume that other players are thinking the same thing.

As if there is any doubt that this team's game is now over, the following happens before we play round 6: We are all informed that there are other groups playing the same game in adjacent rooms. One of those groups is larger than ours. It has already played dozens of rounds and made thousands of dollars. It has enjoyed 90 to 100 percent participation in every round. This is due, in part, to special rules that allow the majority, composed of players who participate consistently, to punish players who withhold their antes by banishing them from the game. This large group has begun calling itself America. The organizers have just begun inviting players from other groups to join America. But only players who have exhibited a perfect record of anteing in their own games are eligible.

Our game is now over, of course. The eight of you are off to America, leaving my new friend and me with our meager winnings. Notice that in just one round we went from a sustainable, profitable state of eight anteing players to inevitable extinction. Viewed from the organizers' vantage point, and from yours as a reader, the outcome was obvious from the beginning. Once additional participants began withdrawing, the group's demise quickly became unstoppable. The team went from a sustainable (solid line) state to an extinct (dotted line) state instantly, without pausing in the warning range (gray line). Why was this so unclear to the other players?

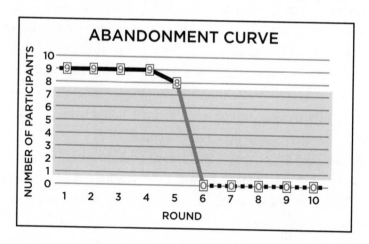

The players shouldering the burden of sustaining Israel's economy, upholding its democracy, and defending its borders are gradually departing for safer shores in the United States. As individuals, they may not recognize the obvious endgame that will play out once most of their community departs. As more Secularist Israelis depart and fewer return, the burden on those who remain in Israel grows. The endgame should be obvious, but Israel's three parochial communities are too busy fighting for their short-term interests to recognize it.

These thoughts were foreign to me until my family's current sojourn in the United States. For eighteen years, I was prepared to sacrifice everything I had for an ideal I believed in, without a moment's hesitation. I had done my thinking in advance. When the alarm sounded, I did not have to think. I would be airborne in two minutes. I might not return, but I was comfortable with that possibility. I was willing to fight even when I did not agree with a given mission, tactically or morally. A soldier cannot pick which of his duties to fulfill on the basis of his personal views. As my eminent instructor understood so well, you either buy the whole package, committing to its totality, or you walk away. I bought the package, and I have repeatedly chosen to keep it.

But looking at that trade today, older, maybe wiser, and, most important, living in an American reality, would I still act without a moment's thought? Will I still be willing to act ten or twenty years from now if my own vision for Israel has become diluted beyond recognition? Will a future me be willing to trade his life, for example, for a democracy on its last legs, undermined by the very people I will have been defending, long since abandoned by those with whom I shared common cause? Twenty years from now, how many Secularists will agree to fight and die for a rising theocracy, eventually to be overrun by its neighbors, most of its defenders having left the table long ago? Should the Secularist die fighting just to delay the fate that awaits minorities in the Middle East for a few short years despite his government's best efforts to hasten it?

These questions might seem premature to many readers. Until recently, they did to me. But ask Israelis living in Palo Alto or New York City if they dropped everything to board a flight to Israel the last time war broke out. Their parents' and grandparents' generations did exactly that in 1967, 1973, and 1982. Some did, and still would, of course, but you will find that most are far less eager to ante up than their parents were. Almost nobody flew home in 2006 or in 2014. Of course, these more recent wars were not perceived as existential by most Israelis. Reserves were, however, called up. Reserve units suffered casualties. There was a time when it was inconceivable for an Israeli reservist to sit at home while his unit was engaged in combat. But many now have done so.

It is not the people who have changed. It is the calculus. I know the people. They are friends from Wall Street, from Boston, from Silicon Valley. They were once among Israel's most dedicated defenders. They served in combat units. They served extra time as officers. They served in the reserves for years. They flew in my squadron. They graduated from the Academy with me. They volunteered. They donated. They still donate. These Israelis are outstanding citizens, as their parents were, but the trade is now a different trade. Ask these truly model citizens how eager they are to go back and fight. Many today find the question difficult to answer. Ask them if they would send their *children* into the fray, to staff checkpoints or patrol casbahs when they would otherwise be getting degrees at UCLA or NYU. Frighteningly for many, that is a much easier question. I will answer it myself in the coming pages.

5

Boiling Point

I joined Squadron 144 in 1994 with two other new F-16 pilots. One had been at the Academy and the Operational Training Unit with me. The other, a transitioning F-4 Phantom pilot, had joined us at F-16 school. We spent our first six months in the squadron's Operational Certification Program, where we would become expert in the specific avionics and weapons systems deployed at 144, learn squadron-specific battle doctrines, and catch up with the regional intelligence narrative that would continue unfolding throughout our service. We would learn to fly with our squadron mates in every possible pairing of pilot and weapons systems officer, and of flight lead and wingman. The intimacy we developed was critical. Like everyone else, I was highly motivated, both professionally and patriotically, but it was this small tribe that I would have in mind when I went into battle.

Knowing one another well made us a more effective fighting force. We would often fly internal training fights with no radio communication, forcing each pilot into his formation mate's head. We studied the conditions under which a specific squadron member was likely to be aggressive and those under which he would be conservative. We noted different pilots' tendencies for complex formation tactics versus straightforward brute-force maneuvers. We learned how some people were instinctively biased toward a detailed battle plan, while others intuitively attached a high premium to flexibility and optionality. We understood one another's strengths and weaknesses intimately and worked together to improve. Over time, we also discovered which pairings within the squadron worked the best.

Our Operational Certification Program was commanded by Yishai, a 144 pilot who had graduated from the Academy two years before me. Yishai had grown up on Kibbutz Sde Nechemia, at the base of the Naftali range in the Upper Galilee, several miles from the Lebanese border. Sde Nechemia was founded by Dutch Jewish immigrants, who had drained the surrounding swampland to create farmland. The kibbutz eventually became a major exporter of water drainage and irrigation products.

Yishai was one of the most gifted fighter pilots I have ever known. In a crowded turning fight, he had an uncanny ability to track each aircraft, friend and foe, and to understand the complex battle narrative as it unfolded. Whether he could see an aircraft or not, he always had a sense of its position, its energy state, and, most important, its pilot's options. He perceived evolving threats intuitively and defused them creatively. He was rarely shot down in training flights. Yishai was also an outstanding marksman. With all of the F-16's sophisticated systems, the one weapon that could never be spoofed or jammed was its cannon. It fired dumb (unguided) 20-millimeter shells at a rate of one hundred rounds per second. If you mastered the art of aiming it within the short windows of opportunity that might open up during a dogfight, it was a very effective weapon. Israeli Air Force F-16s have scored more aerial combat kills than any other nation's. Dozens of these kills were cannon shots. Of course, some marksmen were better than others. Yishai almost never missed.

It turned out that Yishai and I were a strong pairing in the air. We clicked on the ground as well. He would become the closest friend in my Air Force family. Over the next twenty-five years, our lives' paths would diverge as widely as they possibly could. Our views would become so different that the gulf between us encompassed the majority of Israel's bitterly divided communities. But I still consider him a brother.

I met Amber not long after joining 144. She was on leave from Cornell University's hotel school for an internship. Having spent summers in Israel, she was also drawn to the country's exhilarating mission. She was taking a semester to experiment with living there. We were introduced by telephone. I remember driving up the one-way street to the Dan Tel Aviv Hotel, where she was staying. I was looking for parking, assuming I would call up to her room from the lobby. Passing the hotel, I saw a pretty blond girl sitting on the edge of a large planter in a poorly lit area, a short distance from the main entrance. Her legs dangled casually toward the sidewalk. I pulled up to the left curb, realizing somehow that this was Amber, and rolled down my window.

"Amber?"

"Yes. Amber." She slid off the ledge and walked around the front of my car.

Amber had also left a broken family for boarding school at a young age. We both knew what it was like to grow up in transit, to have no home base. We were always on the lookout for an opportunity to put down roots, but we were never able to commit to any patch of earth for long enough. As much as we craved it, permanence felt unfamiliar to us, even unsafe. We both knew how to feign belonging. We were experts at concealing our isolation behind a smile, but we recognized it in each other immediately. We became instant confidants.

Amber went back to Cornell in August, but we stayed in touch through letters and frequent calls. She was evaluating career opportunities at American hotel companies but also seriously considering returning to Israel. It was an optimistic moment. Israel had just signed a peace agreement with Jordan. Regional peace felt like a real possibility.

At the time, I was living in an apartment on King David Boulevard in Tel Aviv with a roommate, Tiffany, an American medical student at Tel Aviv University. In November 1995, I joined some friends from the Academy at a rally in support of the Oslo Peace Accords. These agreements laid out a plan for Palestinian autonomy in Judea and Samaria and the Gaza Strip. Autonomy would evolve into full Palestinian statehood as Palestinian violence was gradually curtailed and negotiators worked toward a final status agreement. The rally took place in the square in front of Tel Aviv City Hall, about two blocks from my apartment. The atmosphere was celebratory, with stirring speeches and performances by popular Israeli artists, the crowd often joining in. The flight crew community at the time was by and large in the peace camp, the segment of the Israeli political spectrum willing to risk territorial concessions for the chance of achieving peace. We met so many friends from the Air Force that the rally became a sort of reunion. After hearing Prime Minister Yitzhak Rabin speak, a few of us crossed Ibn Gabirol Street to get a beer at the small pub at the corner of King David Boulevard.

We did not hear the shots, but police sirens started to blare before we sat down. A limousine careened out of the alley behind City Hall, streaking across Ibn Gabirol Street and up Bloch Street, followed by unmarked Secret Service cars. We could see the crowd in the square across the street dispersing rapidly. Something unusual was unfolding. We did not know what had happened, but we realized that traffic would now be building up and decided to call it a night. We all had early starts at the squadrons the next morning. If something important had happened, we would hear about it soon enough on the news. In the few minutes it took me to walk home, ambulances and police cars sped down King David Boulevard, rushing from City Hall toward Ichilov Hospital. The street was quickly closed to civilian traffic. I turned on the television when I got upstairs. Yitzhak Rabin had been shot after his speech. He was at Ichilov Hospital, in critical condition. I called Amber. It was early afternoon in Ithaca.

"Oh my God. I can hear the sirens. Wait. Let me turn on the TV."

Eitan Haber, Rabin's close adviser and bureau chief at

the Defense Ministry, appeared on both of our screens. I could recognize the entrance to Ichilov Hospital behind him. Tiffany was doing a rotation there.

"The government of Israel announces with shock, and with great sadness, the death of Prime Minister and Minister of Defense Yitzhak Rabin, who was murdered by an assassin tonight in Tel Aviv. May his memory be blessed."

"Oh my God," Amber repeated in a whisper.

Another siren wailed outside my window, then faded and stopped as the ambulance turned in to the hospital entrance. The line was quiet for a few seconds.

"Tal, shouldn't you be calling someone from work right now? Why are you talking to me?"

"No. There is nobody for me to call." I knew why I was talking to Amber. I had adopted a very specific persona in Israel. I was playing Israeli. When I was confronted with a moment that challenged my grasp of the entire enterprise, I would hide my distress. With Amber I had no pretense. We were both trying to reconcile the same intense feelings that drew us to Israel with an Israeli reality that was sometimes too complex for us to understand. This was such a moment. Rabin's assassin had been a Jew.

I stood at the open window looking out at Tel Aviv. The crowds that had reveled in the square just an hour earlier were now flowing slowly outward from the new ground zero in reluctant waves. They walked past the window quietly. They already knew. An occasional empty ambulance cruised slowly up the street without lights or sirens. It was over.

This was not the kind of war I had been equipped to

fight. It was a war I was barely aware of. It was difficult to imagine that a Jew in Israel, one of us, could disagree so fundamentally with his fellow citizens that he would turn to violence. People would later describe Rabin's assassination as the shocking moment when Israel's innocence was shattered. Perhaps we should not have been so shocked. The time bomb of Israel's conflicting visions had been ticking for decades. Reconciling them had not been our top priority. We had always been distracted by something more urgent, the fervent enemies straining at our borders, planning our annihilation. For many of us, 1995 provided the first glimpse of what might be the end of the road we were on.

As Amber prepared for her final round of exams as an undergraduate, Israel went to general elections. Six months after the Rabin assassination, the 1996 election was seen as a referendum on the Oslo Accords. Shimon Peres, Rabin's natural successor, would have the electorate's mandate to move toward a final peace deal, the realization of a dream celebrated in Israeli nursery rhymes, political campaign slogans, radio songs, and Friday evening prayers. Rabin had sung along with the "Song for Peace" at the November rally. The bloody song sheet was still in his breast pocket when he was hoisted onto the operating table.

But it was Benjamin Netanyahu who won the election. By a margin of less than 1 percent, the citizens of Israel voted against what Amber and I saw as the obvious trade. It would have been a bold trade, to be sure. Israelis would be making themselves more vulnerable to Palestinian violence. We would have to weather that violence for a period, hoping for the other side to eventually reciprocate our gesture by ending its incitement, recognizing the Jews' right to self-determination, and committing to living side by side in peace.

For Amber and me, the 1996 election laid bare another fundamental misconception. The risk takers were not the majority, not for now. The hope and courage that had drawn both of us to Israel had lost out to fear. This had no practical implications for me, of course. I was committed. I would have no choice but to try to view the result as a temporary setback. As Churchill had said of the Americans, we Israelis would eventually do the right thing. We just had to exhaust all other options first. But Amber had made no commitments. She had just graduated into a surging U.S. economy. Just as the prospect of a life in Israel was losing much of its luster, Amber's options for a career in the United States were more exciting than they had ever been.

"It's all so fragile," she told me by phone. "You think you are fighting for one thing, and suddenly it turns out it was for something totally different. And you have so much riding on all of this, Tal. You are all in. More than enough for both of us."

But Amber was undeterred. If anything, the election results increased her resolve to return to Israel. There was a long struggle ahead, and she seemed eager for an opportunity to participate in it. Amber came back after graduation and moved into the King David Boulevard apartment with Tiffany and me. I introduced her to the squadron a few months later. Yishai, two other pilots, and I had organized a scuba diving trip in the Sinai, near the Red Sea village of Sharm el-Sheikh.

Amber had earned her scuba license the week before, in a crash course at the Tel Aviv beach. Still uncomfortable managing the cumbersome diving equipment, she was always the last into the water. The guys would bob offshore watching patiently while I stood on the beach tightening her buoyancy vest or reattaching the weight belt she had dropped.

"Go ahead. Don't wait for me! I'll catch up!"

But they waited. Apparently, Amber's drill was more entertaining than the fish or the coral. After a few dives, Amber earned the nickname Handbrake, which rhymes with Amber in Hebrew. This was a mark of affection, and it came much more quickly than I expected it might. Amber and I were lucky to have found each other. We were a rare match, and this was clear to everyone.

We spent our evenings at the Sinai Star, a corrugated tin shack near the middle of the village, which served fresh fish and cheap, cold beer. We ate most of our dinners there, and we spent our evenings playing cards or backgammon with its Bedouin proprietors on rugs laid out on the desert floor. On our first night, I fed some of my fish to the owners' fat black cat, and for the next three or four nights, Gusgus never left my side. At our farewell dinner, I ordered Gusgus his own plate of shrimp, fresh from the Red Sea. Apparently impressed by the closeness of our relationship, Yishai took to referring to me as Gusgus, and he has ever since.

Yishai the kibbutznik seemed almost literally incapable of eating kosher food when another option was available. He ate every exotic mollusk and crustacean that made its way through the Sinai Star's outdoor kitchen. I have never kept kosher, but for some reason I have always been conscious of whether the food I eat is kosher. I favor kosher food in the company of people I suspect might keep kosher themselves. Yishai was part of a community that implicitly valued non-kosher food above kosher food. Nonkosher food was a declaration of his independence from our ancestors in Europe's ghettos. Eating in the company of people who might object was an opportunity to put his defiance on display. This was Yishai's Zionism. Yishai's last name was Shellach, which had been Hebraicized from a European Jewish name, as most of the kibbutz pioneers' names were. Shellach is a biblical word meaning "missile," fittingly (for a member of Kibbutz Sde Nechemia) found in the Book of Nechemia, but when I became Gusgus, Shellach became known as Shellfish.

A few months after the trip to Sinai, I served as Yishai's wing-man on weekend alert duty at Israel's southernmost fighter base, Ovda, near the resort city of Eilat. I liked this particular assignment. At the time, there were no permanently based fighter squadrons at Ovda. It would just be the two of us and a skeletal maintenance crew at the alert hangars. We spent the first few hours in the underground operations room, plug-ging in to the intelligence stream, briefing with the air com-bat controllers who would be accompanying us on alert from their base about a hundred miles north of us, and reviewing weather and other potential flight hazards. After that, we were on our own, quietly waiting for the alert siren to go off. I would spend most of my days reading. After four years of intensive training, I was tentatively beginning to revisit old

interests. I had taken some of my history books from Georgetown and Tel Aviv University out of storage. I reread Bernard
Lewis, Fouad Ajami, and Philip Hitti. *The Arabs in History*
had once been a tedious sophomore slog. Now that I had
interacted with the Arabs and with Islam, these books became a vivid reference point. The people who occupied the
broken states around us had once represented the pinnacle
of civilization. At their peak, during the Abbasid Caliphate,
they had laid the foundations of algebra and modern medicine. Al-Razi's *Kitab al-Mansuri fi al-tibb,* translated into
Latin, would continue to serve as a medical textbook in the
West almost seven hundred years after its original publica-
tion. As Europe descended into centuries of primitive super-
stition and illiteracy, Greek philosophy and theater were
preserved in Alexandria, in Arabic, together with volumes of
original Arabic literature. The tragic Persian love story of
Leila and Majnun, a medieval Romeo and Juliet, appeared
nine hundred years before Shakespeare's birth. The voices of
One Thousand and One Nights, Sinbad, Ali Baba, and Alad-
din, still echo in the Western imagination. Most of this literature would fail to find purchase in much of today's benighted
Middle East.

I sympathized with modern Arab bitterness. Self-
destructive as it was, I understood the Arab compulsion to
blame an external force for the tragic decline of an entire
civilization. The West's colonial legacy and its contemporary
ascendency made it an easy villain from the Arab perspective.
Despite the Jews' chronic failure to gain permanence in European culture, Israel's successes made it an easy proxy for
the Western oppressor in Arab eyes. We were colonists to

them. The inconvenient fact that we did not have an empire from which to colonize, that there was no home country to which we could return, could be ignored, so as not to spoil their bitter narrative. The war against the Jews was an easy political sell in Arab capitals. Whipping up hatred was infinitely easier than taking responsibility for the Arab future. I acknowledged, already then, that our children would be condemned to fight the same war we were fighting.

At night, I would sit outside the ready room under a brilliant desert sky picking out the constellations, characters my father had introduced to me twenty years earlier. Orion the hunter dominated the winter night. In the high desert, miles from city lights, the hunter's left shoulder, Betelgeuse, burned deep red. The arrow formed by using Orion's belt as its base and Betelgeuse (in Arabic, "the home of Orion") as its tip always pointed north. That was a trick my father had taught me so that I could orient myself. Once you knew where north was, he explained, you could walk with confidence—in any direction you chose.

We had eaten dinner in the ready room on Friday evening. I was sitting in my spot, on a plastic chair that had been left there by some previous alert crew, when Yishai came out with two glasses of Turkish coffee, which he brewed in the authentic method, in a small Arabic *finjan* over a gas stove. It was powerful stuff that would keep me up all night, though it did not affect Yishai. He had grown up on it and easily drank half a dozen shots every day. He lit a cigarette and sat on another plastic chair. We were on a short alert, wearing G suits and torso harnesses, but it was still cold in the desert night. The coffee was good.

"How's Amber's Hebrew coming along?" he asked. Amber had been taking immersion classes in Tel Aviv.

"It's good," I said, "but it looks like she's going to be taking a job writing for the *Jerusalem Post* in English, so I'm not sure how much Hebrew she'll need to speak."

"Do you think she is ever going to get it? Do you think she will ever understand what you are doing here?"

"What are you talking about?" I shot back. "She already does get it. What do you think she's doing in Israel? She threw away a great career to be here. Of course she gets it."

"She gets *you*," Yishai said. "That's different. I bet she admires you for throwing away whatever it is that you threw away, but that doesn't mean she's on the same mission."

Yishai was as blunt as any Israeli. If he perceived personal boundaries, he did not heed them. But he also never spoke without conviction. If he didn't know what he was talking about, he wouldn't talk.

"Maybe," I said. "Time will tell. And whatever her reality is today, it might be different tomorrow."

"I don't think so. I think this is about you more than it is about Amber. If you knew you wanted to stay here, you would have found a good Israeli girl to settle down with. You and Amber are great together, but you are with her for another reason. You still want the option. You haven't figured out if this whole thing is for you."

"That's a pretty neat theory, Mr. Shellfish," I replied. "Congratulations. You might even be right. Of course, there is no evidence to suggest you are, but don't let that shake your confidence."

"Let's remember this conversation." He reached into his

shoulder pocket for another cigarette. "I'll bring it up again in a few years. If you go back to America with Amber, even for a couple of years, I say you are not coming back here." Twenty years later, we still talk about that night.

Yishai married Sagit, a lawyer from a moshav near Sde Nechemia. Amber and I would not be married for another few years, but we became very close as couples. We spent our weekends together and borrowed each other's cars and furniture. Amber and I had adopted a Jack Russell terrier in England and named him Ernest. When Ernest was bred, we gave Yishai and Sagit the first puppy in the litter. Our children would be friends from infancy.

After Amber left the *Jerusalem Post* for a higher-paying job at the English edition of *Haaretz* newspaper, we parted with Tiffany, and for the first time, we were living on our own. But as we took shape as a couple, Yishai and Sagit began to unravel. Yishai had been offered an accelerated career track in the Air Force that would require a long-term commitment. The offer forced him to consider his career ambitions from beginning to end. Yishai had been indoctrinated as a child with the stoic ethos of the kibbutz. The principles of self-sacrifice and national service were central to his identity. His natural talent only confined him further. The nation had invested many millions of dollars in his training, and as far as Yishai was concerned, his resulting skills belonged to the nation.

At the same time, he had his own interests. He had a degree in architecture, a field he would never pursue professionally if he signed a long-term contract with the Air Force. He spoke impeccable English, which gave him a clear sense of the world beyond Israel. He was one of those who understood, for example, the better deal on offer for Jews in America. He was adventurous by nature, and he often imagined a life outside the track he had established for himself. We had spoken about the idea of Yishai and Sagit spending a few years in the United States, studying or working. He could easily secure a defense industry job in Washington, or California, or Texas, or pursue an advanced degree at an American university. I encouraged him to consider that option. This would be his last realistic opportunity. I thought he had seen too much to go back to the kibbutz. My voice only added to a rising cacophony. Yishai's overpowering sense of responsibility clashed loudly with his individuality and his ambition. The Air Force, determined to lock him in, played every card it had, sketching out a path that could ultimately take him to the top of the command chain. On the other hand, Sagit had her own ambitions and her own views on what was good for Yishai.

Without discussing the idea in advance, Yishai took a sudden leave of absence from the Air Force—and from his marriage. He left home. For a few weeks, he and I spoke by phone while Amber spent time consoling Sagit. Yishai had little understanding of what he was seeking at the time. He understood instinctively only that he needed some distance and independence from his commitments in order to consider them honestly. He roamed the country alone. We did not know where he spent his days or where he slept at night. He checked in with me by telephone every week or two, but for only a few minutes. Eventually he got rid of his telephone and disappeared completely. I knew he did not want me to look for him. I was part of the noise he was seeking to quiet.

Amber continued spending time with Sagit, helping her through a crisis she would not allow herself to regard as temporary. But a few months after Yishai broke contact, we got a call. He had come home, and Sagit had agreed to take him back. She asked us to come to their house in the north. When we entered, Yishai was wearing a *kippah*. He gave me a long hug, but before he embraced Amber, he apologized that this would be the last time he would ever do that. Yishai was now a religious Jew. He had found a rabbi and was studying to make up for what he described as decades of lost time.

Although his Jewish knowledge was still basic, Yishai described his sudden connection with Judaism as a reunion with a family from which he had been separated at birth. On some unconscious level, he had always known of this family's existence, and without yet knowing any of its members as individuals, he already felt a love from which he would never again want to be separated. He was not replacing us. He wanted all of us back in his life, his family, his friends, the Air Force, even the kibbutz. He was the same person. He had the same warmth, the same earnestness, the same mischievous dry humor that brought a twinkle to his eye. He was back, just with a new side that we would need to learn to accommodate. Before we left the Shellach home, I told Yishai that between us, nothing would change, whether this awakening was temporary or permanent. Nothing other than his squadron nickname. "Shellfish" was not a kosher nom de guerre. He would become simply "the Fish."

Although our friendship remained strong, Yishai's spiritual awakening was not temporary. Over the next few years, he became ensconced in a mystical brand of Judaism. Sagit respected it but did not buy into it at first. She was an independent secular woman, with her own career and her own identity. She had never depended on Yishai to define herself. Yishai observed Shabbat. She did not. If Amber and I wanted to visit on a Saturday, we would call Sagit on her cellphone to coordinate. But over time, the force of Yishai's new Judaism began to fill a void that must always have existed in the family. Sagit learned Judaism by observing Yishai, and she came to value it. She valued the community that struggled with questions of purpose unselfconsciously, immune to the cynicism that pervaded Israeli Secularism. She valued the rituals that bound the community together. One by one, she began to adopt these rituals. Within a few years, I had my final hug with Sagit. Our families began to see less of each other.

Sagit and Yishai went on to have five girls. They moved their oldest daughter, Gaia, into a religious school. Gaia's four sisters have only ever studied at Orthodox Jewish schools. Yishai and Sagit sold their television set and eventually removed all literature from their home other than religious texts and Air Force material. They now live in a community with no secular members. Yishai and I remained close, but we shared fewer and fewer common acquaintances. He stopped spending time with Air Force friends. Eventually, he gave up flying, explaining that the person he became in the air could no longer exist in the same body as the person he hoped to be. Although Yishai is neither a Territorialist nor a Theocrat, he found little to connect him with

the Secularist culture within which our friendship had originally been forged.

Yishai's final role in the Air Force was as commander of a
fighter squadron. Beyond the high professional standards he
demanded from his pilots, his unusual new identity fostered
a unique (for the IAF) atmosphere of Jewish questioning
within his squadron. His spirituality was too big to ignore.
Yishai was too big to ignore. He was not a young dilettante
trying Judaism on for size. If Yishai was asking a question, it
was a question worth asking. Was our traditionally Secularist
vision compelling enough to support the identity of a nation?
Especially this nation? What was it that actually made us
Israeli?

Speaking with Yishai at the time, and with friends who
flew in his squadron, I first understood the need for a new
model to define the relationship between individual Jews and
Jewish statehood. This model would have to tolerate a diversity of approach, even celebrate it. It would not accommodate artificial divides such as the one that some old friends
imagine must exist between Yishai and me. It required a lowest common denominator. The three visions of Israel could
never be merged into one, but they would have to be reconciled.

PART
TWO

| The Code |

6

Stones and Spirits

For those who hope for a Jewish future, the challenge is to offer a model of Judaism compelling enough that the vast majority of Jews, in America and in Israel, will embrace it willingly. This model will have to be *exclusive* enough to delineate membership in the Jewish *nation* clearly. It will have to maintain fidelity to the traditions that define us, but at the same time it will have to be *inclusive* enough to allow *individual Jews* to participate fully in modernity. This is a tall order.

In the summer of 1988, between Exeter and Georgetown, I stumbled on an artifact that would, years later, come to form the core of my conception of Judaism. I had met Dave Aisner the summer before, on that Jewish teen tour. The son of Holocaust survivors, Dave had been raised secular, in a Polish-speaking home in Detroit. He had found religion on his own, as a teenager. He and I had come to Israel seeking different things, but we seemed to have found them in similar places. We stayed in touch, both resolving to make our way back to Israel. We worked during the month of June and saved enough money to spend July and August in Israel, hitchhiking around the country, sleeping on the beach, in youth hostels, or at the homes of Israelis we had met on our summer program.

In Nazareth, we stayed at a Christian youth hostel above a bakery, where we spent long nights talking to Hamud the baker over Turkish coffee and *knafeh*. After two days in Nazareth, we decided to walk to Zippori, an archaeological site Dave had read about, wedged onto a narrow plateau in the mountains a few miles north of town.

We set out before dawn, walking through the darkened alleyways of Nazareth's ancient covered market. We passed the churches and monasteries we had visited on previous afternoons, together with loud hordes of tourists and pilgrims. Now their courtyards were silent, even our footfalls dampened by the humidity of Galilee in August. I have never crossed these stone passages, polished smooth by centuries of sandaled traffic, without imagining the other feet that have passed here, and the illegible lessons of history that must be written in their cracks.

From the Basilica of the Annunciation we climbed north, up the mountain on which the old city rests, passing the Maronite church and cresting the northern ridge at the Salesian monastery just as the monks were emerging from their dormitories. We walked through the al Safafira quarter and followed the highway north for several miles, to the turnoff at the modern-day agricultural village of Tsipori. Morning had already clanked to life when we walked into town. Tractors bouncing down the graveled main street kicked up dust that churned in the day's first hot breeze, blending with the scents of Galilean summer rosemary, cypress, and lavender, a fusion that has since animated Israel in my mind. I can recall it easily, even from the distance of the United States. As we walked past Tsipori's northern greenhouses, contemporary and banal, the town gave way, suddenly and unceremoniously, to the ancient plateau itself, its magnificent Roman-era cardo stretching before us, the central boulevard of Zippori.

Nineteen hundred years before our walk up the cardo on that hot summer morning, the Roman imperial province of Galilee was convulsed in violence, in the final throes of Jewish dominion in the land of Israel. Three successive revolts against the Roman Empire marked milestones on the road from sovereignty to Diaspora. In the first, the Great Revolt of the year 70, the Second Temple of Jerusalem was destroyed, and with it the capital's status as the physical center of Jewish worship. Pinhas ben Samuel, eighty-third and last in the line of Jewish High Priests, was killed during the sacking of the temple. The institution of Jewish High Priesthood ended with his death, and the structure of Jewish governance was demolished.

Jews who had survived the Great Revolt were now scattered across Judea and Galilee. Disparate synagogues replaced the Great Temple as hubs of Jewish congregation. Local rabbis, in hundreds of small communities, replaced the High Priest. Jewish theology and law until that time had been transmitted to successive generations through the

Tanakh, the Old Testament, and through the Oral Law, the indispensable addendum to the Tanakh. The Oral Law was the medium through which written law was translated into practice. In the first generations of Judean dispersion, the Oral Law, no longer under the singular custody of a High Priest, began to evolve in multiple tracks and developed inconsistencies. Independent rabbis handed down individual interpretations, often in isolated synagogues and schools.

The Second Jewish Revolt (115–117 C.E.) and the Bar Kochba (Third) Revolt (132–135 C.E.) ultimately failed. Most of the remaining rabbis of Judea were killed, enslaved, or exiled. The yeshivas were destroyed. Even the compromised Oral Law's continuity was now in jeopardy. By the year 135, only a few thousand Jews remained in Galilee. Yehuda Hanassi was among them.

As an adult, Rabbi Yehuda lived in Zippori. He, and the city, had not participated in the revolt. This fact, together with his close relationships with the Roman leadership, allowed Rabbi Yehuda to live and prosper as a leader of the surviving Jewish community. Yehuda Hanassi's defining act of Jewish leadership was the compilation of the Oral Law into a singular written work, the Mishna, which would enable it to survive dispersion. He may have assumed that sovereignty could be reestablished within a generation or two. Of course, his Mishna and the subsequent commentary known as the Gmara—together the Talmud—would end up serving as a common code of Judaism for the next nineteen centuries, from Siberia to Mumbai, to Casablanca to San Francisco to Buenos Aires. Yehuda Hanassi's prominence in the city of

Zippori, and throughout Judea and Galilee, ensured that his Mishna would be widely embraced among the remaining rabbis, and among Jews living beyond the boundaries of rabbinic authority. It sparked a new mode of engagement. Its internal contradictions and omissions, perhaps intentional, invited the Gmara's dissent, debate, and amendment. Debate would often take place in forums as small as two interlocutors, neither of them a rabbi, in a study format that became known as *hevruta*. The Mishna, and the generations of dissenting commentary and amendment that would come to surround it, were arranged around specific questions of Jewish law, broken into sections, or orders: Zeraim (seeds) mainly deals with agriculture, property, and the economic sustenance of community; Moed (festival) deals with Jewish ritual and its observance; Nashim (women) deals with Jewish family life, including marriage and divorce; Nezikin (damages) deals with civil agreements, their enforcement and their abrogation; Kodashim (holy things) deals with the Jewish community's relationship with God, including sacrifice, blasphemy, and excommunication; and Toharot (purifications) deals with both physical and spiritual hygiene.

Jews throughout the vast, disconnected Diaspora would be debating the same Talmudic questions and refining their answers for millennia. In order to prepare for this engagement, Jewish boys would, of course, be taught to read. They would be taught to debate. They would be encouraged to question. In one generation, at Zippori, Rabbi Yehuda Hanassi transformed Jewish identity. The Jews would no longer be defined in territorial terms. They would not depend on any individual's leadership. Their identity would be imprinted in a code, distributed among all of its adherents. I was not the first to have searched in vain for a legacy in the ancient stones. Our legacy has really resided in Rabbi Yehuda's code and its millennia of permutations. In contrast with the many empires whose ruins dot the terrain surrounding Zippori, Judaism's medium is not physical. The Jewish code runs in the nation itself, and it has followed us everywhere. This code has a name.

Twenty-five years after that morning hike to Zippori, I was speaking at an investment conference in Tel Aviv. As a sponsor of the conference, Clarity Capital had been allowed to set up a marketing booth in the main lobby. We had decided to use the strategic location, where all of the conference participants would pass, to run a behavioral experiment known as the Wisdom of Crowds. Over the course of the day, hundreds of participants were asked to estimate the number of gumballs we had placed in a large glass jar. The winner would be the person whose estimate came closest to the actual number of gumballs. We offered a substantial prize, as an incentive for players to invest some effort in the game. There were 463 gumballs in the jar. Our results were striking, but not abnormal for this experiment.

The average of all responses was just over 461, within 0.25 percent of the actual number of gumballs. The closest individual guess was 467. In the Wisdom of Crowds game, the average guess is frequently better than the best individual guess. Even in cases when an individual player wins a game, he will almost inevitably lose to the crowd when the game is played multiple times.

Interestingly, the crowd's guesses typically include wild misses. Except in extreme cases, even these bad guesses play a role in conjuring the wisdom of the crowd. We have experimented with various objective rules for filtering the crowd's data for outliers, or ridiculous guesses, in an effort to improve accuracy consistently. This is a difficult exercise unless the person writing the rules knows the correct number of gumballs in advance. Even the "bad" guesses, presumably made by "bad" guessers, add to the crowd's wisdom. In many cases, a small group of expert guessers is less wise than a large crowd of diverse guessers. It is as though the crowd is its own intelligent organism, dependent on its members in the aggregate but almost completely independent of any individual member, even the most expert.

Originally designated Vox Populi by Francis Galton in a 1907 article in *Nature,* in which Galton reports on a crowd accurately estimating the weight of a cow, the Wisdom of Crowds has been applied successfully to many real-world problems including predicting election results, professional sports scores, and the commercial success of Hollywood movie releases. It has been used to make complex decisions in large organizations. In his 2004 dissertation on Galton's insight, *The Wisdom of Crowds: Why the Many Are Smarter Than the Few and How Collective Wisdom Shapes Business, Economies, Societies and Nations,* the *New Yorker* science writer James Surowiecki asserts three prerequisites to achieving wisdom in crowds: intellectual diversity, independence of contribution, and a mechanism for aggregation and reconciliation. Of course, for the crowd to function as an intelligent organism, it must also be trying to answer a common question or set of questions.

When considering the unlikely story of Jewish survival in the Diaspora, it is difficult to ignore the neatness of the theory that Crowd Wisdom served as Diaspora Jewry's method of governance, that *this* was the code. The questions that form the framework of Jewish governance were first drafted intentionally, by Yehuda Hanassi, at Zippori. Dispersion created the condition of *independence*. Communities in the Russian Pale, for example, were cut off from the ghettos of Western Europe, or the coastal cities of North Africa, or the colonies of the New World. Each interpreted its Talmud independently. Each amended its interpretations independently.

Jewish communities in the Diaspora were culturally diverse, each influenced by its particular surroundings. Bankers in the Venetian ghetto were affected by their interactions with the Venetian business community, and by the language of those interactions, making their experience distinct from that of Ottoman Jews, for example, or from that of the Jewish communities of Yemen or India. Together, these separated communities formed a mosaic of *diversity*.

Periodic migrations and expulsions over the centuries forced the *aggregation* and reconciliation of ideas that had diverged in isolation. The simple average that we used to aggregate guesses at the number of gumballs in a jar was an unsophisticated operation. This qualitative Jewish reconciliation would have been far more complex, but it served the same function. Jewish communities from Castilla, Aragon, and Granada, for example, each with its separately evolved traditions, were expelled from their lands in 1492. They converged in Amsterdam, in Istanbul, or in the outposts of the Americas in the first decades of the sixteenth century. Together with the Jews of Portugal, expelled soon after, they were forced to reconcile traditions in their newly merged communities. If a Jewish community in Amsterdam was to accommodate the refugees of these once distinct communities, it would have to reconcile their divergent traditions. Four hundred years later, Eastern European Jews of diverse traditions converged on the Lower East Side of Manhattan, beginning a reconciliation among themselves. Within two generations, these communities had almost completely merged with the established German Jewish community of New York, itself having reconciled its traditions with the city's original Sephardic community.

If the model of Jewish history as an exercise in the Wisdom of Crowds had occurred to me as a teenager admiring the mosaic floors of Zippori, it was only as a vague intuition. I had never heard of Crowd Wisdom. But looking out over the yellow hills of Galilee from Rabbi Yehuda's vantage point, I could imagine the moment those hills would become foreign to us for eighteen centuries. Even as a teenager, I was overwhelmed by the improbability of surviving exile and dispersion for so long. It could not have been arbitrary. The Jewish population was too small. It had never been centrally led. There was no pope. Over the many generations of Diaspora, there had been too many opportunities to evolve separately, to assimilate, or just to die out. We *had* evolved dramatically, but we had evolved together. Somehow, we still had a coherent identity after eighteen hundred years. There had to have been a code, and as it governed us primarily in exile, it could not have been in the stones. It was written, instead, in the dispersed nation's consciousness.

ONE MAP, MANY ROUTES

I began pursuing spirituality toward the end of my active military service. As in high school, I was not seeking God. I was not seeking community. I had that. I was seeking orientation. I did not want to be told how to behave; I would make my own decisions, but I did want a sextant against which I could check my position and heading on the map of my own principles.

I read Jewish religious texts and commentary and discovered a labyrinth of ethical questions and answers, erudite interpretations of the answers, and nuanced dissent with the interpretations. I discovered study groups at a Tel Aviv synagogue. Their members read from the same texts and asked many of the same questions Yehuda Hanassi had asked, but each against the backdrop of his or her individual story. We were navigating from different origins to different destinations, but we sought a common orientation, a North Star. I discovered my own compass in our legacy, and I came to cherish it.

But I found troubling moral inconsistencies in the original texts, the Bible itself. Most careful readers do. In chapter 31 of the Book of Numbers, for example, Moses admonishes his generals after their battle with the Midianites. Although they were victorious, the generals had failed to act in strict

accordance with his orders. Moses lectures the officers outside the camp. The orders he had issued before the battle
were to smite every last man, woman, and child of the Midianite nation. The Hebrew army indeed smote all of the Midianite men, and some of the Midianite women and children,
but not all of them.

> So they made war against Midian, just as the Lord had
> commanded Moses, and they killed every male . . .
>
> And the sons of Israel **captured the women of Mid-
> ian and their little ones** . . .
>
> And Moses and Eleazar the priest and all the leaders
> of the congregation went out to meet them outside the
> camp. And Moses was angry with the officers of the
> army . . .

Moses's response:

> **Now therefore, kill every male among the little ones,
> and kill every woman who has known man inti-
> mately** . . .

After the second massacre, while deliberating what to do
with the surviving women and children, Moses turns to God:

> Then the Lord spoke to Moses, saying . . .
>
> levy a tax for the Lord, one in five hundred of the
> persons . . . and give it to Eleazar the priest, as an offer-
> ing to the Lord . . .

> And from the sons of Israel's half, you shall take one
> drawn out of every fifty of the persons . . . and give them
> to the Levites . . .
> **And the human beings were 16,000, from whom
> the Lord's levy was 32 persons** . . . (Numbers 31:26ff)

Was human life not a Jewish value? If you save one life,
it is as though you have saved an entire world, the Talmud
says. Was this not an irreconcilable contradiction, the God of
the Hebrews desecrating a Jewish value, ordering the murder
of innocents? I sought and found many creative interpretations of the passage, but none satisfied me. The order had
come from the Lord himself, which limited the reader's lati-
tude to interpret it.

The Bible's treatment of the Midianites, the Amalekites,
and others suggested a disturbing paradigm for modern Judaism, in which the religion was little more than an empty ves-
sel, an ancient mask worn over the modern face of values
that really took form in Enlightenment Europe. The sanctity
of life was an Enlightenment value. Human rights were an
Enlightenment value, perhaps also originally derived from
the Hebrew text, yet clearly contradicted within that same
text. In this model, the exercise of practicing Judaism and
reconciling it with modernity was simply an exercise in am-
plifying those Jewish themes that reinforced Enlightenment
values while muting, even ignoring, those that conflicted
with modern sensibilities. Judaism, I was beginning to fear,
might essentially be indistinguishable from any other value
system that emerged during or after the Enlightenment—

Pluralism, Empiricism, Americanism—just with different rituals.

Perhaps Reverend Thompson's generic Judaism was more authentic than I had appreciated. Once you recognized the ideals behind the mask, what was the use of confusing matters and calling yourself Jewish? Why not cut to the chase and admit you were simply the moral product of modernity? Reconciling a God who commands slavery and genocide with modern Jewish reverence for human life and dignity seemed needlessly convoluted. Couldn't John Locke, or the U.S. Constitution, or the Universal Declaration of Human Rights serve as the navigation aids I was seeking in Judaism? Uncorrupted by contradiction, would they not be more accurate and easier to use?

It turned out that the Jewish navigation aids worked well. I was just not reading them correctly. The Midianite genocide need not be read as prescriptive. It can be seen, instead, as an important point on a Jewish moral map. The Torah had laid out a vast atlas of human experience. The Talmudic tradition had served as a practical overlay, updating the map and providing the layers of interpretive insight that kept it relevant. The analogue in physical navigation is a globe, the accurate spherical representation of earth that might reside in an office or a home. It is the map, however, and not the globe that we carry in the cockpit and with which we navigate in practice. There are hundreds of map types, each representing a different projection of the globe onto paper. Different projection methodologies—Mercator, Cassini, Gauss-Kruger—can be applied to different navigational tasks. Variables such as distance to be flown, or latitudes crossed on the route, inform their selection. No map is perfect for every application. New perspectives and refinements have emerged continually over the centuries. Marinus, a cartographer who lived in the time of Yehuda Hanassi, just thirty-five miles north of Zippori in the port of Tyre, introduced one of the earliest cylindrical projections. Almost two thousand years later, Google still designs new projections for digital mapping. The actual routes we fly are influenced by our choice of maps.

Optimal routing between two points may change over time as new projections (interpretations) emerge or as other factors shift. The magnetic polarity of the earth, for example, changes gradually but constantly, forcing navigators to periodically update their instruments' magnetic declination corrections. Local magnetic deviations, anomalies in the earth's magnetic field, are also mapped and updated, allowing for appropriate adjustments. Changing political realities affect navigation routes. Instead of taking a direct route, flights from Tel Aviv to Mumbai fly sixteen hundred miles south before turning east toward India, because they are not permitted to overfly the Muslim Middle East.

Even having corrected for these evolutions, navigators do not follow prescribed optimal routes blindly. Transitory factors such as winds aloft, storms, temporary flight restrictions, or even other air traffic influence navigation decisions, often dramatically.

Looking at a U.S. Instrument Airways chart, with hundreds of possible destinations, millions of combinations of origin and destination, and billions of routing options among them, it is difficult to imagine the system functioning without central control. And yet thousands of pilots use the system every day, freely choosing their own destinations and charting their own routes. In most cases, the air traffic control system serves only an advisory function. The result is not chaos, but an exquisite balance of freedom and order. Armed with common maps, charts, and instrumentation, the pilot is both an individual, enjoying personal freedom, and a cell in an organism that functions coherently, efficiently, and safely.

Moral navigation may present more subtleties than physical navigation, but the Jewish approach to it is similar. The Midianites appear on a moral globe, a representation of the earth as it is. The Jewish nation has cultivated, and continuously refines, its own particular system of maps, charts, and instrumentation. This system has bound us as a community while still allowing us freedom to wander. The navigator chooses her own destination, using maps, charts, and instruments to plot her route.

Perhaps paradoxically, the diversity of our individual readings, and our diverse choices of destination, help to define us as a coherent nation. The Jewish Crowd in Diaspora did not receive dogma from above. It wrestled with its own moral governance. It reached conflicting conclusions and reconciled them over time, incorporating new projections and evolving realities, leaving its members to correct for the winds that prevailed in specific eras—and to choose their own destinations.

Once I encountered the theory of Jewish Crowd Wisdom, I began to experience it, both in Israel and in the Diaspora.

Despite distractions, temptations, and a sometimes hostile Israeli government, a segment of world Jewry, including Orthodox, Conservative, and Reform Jews, engages in vigorous debate, between the movements and within each. Crowd Wisdom may be damaged and fading in both centers of Judaism, but its core elements are still in place. These elements may be used to formulate the medicine that could cure the Jews' otherwise terminal condition.

Although I began studying Jewish texts in Israel, I did not attend regular prayer services until a stint working at Clarity's New York offices. Amber and I had gone back and forth on the question of the girls' education for most of the year before we moved from Tel Aviv. Was this primarily an opportunity to immerse them in America for a few years, strengthening their American identities, or a threat to the Israeli identities we had carefully cultivated in them?

We decided to split them up. Ella, having lived in Israel for twelve years, was a fully baked Israeli, conscious of her identity and comfortable with it. She enrolled in a nondenominational New York school. Only the younger girls went to Hebrew day school, with the aim of preserving their Hebrew and continuing to cultivate what we saw as their Jewish identities. After our warm welcome, Amber and I became more involved with the school than we had expected to be. Among the school's community-building functions, there is a weekly morning prayer service that parents are invited to join. I began attending whenever I could.

The congregants were a diverse group of parents. Some were religiously committed, keeping kosher, observing the Sabbath, and supplementing their children's Jewish education with home lessons and religious study groups. Others considered themselves irreligious. Some were not born Jewish but were married to Jews and bringing up their children in the Jewish tradition. Our relationships with Israel were diverse. There were Israelis, American Zionists, people who had no strong feelings about Israel, and even a few I would describe as anti-Zionist. Despite the diversity, there was one thing we shared: We had all made a conscious choice to immerse our children in Jewish community and expose them to a canon of Jewish values.

Reading along in the community prayer book during my first morning service, vaguely familiar with the tune to which the words were set, I realized I understood what I was reading. Until that point, Hebrew's biggest role in my life, by far, had been in flying jets, but Israeli Air Force Hebrew was good enough for the ancient texts. The words *shamayim* (heavens) or *herev* (sword) evoked the same images in my mind as they had in my German Jewish ancestors' minds, in eighteenth-century Hess. Sephardic Jews, arriving in New Amsterdam four hundred years ago, just a few miles south of the school, would have understood them as we did, as would their ancestors in Toledo and Granada. The same Hebrew words had been read on the Russian steppe, in the Atlas Mountains, in pre-Edwardian England, throughout the Ottoman Empire, in Byzantium, and across the Roman Empire. They had almost certainly evoked the same meaning for Rabbi Yehuda Hanassi as they had for me.

The diverse, sometimes conflicted, community assembled in this school chapel was my generation's link in the thirty-nine-hundred-year chain I first envisioned at Exeter, the link Amber and I had closed in Israel. It was not only a chain of knowledge and wisdom; it was poetry, ancient and enduring. The Crowd shared not only a wisdom, but a spirit. The code we carried was not only moral, but emotional. We were stewards of an energy that had existed for so many centuries, shaped by individual realities and shaping those realities in turn. This energy was sustained in the medium of the Crowd. Without the Crowd, it would be lost, the consequences of its demise unknown. I was part of this Crowd. I could not detach myself; nor did I want to.

As always, struggle was embedded in the code. One prayer in the prayer book, the *siddur,* has anchored the service since Zippori, probably even earlier. I knew I could not have been the first to wince at its meaning. As much as the Particularist in me was compelled by the ritual, the Universalist bristled at the passage. I translate directly, and inelegantly, from the Hebrew, as most modern translations soften the prayer's words, blunting its meaning, perhaps for obvious reason. *Aleinu LeShabeach LeAdon HaKol . . .*

> *It is incumbent on us to praise the master of all,*
> *To acknowledge the greatness of the original creator,*
> *For not creating us as the nations of other lands,*
> *And not placing us like (with) the families of the earth,*
> *For not allotting to us what he allotted to them,*
> *Or making our fate like that of their masses.*
> *And we kneel, bow, and give thanks [rituals associated*
>   *with the Priesthood of the Second Temple, suggesting*
>   *the prayer may even have predated Yehuda Hanassi]*

Before a king, the king of kings, the holy one, blessed be
he . . .

The prayer has evolved through different iterations over the centuries, but all versions express gratitude for a clear line segregating Jews from non-Jews. The Universalist rejects these words. They disparage the rest of humanity needlessly. They indulge only the Particularist.

And yet the prayer ends with these words:

. . . we put our hope in you, our God, to soon see the glory of
Your strength, to remove all idols from the earth,
And to completely cut off all false gods,
To repair the world, your divine kingdom.
And all owners of flesh [people] will call your name . . .
And all the world's inhabitants will recognize and know that
Every knee will bend to you and every tongue will swear
its faith to you. [Emphasis mine.]

Judaism has generally seen itself as an exclusive club, as evidenced in the first section of the prayer. Throughout most of its history, it has not espoused the proselytizing ambitions of Christianity or Islam. But in its last section, the prayer aspires to a world in which all people achieve the same footing. Its ambition is suddenly Universalist.

In the early Rabbinic Period of Judaism, after the destruction of the Second Temple, when the prayer may have been written, Judaism was indeed Universalist. Gentiles often joined prayers in Jewish synagogues. Zippori was a cosmo-

politan city in Yehuda Hanassi's time. Jews interacted intimately and harmoniously with their Roman pagan neighbors
on a daily basis. Rabbi Yehuda was said to have spoken Hebrew at home but conducted his public dealings in Greek. In
From the Maccabees to the Mishnah, Shaye Cohen makes the
point that the Mishna itself is full of Greek and Latin words,
and that many of its arguments are structured in a decidedly
Hellenistic fashion. Tension between Particularist and Universalist Judaism is not new. Nor is our perpetual struggle
with reconciling the two. The Aleinu prayer's reconciliation is
temporal. Its present is Particularist, its future Universalist.
But the Aleinu was written at least eighteen hundred years
ago. Where, on its original continuum from present to future,
do we stand today?

If we do not learn to accept, embrace, and honor the active struggle between Particularism and Universalism, neither Israeli nor American Judaism will survive the next three
generations. Today, many Jewish Universalists find insufficient value in any form of Judaism to warrant building their
lives around it. Devout Particularists find the value, but often
only through imposed obliviousness to all that lies beyond
their insular lives. These two communities share virtually
nothing, but a bridging constituency does still exist. Perhaps
like the redactor of the Mishna himself, this bridging community struggles to balance Particularism and Universalism.
It identifies actively with the Jewish People but finds common cause with non-Jews, professionally, academically, and
socially. Its interaction with both worlds feels seamless.

This group includes Modern Orthodox, Conservative, and

Reform Jews. It includes Jews who are not affiliated with any formal religious stream but who embrace the Jewish tribe warmly. Few of its members define themselves as a community, but they represent the common denominator around which Jewry could ultimately identify and unify. They form the core of a movement that could resuscitate the Jewish code.

RECONCILIATION

I became interested in applications of Crowd Wisdom while studying game theory at Harvard Business School. Could Crowd Wisdom reconcile the Bible's treatment of the Midianites and the Amalekites with the set of values that I had identified as Jewish? Could it reconcile the tension in the Aleinu prayer? It was a compelling idea, but I was initially suspicious of my own motives. Was I seeking truth, or just trying to square an inconvenient reality with an ideal I hoped to preserve? There were certainly weaknesses in the analogy. Perhaps most troubling, the gumball experiment features a static correct answer, a discernible truth. All of the data points (guesses) in the average are attempts at unearthing that static truth. The Jewish Crowd was seeking a moving, evolving truth. Were the mathematics of Crowd Wisdom applicable to such a challenge?

Financial markets seek an evolving truth. Their participants aim to determine the value of a security (a stock or a bond), which changes as ambient circumstances change. In a market, millions of participants guess at this value, their individual guesses accumulating to form a security's price. Game theorists will point out that market participants' contributions (guesses) are typically influenced by the contributions of other participants, subverting the Wisdom of the Crowd by removing the condition of independence. This is true in the short term, but over time market prices tend to revert to true value. As described by Benjamin Graham, considered the father of Value Investing, "In the short run, the market is a voting machine, but in the long run it is a weighing machine." Therefore, when the goal is to determine the evolving value of securities prices, the equivalent of the gumball experiment consists not only of taking a snapshot of all of the market's guesses at a given time, but also of viewing the average of those snapshots over extended periods. The act of reconciling diverse estimates of true value is far more complex when inputs are fluid, iterative, and ongoing. The simple average we use in the gumball game is insufficient for understanding financial markets.

Charting is a set of methodologies that financial market professionals use to identify trends in markets. One of the most basic charting concepts is the moving average. The simple moving average allows the trader to see through the clutter of random short-term movements. It is calculated by adding up the prices (end-of-day prices, for example) of the security being analyzed for the entire time frame (look-back period) of the moving average (say 100 days), and dividing that sum by the number of days (100). This calculation is updated at the end of each day by removing from the average the value that was added 101 days ago and introducing the value added today. The result is a smoothed trend line that marks the trajectory of the price of the security.

GE General Electric Co. NYSE stock prices (March 2012–March 2014)

Moving averages reduce the noise associated with the drama of individual daily price moves, making trends more apparent. The longer the look-back period, the smoother the trend line (the less effect any individual price move will have on the moving average).

Consider the month of April 2013 in the General Electric stock chart above. Looking only at end-of-day prices over this period, you might conclude that a negative trend is forming. Now look back along the moving average trend line. You can see that this sort of dip has occurred a few times in the recent past, even as the longer-term trend remained decidedly positive.

Look at late October 2012, when the share price drops sharply over a few days. Is this the beginning of a downward trend, or just a blip you can ignore? Technical charters might cite one of many rules of thumb asserting that in periods during which the security's actual price is higher than the moving average, the trend will typically continue to be up (and vice versa). Look at the points marked with arrows and note that the moving average usually acts as a sort of support, or a floor, for the security's price. This does not always work, of course, but it is a common pattern that you would have trouble recognizing if not for the moving average, which acts as a long-term reference against which we can interpret shorter-term occurrences. The longer the history of a security, the more data the trader has to work with, and the more analytical tools he may apply to his evolving understanding of the security.

Could the evolving Jewish moral code be a representation of a continuous moving average of more than three thousand years of religious, cultural, and moral data points? If so, the erratic impulses of specific eras would rarely represent a useful history of communal wisdom; they would just be points in a moving average. The living commentary of the Talmud, however, could be viewed as a trend line. Discrepancies in time and place would create the human diversity that catalyzes an interplay of ideas, contributing wisdom to an evolving Jewish Moving Average. As with moving stock averages, the Jewish texts are a documentation of the evolution of our Moving Average. Broad and conflicting participation in the exercise of debate and commentary are critical in maintaining the momentum of our evolution.

Judaism's dynamism has always been driven by the Crowd. Talmud has not been its only medium. Jews have been reciting the Aleinu prayer, for example, for at least two thousand years. But the Aleinu is not the same prayer it was two thousand years ago. It has been edited many times, editions gradually aggregated and reconciled as communities migrated and converged. The concept of *tikkun olam,* which features in the prayer, has evolved with it. The meaning most Jews ascribe to *tikkun olam* (repair of the world) today was invoked by Jewish social activists in Europe and the United States in the first half of the twentieth century as a call for human (versus strictly divine) action to bring justice to the world at large. In its earlier forms, the prayer appears ambiguous regarding the questions of what exactly must be repaired, and who (God or humanity) is to do the repairing. The word *tikkun* itself has evolved over time. *Tikkun* spelled with a *kuf,* indeed meaning "repair," features in almost all Jewish prayer books today. But in some versions of the prayer, including in Rabbi Saadia Gaon of Tiberias's tenth-century *siddur,* the word is spelled with a *kaf,* meaning "establishment" or "binding together." Almost three hundred years after Saadia Gaon, Maimonides tied *tikkun olam,* with a *kuf,* to relations between Jews and non-Jews in Córdoba, asserting an explicitly human role in its implementation. In Jerusalem, three hundred years after Maimonides, the Kabbalist Rabbi Luria included *tikkun olam* in his mystical meditations on the singularity, creation, sustainment, and repair of the universe.

Those who assert that the modern interpretation of *tikkun olam* somehow contradicts an age-old, unwavering interpretation seem not to be considering how many times the term's meaning has changed over the centuries. All of these changes were influenced by big ideas, such as democracy, Christianity, the scientific method, capitalism, and human rights. They were steered by events like the Roman exile, the rise of the Spanish Empire, the Renaissance, American independence, the Equal Rights Amendment, and Israeli independence. No single contributor can provide a comprehensive and lasting reflection of Judaism. Each is just a data point, sometimes dramatic in its short-term impact but eventually smoothed by the friction of time, shaped against the backdrop of preceding and subsequent events.

It would be natural, in retrospect, to emphasize those data points that have been most reflective of the Moving Average trend line as we see it from today, and to deemphasize those that have not—as we do with the Midianites. Asked to recall the Ten Commandments, for example, more people I polled remember the sixth, *Thou Shalt Not Kill* ("murder," in the original Hebrew), than the ninth, *Thou Shalt Not Bear False Witness Against Thy Neighbor*. The sixth commandment is more consistent with current sensibilities, as guided by the Moving Average, than the ninth. Indeed, the sanctity of life featured in the Ten Commandments of antiquity, and was subsequently reinforced through centuries of more recent data points guiding the Jewish Moving Average, making it the central Jewish value that it is today. Episodes like the genocide of the Midianites have not been repeated in the last three thousand years. The sensibilities that may have enabled it at the time have not been reinforced in more recent data points and, as a result, have faded from the Jewish Moving Average. This is an honest exercise. The reason we do not emphasize the Midianite passage in the Bible is not that we are ashamed of it in light of our finer modern sensibilities. It is because the slaughter failed to become a trend in Judaism. It certainly remains a data point in the Moving Average, but has become decreasingly representative of it.

As a reminder, the Ten Commandments are:

1. I am the Lord your God.
2. Thou shalt have no other gods before me.
3. Thou shalt not take the name of the Lord your God in vain.
4. Remember the Sabbath day, to keep it holy.
5. Honor thy father and thy mother.
6. Thou shalt not kill.
7. Thou shalt not commit adultery.
8. Thou shalt not steal.
9. Thou shalt not bear false witness against thy neighbor.
10. Thou shalt not covet.

Age confers neither legitimacy nor weight upon a moving average. Despite protestations from much of the religious hierarchy, in both Israel and America, there is no clear justification for attributing more weight to the old data points than to the new. And despite protestations from Judaism's most radical reformers, there is no justification for attributing more weight to the new data points than to the old. The average is only moved by the accumulation of data points over time. As a singular point, Yehuda Hanassi might eventually prove as consequential as Moses, Theodor Herzl as important as Ibn Gabirol. The evolution of Judaism did not end with the biblical prophets. As long as there are Jews in the world, the Moving Average must continue to be shaped; without new data points, a moving average becomes irrelevant. The shaping *must* continue if Judaism is to remain relevant, and relevance is a precondition for survival in a world of free and open affiliations.

I attended a conference in Spain in 2010 where I had the opportunity to hear Rabbi Sholom Lipskar speak. Rabbi Lipskar founded The Shul of Bal Harbour in Miami Beach, a highly successful Orthodox synagogue with a very large and enthusiastic congregation. Rabbi Lipskar is an adherent of Chabad, probably the best known and most popular Hasidic movement in the world today. The movement is intentionally inclusive, with extensive outreach, seeking contact with any and all Jews. This inclusiveness has, by necessity, influenced Chabad ideology. Chabad emphasizes Jewish spirituality and Jewish community as strongly as Jewish practice. A Chabad rabbi will certainly keep the Sabbath, but will typically not shun a congregant for driving to synagogue on Shabbat.

Rabbi Lipskar spoke about The Shul's position on homosexuality. In the Chabad tradition, all Jews are welcome in the congregation. But Judaism explicitly forbids homosexuality. The rabbi reconciled this conflict by explaining that everybody in the congregation sins. One congregant might not keep kosher, and another might break the Sabbath, but they are still welcome at The Shul. By the same token, gay congregants should be welcome despite the sin of homosexuality.

Speaking with the rabbi over dinner later, I pointed out that gay members of his congregation might not find his reconciliation so satisfying. Failing to observe the Sabbath is not a central component of most people's identity. It is simply a choice they make. Being gay is central to the gay congregant's identity, not a choice. It is who he or she is. The notion that a permanent and central feature of a person's identity must be regarded as sinful is offensive.

But I was looking at Rabbi Lipskar's policy as a snapshot. I had failed to see it in the context of a trend. Chabad estimates that one million Jews attend Chabad services annually, making it one of the most significant movements within Orthodox Judaism. Consider how far Rabbi Lipskar stood from his tradition's starting point on this subject, Leviticus 20:13, which reads (my translation and emphasis): *And a man who lies down with a male as one lies with a woman, both have committed sacrilege.* **They shall be put to death.** *Their own blood is upon them.* I saw little room for interpretation in this verse. Like the slaughter of the Midianites, it is God's word, and it is a command. But this Orthodox Jewish leader welcomes gays into his congregation, and is willing to engage in public debate over his policy.

Reconciliation of diverse and conflicting ideas is a process that takes time. The resulting metamorphosis of practice also takes time. The example Rabbi Lipskar was illustrating was part of an exercise in moving averages. The rabbi was reconciling voices from a large crowd. The legacy he inherited from his ancestors was a prominent voice in that crowd. It is that voice which kept this measured evolution from turning into an impulsive chase after the latest trend.

That impulsive chase is what I was essentially proposing at dinner. I understand that today. I should have then. I had been taught the power of the crowd, and the compromises involved in wielding it, years earlier. A formation of four fighter aircraft is far more potent in a dogfight than four individual aircraft. Given the choice, you would rather fight the four individuals than the formation, which fuses information gathered by four different pilots, each viewing the fight from his own unique vantage point, to construct and share a comprehensive picture of the battle. Each member's maneuvering in space is coordinated with the others. Like a wolf pack, they work together to dictate the geometry of the fight, limiting their adversary's options and robbing him of initiative. To this day, a central principle in air combat doctrine is that an aerial force should aim to coordinate temporary numerical advantage within a segment of sky as a prerequisite to entering fights.

Of course, for all its potency, the formation is also constrained in its ability to maneuver. The independent pilot, unencumbered by team members, is free to turn, climb, or break at his own discretion. He can initiate a maneuver and change his mind seconds later in favor of a new maneuver. The formation member must take his three teammates into account before deciding on a course of action. This limits his choices. Once the formation enters into a maneuver, its members are committed for some time. At any given point in the fight each individual member of the formation might have a better move available to him as an individual, but by maintaining tactical discipline, and forgoing what might best serve the individual, he and his teammates achieve a far more powerful effect.

Judaism will lose its communal potency if its members lurch impulsively after ever-changing sensibilities. It will break apart if each individual indulges only his own individual moral views. Community can function only if a critical mass of its members defers, at least partially, to the momentum of a gradually evolving moral framework. Rabbi Lipskar's approach was both an expression of fidelity to the gradual evolution of Jewish practice and a wise acknowledgment of the Jewish community's responsibility to embrace its members' individuality to the extent possible.

In order to remain relevant, Judaism must continue to evolve. Some, in the United States and in Israel, resist this evolution. The Israeli religious establishment has employed the sovereign power of the Israeli state to inhibit it. But even the establishment must concede that the rules it often dogmatically enforces have evolved over time, as a moving average does. The biblical prohibition against cooking a calf in its mother's milk has evolved, over many phases and modifications, into a set of rules that today includes the separation of chicken and goat-milk products—neither of them related to calves or to cows' milk. For some, rice is currently kosher for Passover. For others, it is not. We do not slay prisoners of war or homosexuals today. We have evolved.

No event in modernity makes the case for ending this evolution. Some, who argue that there are no longer any great scholars with the authority to amend Judaism, miss the point that Jewish evolution *must* continue as new realities force it to. It was only 200 years ago that Judaism confronted steam-powered travel. It was only 130 years ago that Judaism contended with electric light. Both presented halachic challenges that were debated vigorously. The practices that emerged from these debates have evolved over many decades, and continue to evolve.

And yet the process of incorporating the new data points that drive the evolution of Judaism is broken, both in the United States and in Israel. Too much of the diverse crowd of Jewry has stopped participating in the process of generating wisdom. In the coming years, Judaism will be forced to adjust to human progress at a faster rate than ever before. Advances in medicine, automation, and transportation will raise questions that Judaism has never answered. Human progress is not ending; it is accelerating, and Jewish evolution must keep pace if Judaism is to survive.

DIVINING THE CODE

Amber and I occasionally discuss where we should live during our next stretch in Israel. In the few years before our family's current New York stint, we lived in Herzlia, a suburb just north of Tel Aviv. Herzlia was wonderful for us in most respects. Our kids could bike around the neighborhood safely at any time of day or night. We were happy with the kindergarten and elementary schools they attended. After putting the girls on their school bus every morning, I would walk down the steps to the beach to swim or surf in the clear Mediterranean water, even in the winter. I would be in my Tel Aviv office within twenty minutes of leaving home. I would work late, often meeting Amber for a dinner with friends or a concert in Tel Aviv, and still be home by midnight.

Although we miss that life, we do not plan to live in Herzlia again. We have found that when we spend time in Israel as a family now, most of the friends we visit live in another

Tel Aviv suburb, Raanana. Raanana is not on the beach. Its commute to Tel Aviv grinds through notoriously heavy traffic. But Raanana has something that Herzlia lacks: a real community. Many Raanana residents whom we know live there primarily because their friends live there. We feel we are part of this community, which might strike some people as odd, not just because we do not live there, but because the majority of its members are Orthodox Jews. Their homes are kosher, unlike ours. Their neighborhood restaurants and grocery stores are kosher. They attend synagogue together on Friday evenings and Saturday mornings. We do not. Our family's weekend activities typically involve breaking the rules of Shabbat.

In Israel for the summer, Amber and I recently spent a Saturday afternoon at the Raanana home of Rabbi Seth Farber and his wife, Michelle. Seth, an author and historian, runs ITIM, an organization that helps Jews to navigate Israel's religious bureaucracy. Michelle presents a podcast on Jewish theology. While we were there, friends from the neighborhood occasionally stopped in unannounced and joined the discussion Seth and I were having about this book. Some were people I knew; I had worked with one in Israel's technology sector and had been involved with another in a social endeavor. All of the Farbers' guests were Jewishly knowledgeable, and some had serious religious educations. All were Modern Orthodox Jews. But all of them also fit under the umbrella of Secularism as I define it. Although these people obviously respect and embrace Jewish Orthodoxy, they find the idea of forcibly imposing it on others repellent. Amber and I had arrived at the Farbers' house by car on Shabbat and, although none of their guests that day drive on Shabbat, the fact that we did bothered nobody. The Raanana community engages comfortably in multiple worlds that many other Jews regard as distinct and unmixable. Their career paths are as diverse as any community's that I know; they include attorneys, biologists, software engineers, military officers, doctors, and artists. Their approach to Judaism incorporates the struggle between Universalism and Particularism. They grapple with the texts. They grapple with one another's views.

The Raanana Jewish community I am describing extends to other towns and cities, in Israel and in the United States. Its Jewish education provides a foundation for debate around the questions that Yehuda Hanassi laid out in the Mishna. Its diversity, and its openness to struggle with these questions, makes it a wise crowd. It is this community that inspired an exercise that might help make it possible to begin inferring and articulating the Jewish Moving Average as it stands today. We may each have a sense of a list of values and sensibilities that define Jewishness today, but is there a definitive, objective method for producing a common list?

Over a period of two years, while writing this book, I proposed the challenge below to a diverse selection of Jews, starting with members of the Raanana community but ultimately including Israelis and Americans, Orthodox, Conservative, Reform, and religiously unengaged. All respondents, young and old, women and men, believed that the survival of the Jewish People has value. All had some sense of Jewish history, claiming some degree of knowledge and some context for imagining the evolution of Jewish sensibilities over history. The challenge:

> List up to ten identifiers, principles that, *in aggregate* (not individually), form the de facto pillars of contemporary Jewish identity. Your list must be exclusive enough to distinguish the Jewish value system from other value systems (like Americanism), but each *individual* tenet must be inclusive enough to be agreeable to at least 75 percent of adult Jews worldwide (to the best of your knowledge). Of course, your list is not meant to be an exhaustive guide to Judaism for each individual Jew. Other values might be layered on top of your foundation by Jewish individuals or by Jewish communities. Keeping kosher, for example, might not meet the 75 percent requirement, but could still serve as a defining practice to a large minority of Jews.

The results of this experiment revealed considerable overlap in the top five values:[*]

1. Justice
2. Education

---

[*] Responses were solicited in free text rather than multiple choice, in order to avoid leading the respondents. My interpretations necessarily introduce some semantic ambiguity and subjectivity. A broader survey, discussed later in the book, will be conducted using Natural Language Processing tools to more objectively classify participants' inputs.

3. Challenge and dissent
4. Ritual and tradition
5. Community

Many readers, particularly Jewish scholars, may find this exercise a folksy and superficial attempt at dumbing down a rich and complex canon. Please bear with me for a few more pages, as I believe you will find value in the interplay among the tenets in the list. I think you will also find value in the exercise, perhaps more than in the list itself. Let's begin by stepping into the debriefing of that tragic 2002 Shchadeh operation.

7

Commander in Chief

We were summoned to the base auditorium for a closed-door debriefing on a humid afternoon about a week after the Shchadeh raid. All of the base's air crew members, active and reserve, had been invited to participate, and from what I could see, practically all were present. I was a reservist and had come in from my office at Giza, an investment firm in Tel Aviv. Dan Halutz, IAF commander in chief, took the stage and began with a personal debriefing. He provided background on the target. He shared intelligence material establishing Shchadeh's central role in specific terrorist attacks, past and pending. He referred to details of the judicial process that had cleared the strike. He reviewed the previous aborted attempts to target Shchadeh and pointed out the terrorist attacks that had been launched under Shchadeh's command since the first aborted attempt—including the bombing that killed young Galila Bugala. He reviewed the intelligence data available to the controllers on the night of the raid and presented his best understanding of the failures that had led to the tragedy, both within the intelligence network and along the operational command chain, including his own. He presented alternative tactical plans that had been considered, and reviewed the benefits and risks that each of them had posed. He asked us to consider, in light of the carnage this man would have gone on to inflict, whether there was *any* number of civilian casualties that might have been tolerable. When the floor opened to comments, they came sharp and direct, ranging from the quality of the intelligence briefings to Halutz's misreading of public sentiment.

We varied in age, from midtwenties to late fifties. Some of us were active duty pilots, others reservists—academics, physicians, lawyers, and technology entrepreneurs. Some were career officers. Some, like me, considered our moral dilemmas from the distant vantage point of professional lives lived partly overseas. Some experienced them from up close, in glaring relief. Some had families who had been victims of terrorism. Some came from the towns and farms enduring regular rocket and mortar bombardment from Gaza. One, a physician, had treated Arab patients from the Gaza communities affected by the conflict. Many had siblings, friends, or even children in the infantry units that would eventually be assigned to fight their way into Gaza, house by booby-trapped house, if we could not protect our citizens from the air.

As evening turned into night, criticism of tactical details turned into challenge of entire battle doctrines. Some comments reflected the personal and societal dilemmas endemic to this type of war. Some presented arguments for alternative strategic responses to our challenges, employing economic tools, new media schemes, diplomatic initiatives, or alternative uses of force. One or two participants tentatively invoked theoretical scenarios in which members of the air crew community should refuse to follow orders. (The pilots' letter my old instructor would sign had not yet been published.)

I was familiar with the taste of adrenaline under my tongue. It was an early warning system, sometimes triggered moments before I became explicitly conscious of danger. I could taste it now. Within a few seconds, a deep baritone rose from the rear of the hall, its force challenging the constructive tenor of the discussion. By the time the first sentence had been spoken, we were in a different conversation. It felt as though the temperature in the room had risen. The voice belonged to one of our oldest reservists, a man who had flown in one of the two indomitable Phantom squadrons that had lost nearly half of their aircraft and crews in the chaotic first two days of the Yom Kippur War. He had served with distinction for decades. Today he was a grandfather, at the sunset of a long reserve career. Responding to another pilot's description of a theoretical but morally precarious operational scenario, he declared purposefully, unambiguously, "I would sit in jail before flying that mission." I remember turning in my seat, trying to catch the expression on his face and on the faces of the younger people seated around him. Had they also heard the gauntlet drop? Had they understood its significance? The Air Force was charged with a critical mission, in which failure carried deadly consequences for an entire nation. This was not a thought exercise. Could we afford to openly express views that would call the entire command chain into question? This was an open forum, not a private conversation. How many of us could share the reservist's view without threatening the reliability of the system on which our nation's survival depended? I was sure that in many military organizations around the world, the discussion we were having would warrant mutiny charges.

I searched Halutz's face for a reaction. He was calm. Aside from my own racing pulse, the entire room seemed calm. Halutz, a comrade in arms who had fought shoulder to shoulder with this man for years, put his pen down and looked the old pilot in the eyes. "I feel the same way. But we need to face this feeling in light of our alternatives." He described his own personal struggle to identify a line between defense and murder. He spoke in detail and with humility. He deliberated aloud, laying bare the personal map of his own unanswered questions, asking the same of the old pilot, and of the rest of us, taking the time to understand the diversity of responses.

This had ceased to be a tactical debriefing. We were probing the fundamental questions that defined our lives' mission, our identity, exposing our most intimate red lines. There was no hiding, not even for our commander. I watched as a cornerstone of my own culture unveiled itself. It was not the first time, but it hit me harder than it ever had. Truth was our ultimate authority. The doors were closed, hierarchy locked outside. Our challenges of one another stood and fell on merit alone. Nobody could hide behind the shields of rank, experience, or courtesy. There were no taboos. We were all accountable to one another, our commander included.

The crowd seemed to understand the inherent risk in the exercise but stayed true to its goal—the truth.

We continued to take apart and reassemble a mosaic of interdependent imperatives, moral, judicial, operational, and personal. There were no simple answers, but we shined a bright light on the complexity of the questions and painstakingly forged a common understanding of the moving parts of the challenge facing us. Not every issue was resolved, but every issue raised was engaged through debate. No point was left unexplored.

The result was a set of compromises representing our own balance between idealized visions of a just world and the imperatives dictated by our responsibility to a nation. Our compromises were necessarily subtle. The enemy's doctrine of firing on our civilians from behind his own did not negate our responsibility to our civilians—or to his. There would be no perfect answers, only optima, and these would change over time. No strategy would ever get them perfectly right, but we would continue struggling for an optimum. We would continue to have a hand in our strategy's evolution, and we would take ownership in its results.

Dan Halutz had not handed down wisdom from above for mandatory consumption. He had officiated over a process that accepted wisdom as diffuse. Dan's personal positions had registered just as those of any other senior member of the community had. His leadership role was primarily as facilitator of the exercise. On most issues, the combined wisdom of the participants was greater than that of the commander, or of any individual. The architecture of the debriefing was Talmudic. The questions were shared. The answers were independent. The process was structured. We were standing, unconsciously, on centuries of Jewish tradition, and Dan Halutz had submitted to that tradition.

Most of us still resented the mission, and the exercise did not satisfy everyone. Indeed, twenty-seven of us resigned. But the rest of us would fly into battle the next day having heard from our community and having been heard. We had been relieved of the paralyzing doubt of unexplored eventualities and unclear consequences. We knew we would never have perfect answers, but through some invisible cognition, the community's combined struggle for an answer had come close, likely as close as we could ever get. This is how Diaspora had worked. This was the code. Sovereignty had not killed it after all.

For almost two thousand years, Jewish wisdom has been refined, adapted, and propagated through a network, not distributed from above. The process of adapting and refining wisdom may have been as important as the wisdom itself. That exquisite process became so entrenched in the Diaspora as to be automatic. We eventually ceased to appreciate its centrality and forgot the subtleties that made it work. This is the danger posed by the end of Diaspora. Under certain circumstances, crowds can be decidedly unwise. They can be random gatherings of individuals, generating no special wisdom or, worse, destroyers of wisdom. Exuberant market bubbles and their subsequent devastating collapses are the work of crowds. The mob, a dynamic instinctively familiar to

the historically attuned Jew, is separated by only a few subtleties from Crowd Wisdom. Had the Jews lost Crowd Wisdom
with the loss of Diaspora?

No. Not yet, at least. Although the preconditions for Crowd
Wisdom, articulated so succinctly by James Surowiecki—
a common set of questions, independence of responses, diversity among respondents, and a mechanism of aggregation—have
begun to fall out of place, we have not crossed the threshold
into inevitable extinction. There is still time to change course.

PART
THREE

| The Medicine |

8

The Wisdom Machine

Consider the idea that the Wisdom of Crowds that governed Jewry in the Diaspora might be reinvigorated to serve post-Diaspora Jewry, that the architecture of dispersion, which was so central to the wisdom of the Jewish Crowd in the Diaspora, might be replaced with technology. The five-tenets survey was a rough experiment designed to demonstrate that the Crowd may still exist. There is a better process in development, which involves technology, and, fittingly, it is being developed in Israel. In *The Wisdom of Crowds,* Surowiecki offers Google's PageRank algorithm as an Information Age application of Crowd Wisdom to the complex challenge of searching the Internet. PageRank maps the links between Internet pages in order to establish the relevance of a given page to a particular search. The more pages that link to the given page, the higher its ranking in the search results. The top-ranked search result is the page that received the most "votes" from the Internet at large. In this sense, Google Search functions like a market, with a crowd of buyers and sellers, their opinions aggregated to predict the value (or ranking) of a security (or webpage). Google takes the approach a few steps further than the market does. In the market, every dollar gets an equal vote in setting prices. "Dumb dollars" influence the market's results just as much as "smart dollars" do. Picture an index fund blindly buying or selling every single stock in the index versus an investor who has devoted time and resources to researching a specific stock. Each gets the same number of votes. Should "smart guesses" get more weight than "dumb guesses"? In our gumball experiment, equal weighting seemed to work best, as it had for Francis Galton, averaging the Crowd's guesses to determine a cow's weight. But Google found a method of identifying and weighting "smarter" votes that dramatically improved its results. This method itself relies on Crowd Wisdom. PageRank, having ranked the *importance* of most pages on the Internet in accordance with the number of other pages linking to them, attributes more "votes" to an important webpage than to an unimportant page. The "important" pages are considered more relevant, and so get more votes. It works.

Waze, acquired by Google in 2015, is an Israeli company that applies the Wisdom of Crowds to mapping the world's roadways and optimizing navigation for drivers. The Waze "crowd" consists of the millions of drivers who use the application while driving. If ten "Wazers" are driving on a stretch of highway at an average speed of 60 mph, the wisdom that Waze generates includes the fact that this particular stretch of highway is flowing traffic-free. If there is suddenly an accident ahead of them, all ten drivers' speeds will quickly decline, suggesting that there is now traffic on this stretch of highway. If only one driver's speed had declined, that might not suggest traffic buildup. That driver might have pulled over for a rest, for example. But a decline in the average speed clearly suggests traffic. If you now begin a drive that would normally take you over that stretch of highway, Waze might redirect you to a different route, one whose flow has also been established by the crowd of drivers. The Waze crowd also identifies road closures and new roads. By relying on the Crowd, it does so faster and more accurately than any other technology.

Imagine a machine designed not for Internet searching or road navigation, but for applying the wisdom of a large crowd to answering a broad array of questions. This machine's inputs would consist of the textual opinions, insights, predictions, and prescriptions of the subject community. The machine would rank the input of the community's various members by means of an objective logic, perhaps similar to PageRank's logic. It would continually aggregate and reconcile these inputs into a constantly evolving Crowd Wisdom. The machine's output would be tools for community governance and self-definition.

Rootclaim was founded by Saar Wilf, also the founder of Fraud Sciences, which was acquired by PayPal. Rootclaim applies the Wisdom of Crowds to divining complex truths. As of this writing (2017), the company aggregates a decentralized array of diverse, independent inputs, which are used to establish the veracity of media news reports and to calculate the probability of hypothetical scenarios having played out.

GOD IS IN THE CROWD

For example, Rootclaim might weigh the probability that the Assad government of Syria was responsible for deploying chemical weapons on Syrian civilians against the probability that rebel groups or foreign actors deployed the weapons in false-flag operations. The software could question the causes of a Malaysia Airlines flight's disappearance in the Indian Ocean. Was it pilot error, pilot suicide, or terrorist hijacking? Where, precisely, did the aircraft go down? Rootclaim works like Google's PageRank in that it attributes different values to its different input sources.

Fact verification is Rootclaim's first-generation application, but Saar Wilf believes that future generations will be capable of scoring the relative attractiveness of different ideas and policies against legal and ethical frameworks and, eventually, of shaping these frameworks into a moving average of communal values and sensibilities that could drive decisions. Other technology companies, some of them also in Israel, incorporate new and evolving approaches, such as blockchain technology, to intelligent voting or Crowd Governance applications.

The Wisdom of Crowds may ultimately reclaim its role in Jewish self-governance not through Diaspora but through technology. Transcending physical boundaries, technologies like Rootclaim's could play the role that Diaspora once claimed in aggregating diverse, independent inputs to establish Crowd Wisdom. In a rapidly changing world, technology may prove a superior medium for establishing and maintaining a coherent Jewish communal voice.

9

The Jewish World Endowment

My survey reached relatively few people. That group was self-selected, in that all of its members were already engaged in questions of Jewish continuity, and all claimed significant knowledge of Jewish history and tradition. This undoubtedly influenced the survey's results.

Those results will also reach only a limited segment of world Jewry—the readers of this book. Even if the book is successful, it will not have directly touched the majority of Jews. This limits the results' usefulness. Successful governance by the Crowd also demands awareness and buy-in by those governed. We all should be able to understand the policies that govern us, and to understand how they are drafted and amended. And we should all be able to play a role in that process if we choose to.

A community education effort would allow us to meet the dual demands of increasing awareness and broadening participation in Jewish Crowd governance. Imagine the following proposition: You and your spouse are approached, after the birth of your first child, by a representative of an organization called the Jewish World Endowment—a sort of Birthright 2.0. The program she describes requires that you begin committing 1.25 percent of your pretax income each year, for each child, to the Endowment, beginning when the child is five years old. Remaining current on your commitment ensures membership in the Endowment. The benefits include:

1. Two years in a Jewish summer program. One summer is on a U.S. campus, the other on an Israeli campus. Campers from the United States, Israel, and the rest of the world attend together. Aside from summer-camp-like outdoor activities and sports, the program's content is an exploration of Jewish identity—history, tradition, and culture. Religion is not imposed on campers beyond two basic common denominators: The food served at camp is kosher, and there are no organized activities that necessitate breaking Shabbat. Orthodox, Conservative, and Reform religious guidance is provided to anyone interested but is not mandatory. All campers welcome the Sabbath together with a common service and a common meal.

2. Two months' participation in a Tikkun project, in the last summer of high school or after high school graduation. Tikkun projects are accredited, but not managed, by the Jewish World Endowment. They include a range of missions, from local assignments that require only basic skills, such as vol-

unteering to read aloud to residents of a home for the elderly, to international missions requiring specialization, such as teaching computer coding in the developing world or volunteering to support the IDF's international disaster relief unit. Successful projects would lead to voluntary participant engagement long after the initial two-month commitment. They would mix Americans, Israelis, and Jewish participants from other parts of the world.

3. A scholarship covering full undergraduate university tuition. In keeping with the Jewish value of education, every Jewish young person in the world would enjoy the privilege of a university education, in the institution and subject of his or her choice (assuming admission), tuition-free. Participants who have served the Jewish People for an extended period, in the framework of the IDF or a multiyear community service program, would benefit from an additional living stipend.

What is an exploration of Jewish identity? Who decides what the program participants will be learning? The Crowd. The curriculum would be based on our own wisdom, our own answer to the question "Who are we?" The following is a summary of people's commentary on their own responses to the values survey. Of course, this is only a starting point. The values survey is a simple and unscientific demonstration of what it might look like for the Crowd to define itself. The Wisdom Machine would provide a far more nuanced, objective, and of course dynamic answer to the question "Who are we?"

JUSTICE

TZEDEK

In the era of Babylonian Exile, Rabbi Hillel was approached by a heathen who challenged him: "Make me a proselyte [that is, I will convert to Judaism] under the condition that you teach me the whole Torah while I stand on one foot." Hillel's response was "What is hateful to you, do not do to your neighbor. That is the whole Torah. The rest is commentary." While conventional notions of the details that constitute justice in legal and ethical senses have evolved over the centuries, the Jewish notion of justice has carried certain distinctions.

First, it is a value to be sought *in this world* rather than in the next. The concept of an afterlife is not developed in Jewish liturgy. Christianity and Islam both offer colorful descriptions of the afterlife, and both make explicit reference to a justice system that affords accommodation in the afterlife for injustices suffered, sacrifices made, and good and bad deeds performed during this life. In Jewish theology, the balance of justice is to be restored in this world.

Second, justice is a human affair. Unlike Catholic confession, which is between man and God, or Islamic justice, which is adjudicated in accordance with the static rules of Sharia, Jewish justice is sought between individuals. On the days before Yom Kippur, the Jewish Day of Atonement, we seek forgiveness for our transgressions directly from the people against whom we have transgressed before seeking pardon from God.

Third, Rabbi Hillel's Torah injunction carries a characteristically practical nuance. Compare Hillel's admonition, *What is hateful to you, do not do to your neighbor,* to the Golden Rule, *Do unto others as you would have them do unto you.* The selflessness of the latter elevates it to a theoretical ideal. There are many things we would have all people do unto us that we simply could not do unto all people. Hillel's is a practical code of behavior, formulated to be enacted rather than pondered. Judaism values orthodoxy of practice above orthodoxy of belief.

Fourth, the conceptualization of justice is subject to individual interpretation. Individuals must struggle with it. Judaism lacks the hierarchy of many other religions. There is no Jewish pope. Practitioners of Jewish ethics are free to grapple—indeed, are compelled to grapple—with the concept of justice, as we did very openly in the Halutz debriefing. Israelis citing justice in the survey in fact often referred to the Ten Core Values in the Israel Defense Forces' Code of Ethics, which include, among other ideals, the sanctity of human life, including that of an enemy. Of course, this value often conflicts with the principle of *self-defense,* and with the IDF's mission of protecting Israeli civilians. In a conflict in which enemy combatants regularly exploit their own civilian populations as cover, this tension is so nuanced that static, heuristic guidelines for defending the value *human life* in all scenarios are impossible, despite the persistent efforts of IDF ethicists and legal experts. The tension is largely pushed down to individual battlefield decision makers, combat officers, and soldiers like those in the Halutz debriefing. This policy of decentralization relies on a common appreciation of the *spirit* of the value. Note that the word "code" in the IDF

Code of Ethics translates literally from Hebrew not as "code," but as "wind" or "spirit," acknowledging the fluidity and subjectivity implied in dilemmas of justice. Of course, a diversity of views prevails among operators, which can sometimes result in inconsistency in decision making amid the complexity and fog of battle. This occasionally leads to emphatically nonconsensus decisions, requiring review and occasional adjudication and censure.

But there are also meaningful benefits to a Crowd-driven approach to justice. It stimulates ethical innovation throughout the ranks. Consider the tactic of "roof knocking," proposed by midlevel officers and instituted by the IAF in 2014. Tactics for contending with enemies intentionally embedded within the civilian populations they claimed to represent had evolved considerably since the days of primitive satellite books and dumb bombs. The IAF had devoted increasingly sophisticated intelligence resources to the challenge and had developed new generations of precise munitions with small warheads and intelligent fuses, designed to localize and contain kill radii. The enemy—Hamas, in this case—also innovated, basing command centers and weapons depots in underground tunnels directly beneath civilian homes, hospitals, and mosques. Tunnel entrances were often positioned inside these dwellings.

"Knocking on the roof" consists of a warning shot. When the presence of civilians within such a structure is suspected, an aircraft launches a purpose-designed, precision-guided projectile, with no explosive warhead, at a predetermined corner point on its roof. The projectile's impact produces a loud thud without endangering the structure's occupants.

The tactic is deployed in conjunction with aerial distribution of warning leaflets that explain the IDF's intent and define safe zones in the vicinity of the target area. These leaflets are dropped in advance, accompanied by telephone calls or text messages to the structure's likely occupants in the minutes before a "knock on the roof."

It is the midlevel officers who designed this tactic who initially weighed its practical costs against its moral benefits. Roof knocking is financially expensive, of course. Consider the cost of the intelligence effort required to retrieve mobile telephone numbers for the occupants of a specific building in enemy territory. It is also tactically costly, tantamount to providing the enemy with precise information on your intentions immediately before acting on them. The tactic is also risky. It endangers Israeli Air Force flight crews by alerting the enemy to the timing and location of their activities. Still, when executed successfully, roof knocking offers moral benefits that the Crowd perceives as outweighing these practical costs.

The entire command chain is empowered to make this calculus, allowing ethical innovations like roof knocking to emerge from within the ranks rather than being passed down from the top of the IDF hierarchy. Such innovation makes IDF doctrine materially different from that of many other military forces. During the Russian war in Chechnya, entire neighborhoods in the city of Grozny were simply leveled by Russian artillery—civilians and all. Even American and British tactics in the Iraq and Afghanistan wars tend to favor efficacy and troop safety over moral concerns. Operators are generally not charged with producing such innovations. In these countries, military policy is dictated from the leadership much more directly than it is in the IDF.

Despite the costs, despite the risks, despite wide consensus in Israel that European and UN condemnation of the IDF is inevitable no matter how delicately Israel defends itself, roof knocking enjoys broad approval among Israelis. The tactic represents a successful use of the Crowd in crafting a just policy. It gives the individual IDF operator an important tool with which to subtly negotiate a complex moral calculus, guided by his own understanding of the admonition *What is hateful to you, do not do to your neighbor*. For a Jewish army, that is a winning trade.

SOCIAL ACTION

Tikkun olam (repair of the world), in its contemporary interpretations, pertains not only to the Jewish world. Its current popularity aside, *tikkun olam* is not a new tradition. Terminologies have changed over time, but Jewish engagement in what modern *tikkun olam* adherents would describe as world repair has been a staple of Jewish history from Abraham's time to our own. It has been most evident in periods when Jews were empowered to act outside their own communities, as they are today. As soon as they achieved relative empowerment in the United States, at the turn of the twentieth century, Jews began serving as agents of social repair beyond the Jewish community. Cofounded by Julius Rosenwald, Lillian Wald, and Rabbis Emil Hirsch and Stephen Wise, the NAACP's original leadership was composed mainly of Jews. The Association's 1914 board included Jacob Schiff and Jacob Billikopf, and its chairman was Professor Joel Elias

Springarn. Felix Frankfurter, later to become a United States
Supreme Court Justice, cofounded the American Civil Lib-
erties Union in 1920. Jews have stood at the fulcrum of all
the social movements aimed at repair in the country that embraced them, from women's suffrage to the War on Poverty to
gender equality.

Jewish engagement in social repair is not just an American phenomenon. South African Jews played as pivotal a role
in ending apartheid as American Jews did in civil rights, serving in the leadership of the antiapartheid movement and
often paying a high price for their engagement. Some paid
with their lives. Nadine Gordimer authored much of Nelson
Mandela's often cited 1964 Rivonia trial defense speech. Ar-
thur Chaskalson, the chief justice in postapartheid South
Africa, served as Mandela's defense attorney at Rivonia.
Denis Goldberg, Mandela's codefendant, was sentenced to
four consecutive life sentences.

Today, 76 percent of American Jews surveyed report having made a charitable gift in the last year. Even Jewish households earning less than $50,000 per year are more likely than
not to give to charity. And, interestingly, although 92 percent
of American Jewish donors donate to non-Jewish causes, the
strongest determinant of Jews' propensity to give is their level
of engagement with Jewish community. Observing Jewish
rituals, being married to a Jewish spouse, and having Jewish
friends all increase a Jew's likelihood to donate to *any*
charity—Jewish or non-Jewish.* The Hebrew word for philanthropic giving, *tzedaka*, finds its root in *tzedek*—justice.

---

* Connected to Give, October 2014, Facebook.com/ConnectedToGive.

The tradition of *tikkun olam* thrives in Israel as well. Small and embattled as it is, Israel consistently rallies to the support of people in need around the world. During natural disasters, the IDF Homefront Command deploys a Field Hospital Unit to the most stricken zones. Even in distant locations, such as Haiti or Japan, it is usually the first mobile hospital unit on the scene and has become a staple of international emergency aid efforts. The World Health Organization classifies relief agencies for purposes of positioning and provisioning in disaster areas. The IDF unit is the only organization in the world to hold the highest Type III certification. Although Israeli aid is typically rejected by Muslim governments, including Iran's and Malaysia's, the Israeli government extends individual aid to their citizens when it can. Thousands of wounded from Syria's civil war have been treated in Israeli hospitals, despite the currently severe fiscal strains on Israel's healthcare system. Syria, of course, is in a permanent state of war with Israel. Many Syrian citizens, including some bound for treatment in Israel, regard Israel as their enemy.

Dozens of Israeli NGOs operate around the world, offering aid to millions, including citizens of enemy countries. Save a Child's Heart provides pro bono cardiac surgery to children, including Iraqis, Syrians, and Gazan Palestinians. Israid provides relief services to refugees from across the Middle East. Innovation Africa lights villages and provides irrigation technologies in Uganda, Rwanda, Tanzania, and Kenya.

Some have charged that these Israeli government and

NGO efforts are driven by ulterior motives such as enhancing Israel's public image. Popular conspiracy theories based on this charge have taken root, particularly in Middle Eastern countries that have contributed nothing to these aid efforts themselves. These conspiracies find disappointing purchase in the democratic West as well. One theory, evoking the medieval blood libel by claiming that Israeli teams harvested the organs of Haitian children during the post-earthquake IDF rescue operation in that country, was shamelessly endorsed by a member of the British Parliament. Of course, by undermining the people actually providing aid, these conspiracy theorists, were they successful, would be harming the very victims who need it.

The IDF Field Hospital Unit turns away reservist volunteers on every one of its oversubscribed missions. These volunteers report for duty because they believe it is the right thing to do. But far more important than the reason they report for duty is the fact that they do. They are driven by a Jewish sense of justice, a value to be pursued in this life, the success of that pursuit measured primarily in practical results.

EDUCATION

Stripped of both a geographic base and an organized hierarchy after the Roman exile, Jewish identity and practice centered on a written code. With no centralized leadership, Jewish learning and debate fell to its practitioners. This demanded the capacity for abstract thought. Comfort with abstraction is part of what some have termed "Jewish thinking." Jewish holidays are infused with symbolism that demands interpretation. Children are at the center of this exercise; it is part of a Jewish education. The Passover Seder, which recounts Israel's exodus from slavery in Egypt, admonishes us to consider each successive generation of Jews as having itself left the land of Egypt. It asks us to consider what freedom means to us. What would we be prepared to sacrifice for it? It asks us to consider the arguments that Moses's dissenters raised during the Exodus. Who would those dissenters be today, and what would their arguments be?

There is a set of questions at the Passover Seder that the youngest participant at the table is asked to read aloud. Engagement with the texts requires literacy, which has traditionally been taught at a young age, even in periods during which most of the world was illiterate. As discussed earlier, Jews were typically literate in three languages—Hebrew for the texts; one of the Jewish languages of exile, Yiddish or Ladino for example, for intracommunity discourse; and the region's lingua franca for extracommunity dialogue and interaction. Often barred from participation in professional guilds and from land ownership in Europe, Jews in many geographies found a living in finance. This required education in a fourth language—mathematics.

The Jews have consistently embraced education as an essential communal resource. Jewish families have traditionally invested in education, even at the expense of other resources. This investment is an inseparable component of Jewish culture, a Jewish value. The value has remained in place even as the conditions that inspired it have faded.

CHALLENGE AND DISSENT

In the Book of Genesis, when God tells Abraham of his intention to destroy the city of Sodom and all of its inhabitants, Abraham challenges him on the morality of his decision and begins a negotiation with him for the lives of the people of Sodom. At first, Abraham proposes that God agree to spare the city if Abraham can find fifty righteous souls in the entire population. When God concedes, Abraham presses him further, asking to lower the threshold to forty-five righteous souls, then forty. Eventually they agree that if Abraham can find just ten righteous souls in Sodom, God will spare the city. Abraham is not arguing with the Almighty out of personal interest. Remember that this is the same man who had unquestioningly bound his own son, Isaac, to the altar for sacrifice at God's command. This is an objective moral argument. Abraham argues morality with the creator of morality himself. God engages willingly in the argument, even conceding victories to Abraham.

Authority and truth are separable themes in Judaism. The structure of Jewish theological practice reinforces this notion. No one individual, or group of individuals, is meant to impart dogma to the undiscerning masses in sermons, edicts, or fatwas. Jewish learning is organized around the *hevruta,* people young and old huddled around a text, itself often expressing a dissenting opinion, debating the nuances of its meaning. Judaism is a religion of challenge and dissent. (Of course, the modern Rabbinate is a glaring exception.)

The tradition holds in secular Judaism as well. Almost always small in number and usually disempowered in the Diaspora, Jews have habitually challenged authority. From Jesus to Karl Marx, they have stood as exemplars of dissent, often at great personal cost. It is the culture of dissent that enabled an assembly of fighter pilots to criticize their leader's decisions so vigorously in an open forum. That culture facilitated their leader's abdication of the shield of hierarchy in favor of merit as a tool for resolving their arguments. They were able to shelve the chain of command temporarily without threatening our own governance. Dissent is a Jewish value.

TRADITION

Michael, a friend of mine who grew up in a kosher home in an American Jewish community, lived within wider American society for the first time when he went off to college. He began to experiment there. He dated non-Jewish women. He studied comparative religion and spent his time outside the framework of campus Jewish life. Michael did continue to eat only kosher food, but as nobody around him did, he naturally began to question that resolution as well. For some reason, the dietary threshold was more difficult for Michael to cross. He shared his thoughts with several confidants, including his liberal, open-minded parents, hoping to gain clarity.

In a telephone conversation, his mother helped him think it through. "We raised you to be curious and to challenge," she told him, "and we are proud to have succeeded. You are your own man, endowed with all of the moral tools to guide you to your *own* decisions. So, if you want to be the first link in our family's thirty-nine-hundred-year chain to actually break, there is nothing we can do to stop you." That conversation took place twenty-five years ago. Michael has stuck with kosher food.

Tradition was the value that Michael's mother was emphasizing to him. In order to maintain a coherent identity, any group requires a common set of beliefs or practices distinct to it. Judaism, specifically, is bound together more by practice than by belief. Data extrapolated from the 2013 Pew study reveals that a majority of American Jews do not believe in God. Only 77 percent of Modern Orthodox Jews—Jews deeply committed to Jewish practice, including strict Sabbath observance and total adherence to dietary laws—report belief in God. Even among Haredi Jews, cloistered in isolated Ultra-Orthodox communities with almost no interaction with non-Haredi people and with tight restrictions on television and media consumption, there are pockets of nonbelievers brazen enough to admit their doubts in a survey (albeit only 4 percent).

Jewish tradition is not about belief. It is about practice. It includes life milestones such as the Jewish wedding, the *brit* or birth covenant (circumcision), and the bar mitzvah and bat mitzvah ceremonies; annual traditions such as the Jewish holy days, the Passover Seder, and fasting on Yom Kippur; and family observances such as the Sabbath dinner. It includes ongoing traditional practices such as Jewish education of some kind, or engagement with Israel. A majority of Jews today, perhaps more than 75 percent, observe most of these traditions in some form.

Some Jews additionally practice Hebrew language study, Sabbath observance, kashrut, and other traditions. Some members of the Haredi communities in the United States and in Israel dedicate their lives to refining their understanding of Jewish religious law (Halacha) and struggle constantly to perfect their compliance with it. Without these custodians of Jewish tradition, all of world Jewry might lose the anchor of its Moving Average. The current state of enmity that prevails between various streams of Judaism prevents many from appreciating the critical role that Ultra-Orthodoxy plays in Jewish continuity today. Ultra-Orthodoxy may even contribute to Jewish moral innovation. Many members of the Reform and Conservative movements might actually be emboldened to pursue religious reform specifically because the Ultra-Orthodox anchor is in place. By limiting the pace at which the Jewish Crowd may drift, Ultra-Orthodoxy may paradoxically be enabling experimentation and risk taking in Jewish practice.

Most Jews are generally aware of the breadth of Jewish tradition, and of its distinguishing role in Jewish identity. Tradition forms an important bond between Jews, whether they practice it regularly or not. Reestablishing open and robust dialogue among the streams of Judaism will be critical to halting Jewish decline. These streams are alienated from one another today, but working together, they could create vital new meaning for the Jewish People. Rapprochement can begin only through mutual acknowledgment of each stream's contributions to the vitality of Jewry as a whole.

COMMUNITY

Jewish commitment to community has been a critical factor in Jewish continuity through its long Diaspora. The lengths we have gone to preserve community have been unambiguous features of Jewish life. The concept of a *minyan,* the quorum of ten participants required to properly exercise certain religious rites, such as mourning a death, is an acknowledgment of community's centrality. In a religious sense, Orthodox Jews cannot fully function in populations of fewer than ten Jewish males.

Over the centuries, Jews from disparate corners of the earth have rallied to one another's rescue in times of distress and succor in times of recovery. The practice is enshrined in the concept of *pidyon shvuyim* (redemption of captives), a Talmudic Great Mitzvah. It has never been abandoned. Consider the intensity of the American and Israeli Jewish communities' struggle on behalf of Soviet Jewry in the 1970s and '80s, or of Ethiopian Jewry in the 1990s. Consider Zionism itself, the ingathering of Jews from around the world, all welcome regardless of ability to contribute or sustain themselves financially. Israel absorbed one million Russian immigrants between 1990 and 1992, a number equivalent to 20 percent of its entire population. These immigrants arrived without financial resources; few spoke Hebrew or would be able to function professionally in Israeli society for years. I remember hearing professionally skilled string ensembles playing on street corners in Tel Aviv in those days. A joke at the time asked, "What do you call a Russian immigrant coming off the plane without a musical instrument? A pianist." Many considered Israeli society, and the Israeli economy, too small to absorb the talent, but these immigrants were ultimately integrated.

In the 1940s and early 1950s, Israel absorbed 800,000

Jewish refugees exiled from newly sovereign Middle Eastern countries such as Iraq, Syria, Lebanon, Egypt, Jordan, Morocco, Algeria, Tunisia, and Libya. That number was equivalent to nearly 40 percent of the existing Israeli population, an enormous integration challenge that would persist for decades. The immigration put a massive strain on Israeli society, mostly borne by the immigrants themselves, like Fouad from the grocery store, but the country ultimately absorbed it, and Jews worldwide supported the absorption unquestioningly. Israel has continued to absorb waves of Jewish refugees, notably from Yemen, Romania, and Ethiopia. As French Jewry has grown increasingly anxious in recent years, the community's emigrants have found harbor mainly in Israel. It is difficult to find parallel community bonds among other religious or ethnic diasporas.

American and Israeli Jewry still share a powerful affinity. Their bond may not be as strong as it was a generation ago, but as long as it exists, the possibility of strengthening it does, too. If community is indeed a key tenet of Judaism, we have no choice but to strengthen it. Without community, there is no Judaism.

Exposure to Judaism through summer camps, volunteer programs, and university scholarships is within the proposed endowment's reach from a financial perspective. Of course, the free education component is more than a Jewish value. Education strengthens our community. It is also a carrot intended to encourage engagement in it. For the vast majority of couples, the Jewish World Endowment would be an outstanding college savings plan. Break-even household incomes for participation are more than $700,000 for a family with three children. (That is, for parents earning incomes lower than this, the program makes sense on a purely financial basis.) This is made possible, of course, by the 1.25 percent pretax participation of the highest-income members of the Jewish world, many of them already community leaders with philanthropic budgets far larger than 1.25 percent of their pretax income. Those leaders who are passionate about Jewish continuity, and about taking ownership of the Jewish future, would be necessary participants in the Jewish World Endowment.

Most families should be in a position to recognize the Endowment plan's financial value immediately. Very few parents of a five-year-old child can be confident they will be earning average incomes above the break-even level over the next thirteen years, as their child matures to college age. And if they do, that will have been a positive outcome, like a life or disability insurance policy that is never exercised because the policyholder remains in good health. Like insurance, the program would be an asset with real financial value.

The lowest common denominator may be financial, but many families would be motivated by nonfinancial factors to seek new, more inclusive forms of engagement in Jewish community. Hebrew day schools are beyond the financial reach of many families. Other families are not disposed to parochial education, which often comes at the expense of general secular education and a multicultural social environment. Synagogue attendance serves as a solution for some, but the numbers demonstrate that its appeal is limited for most Jews. The Endowment could serve as a vehicle for engagement that attracts much broader segments of the Jewish population.

For many who are not already motivated by community, the very act of engagement in the program, including having financial skin in the game and committing their children's time to an explicitly Jewish enterprise, may lead members to engage. A premium-paying family's propensity to connect with the Jewish community, through traditional channels such as Sunday school, synagogue, community center, time in Israel, or other means, is likely to rise.

This is not meant to serve as a detailed blueprint for the next big project in Jewish social action. The Jewish World Endowment should be seen as an experimental concept. Its mission would be to fuse the world's two large Jewish communities by reanimating and invigorating their common Judaism. It should empower us to collectively navigate the new threats to our survival, and the new opportunities to cultivate communal purpose. It is, most importantly, an inclusion mechanism, designed to maximize participation in the global Jewish Crowd Wisdom experiment.

10

The Presidency

The Wisdom Machine, the technology platform for soliciting and aggregating the wisdom of our Crowd, and the Jewish World Endowment, the educational framework that informs the Crowd's participation in its self-definition, form two legs of a tripod on which future Jewish governance can rest. The third leg must provide an executive function, a process that will ultimately translate the Crowd's legislation into policy.

This process should be managed from Israel, the official guardian and custodian of Judaism's holy sites, and the Jewish nation's refuge of last resort.

But location must not form the basis of hierarchy. All Jews must be equal partners, not only in legislating the future of Judaism but in executing it. The challenge is to propose a mechanism for Jewish governance that places Israel at its center but offers all of global Jewry an equal seat at the table. This sounds like a tall order, but many of the key components of such a mechanism are already in place. They include the existing organizational structures of Jewish communal life in the United States, the UK, France, and the smaller centers of Jewish life. They include global organs such as the Jewish Agency. Most important, they include the sovereign government of the State of Israel.

Israel is a country with two separate missions. First, it is a state like any other, whose mandate includes providing its citizens with healthcare, education, welfare, defense, infrastructure, and the rule of law. Its second mission is special. Israel is the self-proclaimed nation-state of the Jewish People. This title dictates, among other roles, that Israel serve as the one guaranteed harbor for Jews seeking refuge, wherever they are. Israel's safe-harbor mission is embodied in the Law of Return, which grants automatic citizenship to any Jew requesting it. Israel extends additional rights to all Jews, claiming to represent them whether they choose to exercise their rights or not. Israel's foreign intelligence service, the Mossad, has a sizable unit dedicated exclusively to Diaspora Jewry. Throughout its history, Israel has acted internationally on behalf of noncitizens in a way that no other country would. It facilitated the waves of immigration we discussed earlier. It has helped to coordinate security with European governments for the Jews of France, the UK, and other countries. These Jews are not Israeli citizens, but the nation-state of the Jews takes responsibility for their welfare. This is Israeli policy, and it has been since before Israel's independence.

But non-Israeli Jews have no hand in defining or protecting their rights in Israel. They have no representation in the

Israeli democratic process. Their rights rest exclusively in the hands of Israeli citizens—both Jews and non-Jews. World Jewry does not get a formal say in its own representation. It does not get a vote in deciding how the resources of the nation-state of the Jews are allocated on the Jews' behalf. World Jewry cannot opine on whether a Jewish crisis in France should take precedence over one in England. It has no representation with regard to the Law of Return and its possible amendment. Importantly, it has no role in defining the Jewish character of the state of the Jews—purportedly their own state. Which Jews should have access to Jewish holy sites? Which rabbis' conversions and marriages should be recognized by the Jewish State? The mismatch between Israel's ambition to represent all Jews and its governance, which leaves non-Israeli Jews unrepresented, is the result of the muddled approach the Israeli government has taken to Israel's dual functions since its inception.

Many in both Israel and the United States feel that this lack of representation is appropriate, maintaining that only people who pay taxes in Israel, serve in the Israeli military, and subject themselves to the realities of life in Israel deserve representation through their vote. I agree that this is true with regard to Israel's first mission—that of a nation among nations. American Jews have no business determining Israeli fiscal or defense policy. But lack of representation for Diaspora Jewry as it regards Israel as the nation-state of the Jews is unreasonable, needlessly alienating, and ultimately undermines Israel's raison d'être. If Israel is to continue claiming to represent all Jews, and to continue demanding worldwide

Jewish support, it must give all Jews representation in the matters that impact them directly. These are:

1. the Law of Return;
2. Israel's Jewish character; and
3. Israeli government actions in Jewish communities beyond Israel's borders.

These demands are not only logical and fair to the Jewish Diaspora; they are squarely in *Israeli* Jews' interest. If American Jews cannot find emotional purchase in Israel *as Jews,* they will not be part of the franchise. As we have noted, this divergence will end tragically for both communities. But we can stop the trend, and even reverse it, with a structural change.

Israel is governed as a parliamentary democracy. The Israeli government is led by the elected prime minister and the cabinet of ministers he or she assembles through coalition negotiations. Each minister (the defense minister, for example) is responsible for policy and for executive decisions in his or her ministerial domain. The system is modeled after British parliamentary democracy, but Great Britain is only a nation among nations, claiming no responsibility for people of foreign nationality even if they are of British lineage.

Unlike the parliament, the Israeli presidency is a figurehead role, similar to that of modern-day European monarchs. Israel's president has few real powers—legislative, executive, or judicial. He or she serves as a sort of nonsectarian diplomat in chief, an advocate for domestic unity, goodwill, and neighborly relations among Israel's disparate ethnic and religious constituencies. The role has no teeth. If it were to be abolished tomorrow, little would change in Israel. But if we were to allocate Israel's two missions to two distinct and separate governance structures, the Israeli presidency could become a vital resource.

Mission 1, running a modern country, would continue to be managed by the elected government—elected by Israeli citizens. It would continue setting policy in all regular matters of state, from education to defense.

Mission 2, maintaining the nation-state of the Jews, would fall to the presidency. The president would have executive power over the policies that allow Israel to make that claim, policies that impact all Jews. These would include actions on behalf of Jewish communities beyond Israel's borders, administration of Israel's Law of Return, and responsibility for Israel's Jewish character, including custody of Israel's Jewish holy sites. Non-Jewish (Muslim, Christian, Druse, Baha'i, or other) holy sites would still be administered by the elected government's Religious Affairs Ministry. The presidency would be the office responsible for defining exactly *who is a Jew* for purposes of *full* Jewish citizenship in Israel, including marriage and burial rights. The presidency of Israel would be the convening point for Jews around the world to debate fundamental questions of Peoplehood.

As this office would represent the *Jewish* interests of Jews globally, Jews in the Diaspora would be entitled to vote for their president. Elections for the government of Israel would remain open only to Israeli citizens—Jewish and non-Jewish. Elections for the presidency would be open only to Jews—

Israeli and non-Israeli. The president of Israel would be, in effect, president of the Jewish People.*

Many, particularly readers in Israel, will balk upon reading this. It represents a radical departure from the status quo. It usurps political power from various institutions in Israel, among them the Rabbinate, the Religious Affairs Ministry, and the Interior Ministry.

But I challenge readers to weigh the costs and benefits of the status quo against those of global Jewish representation. This is not just a question of moral justice, but of practical survival. All Jews should feel ownership of Israel as a national asset. Even if its execution has been imperfect, this was the idea from the beginning. This is a partnership of us all. Denying this would strip Israel of its legitimacy. If Israel is to be a Jewish asset, all Jews must have a seat at the table where Israel's Jewish character is set and maintained. More practically, if the currently widening rift between American and Israeli Jews becomes a permanent split, Israel's survival is thrown into serious question. We all have a very practical stake in creating ownership in the enterprise. And with ownership comes responsibility.

As the new presidency would serve global Jewry, its candidate pool should not be limited to current citizens of Israel.

---

* Some have pointed out that Israeli Jewish participation in presidential elections would, at least initially, be much higher than Diaspora Jewish participation. While it is unclear that this would affect actual election results, if this is indeed a concern, vote counting could be normalized to reflect a set balance (say 50/50) between Israeli and Diaspora votes. This would correct for the results of any numerical bias toward Israeli Jewish voters. It would also provide added incentive for Diaspora Jews to vote, as each Diaspora Jewish vote would carry more weight.

People already uncomfortable with the idea of global elections will likely be alarmed at the idea of a non-Israeli president of Israel, but there is precedent. Albert Einstein, for example, was offered the Israeli presidency in 1952. Other foreign citizens have been offered, and occasionally have accepted, key leadership roles in Israeli governmental and quasi-governmental institutions. In 2005, the Israeli government cast a wide international net in its search for the most qualified Central Bank governor it could attract, nominating the American citizen Stanley Fischer. Like the Central Bank governor, the president of Israel should be the most qualified person in the world for the job. Qualifications for the new presidency should include an intimate understanding of both U.S. and Israeli Jewry, and credibility in both communities.

Reforming the presidency would necessitate an overhaul of the office's resources. Today's Israeli presidency requires no technocracy to execute its ceremonial functions. In any nonceremonial matters, it serves primarily as a rubber stamp for recommendations made by government ministries. The expanded presidency would require a robust infrastructure. It would, in essence, be taking over some of the key functions of today's Chief Rabbinate along with some ministerial functions. Most important, it would:

- Administer Judaism's holy sites
- Manage the relationship between the State of Israel, Israeli Jewry, and global Jewry. This includes:
  - Setting standards for conversion to Judaism for purposes of the Law of Return and Israeli State recognition in matters of birth, marriage, and burial in state cem-

eteries. Of course, individual Jewish communities and their institutions, in and out of Israel, would be free to recognize or reject any individual conversion, but these rejections would have no bearing on State recognition.

- Setting the standards for determining Jewish provenance for purposes of the Law of Return, and Israeli State recognition in matters of birth, marriage, and burial in state cemeteries
- Administration of the Jewish World Endowment

The office would require senior representation of the major streams of Judaism: Reform, Conservative, and Orthodox. It would require at least one dedicated representative of American Jewry, at least one dedicated representative of Israeli Jewry, and one representative of the remaining Diaspora. It would require theological authorities and intellectual leaders. It would require seasoned legislative leadership to interface with government. It would require outreach resources to establish and maintain ties with Jewish communities around the world, especially youth. It would be the elected president's prerogative to nominate these leaders, choosing from the most qualified available professionals in the world. Nominations would aim to represent the two major centers of contemporary Jewish life with equal weight, and to minimize partisanship.

A NOTE ON CONVERSION

The vicious math behind the decline of American Jewry works only if we treat intermarriage as a loss. But we could treat many intermarriages as opportunities to add new members to the nation. This approach would not be unprecedented. It is enough to note the mostly light complexions of Northern European Jews versus the mixed complexions of central European Jews versus the darker complexions of North African and Middle Eastern Jews versus the uniformly dark complexions of Jews of Yemenite or Ethiopian extraction to conclude that our people has practiced inclusion by intermarriage and conversion over many geographies in other periods. The standards for conversion to Judaism have been fluid over the centuries, and have often borne little resemblance to the draconian demands of the frequently fickle Israeli Rabbinate today. Maimonides wrote in the twelfth century, "A proselyte whose motivations were never considered or who was never informed about the Commandments and the punishments for transgressing them, but was circumcised, and immersed in the presence of three laymen . . . He is a valid convert according to Jewish law."*

Not everybody has to agree with Maimonides. As discussed, dissent is central to Judaism. We do, however, need a common standard for recognition of a conversion as far as the State of Israel is concerned. In fact, that is the only standard that matters for the purposes of Jewish Peoplehood. If a non-Jew decides to convert to Judaism in America today, she is certain to be able to find at least one rabbi who will perform her conversion and at least one rabbi who will reject it. As far as she is concerned, however, her conversion need be recognized only by her converting rabbi's congregation. The

* Issurei Biah 13:17.

opinions of other rabbis and other congregations are irrelevant to her, as these rabbis lack any means of influencing her life. Postconversion, she will simply join a congregation that welcomes her and avoid those that do not. Of course, this is not the case in Israel, where the unelected Chief Rabbinate speaks for the State and purports, by extension, to speak for the Jewish People.

If the presidency is to speak for the Jewish People, it cannot view conversion as purely an Orthodox religious act. Indeed, many sincere converts will not lead Orthodox religious Jewish lives—just as most born Jews do not. If a non-Jewish woman converts upon marriage to a secular Jewish man, it is unrealistic to expect her to adopt a strict halachic lifestyle while her husband continues to live his secular lifestyle. Her lifestyle is much more likely to reflect his. But as far as the State of Israel is currently concerned, she is not Jewish, and therefore the couple's offspring are not Jewish. They will not enjoy the full status of citizenship in Israel. Unwelcome, they will most likely turn away from Israel. They may turn away from Judaism entirely. We have lost them, and we have lost their children.

If the elected president were to be the arbiter of conversion standards, he or she would be answerable to world Jewry and would be challenged to author conversion standards that would satisfy and enfranchise world Jewry, most of whose members (and I include Israeli Jews) do not adhere to any version of strict halachic Judaism, certainly not the Rabbinate's monopoly version. Under a new paradigm, the nation-state of the Jews would embrace the converting woman referred to above under circumstances agreeable to a majority of engaged Jews (which could be defined as those who vote). The world Jewish population might grow rather than shrink. Critically, the bond between American and Israeli Jewry would strengthen rather than weaken. No rabbi would be forced to accept this conversion; as in the United States or in Europe, any Israeli rabbi could rule any conversion "not Jewish enough" for his congregation. But such a rabbi's authority would be limited to his own followers. For purposes of full citizenship in the State of Israel, the nation-state of the Jews, this conversion would be valid.

I do not suggest that conversion benchmarks be as lax as possible. In fact, there may be reason to set a higher bar in a post-Diaspora world than there was in the Diaspora. The problem with Maimonides's broad-tent view on conversion today is its vulnerability to abuse under Israel's Law of Return. If conversion were too easy, Israel would quickly be overrun by new converts motivated not by spiritual compulsion or loyalty to the Jewish community, but by the prospect of economic betterment. Worse, mass disingenuous conversion could be used to cynically manipulate the Law of Return to subvert Israeli democracy.

The standards adopted by the presidency would have to take these challenges into account. Conversion need not demand an Orthodox religious lifestyle, but it cannot simply be an act of convenience. These standards would naturally evolve over time, as all Jewish practice has, but one paradigm might be naturalization.

A person born in the United States or to Americans is an American. She is not required to know anything about the United States or about being American. She makes no specific commitments, other than paying taxes. In this sense she is like a Jew, recognized as Jewish because she was born Jew-ish. Like the born Jew, the born American's identity is not challenged even if she is totally ignorant of American values, makes no commitment to the American people, and behaves in a manner that nobody would recognize as American.

But in order to *become* an American, you need to clear a bar. You need to pass a citizenship exam that confirms famil-iarity with what we Americans define, democratically, as the fundamental tenets of Americanism. That requires learning. Study is a commitment. You also take an oath of allegiance to the United States and commit to taking on the specific re-sponsibilities of citizenship. The path to gaining U.S. citizen-ship is open to individuals married to Americans, but it can also be gained, without marriage, after a prolonged period liv-ing among Americans, having demonstrated a long-standing desire to be an American.

The lowest-common-denominator tenets of Judaism, de-rived from an ongoing exercise of Jewish Crowd Wisdom, could serve as the basis of a canon of knowledge, and a set of commitments, required of new members of the Jewish Peo-ple. Some minimum period of engagement in the process could also be required as a demonstration of a genuine desire to become Jewish. This ongoing exercise would be adminis-tered by the office of the presidency.

The expanded presidency would represent one of the most important leadership roles in the world today. It would be the forum for planning and maintaining a new Jewish architec-ture, different from the global democracy imposed by Diaspora for nearly two thousand years. This democracy would be managed intentionally and actively by its own members, and facilitated by technology, which has become an essential feature of our lives. Fittingly, much of this technology is being developed in Israel.

The president's mission would not be limited to survival. Empowered to make decisions collectively, the Jewish People will achieve a higher level of cohesion and of self-determination than it enjoys today. I hesitate to predict the outcome. That will be determined by the Crowd, but it is likely to include the marshaling of this people's collective potential in ways it has not been marshaled before. This will benefit not only the Jews, but all of humanity.

11

Conclusion

I was sitting in our New York dining room with my patient editor, Claire, working on what we hoped would be one of the last drafts of this book, when Ella, now fifteen years old, began practicing the piano downstairs. Claire and I took a moment to appreciate the gentle rendering of Gershwin's "Summertime." I thought about Ella's life. I had heard a calling when I was a teenager, and it has given my life focus and meaning. Ella was lucky to have recognized her own calling at an even younger age. She dreams of leaving the world a bit more equitable, a bit more optimistic, and a bit happier than she found it. Having worked with children in need for several years already, she is now writing a children's book intended for young refugees. The book teaches emotional coping strategies to help children in hopeless circumstances to preserve their ambition and their optimism. These strategies are woven into the book's narrative. Three years ago Ella dedicated her bat mitzvah to raising money for a large orphanage called Kayango, in rural Uganda. She used the money to install solar power, lighting, and Internet service and to provide school supplies and basic provisions for 450 children. We traveled to Uganda with Ella to help coordinate the final stages of delivery and installation. Ella had committed to teaching a multiday computer workshop for the teachers at Kayango, with the goal of establishing a permanent email link with the orphanage.

We arrived to find conditions worse than we had imagined. Many of the children were infected with chronic diseases, including HIV and malaria. Some had been victims of violence. Ella kept up a brave smile during the day but cried herself to sleep every night. Amber and I debated whether we had made a terrible mistake in allowing our twelve-year-old to be exposed to so much reality so suddenly. But every morning Ella collected herself and marched into Kayango with a big smile, and with hugs for the children. She taught her computer class and succeeded in coaching a few members of the administration to the point where they could communicate by email. She is still in touch with the faculty at Kayango. Ella is lucky to have found an identity that brings meaning to her life. Amber and I wish the same for Mia and Lily.

All three of our girls are Jewishly committed. It is important to them that we celebrate Shabbat and the holidays together as a family. Ella has taken pains to keep her Hebrew up after three years living in the United States. She sees a link between her social endeavors and her Jewishness. Judaism is the compass that helps her navigate her course. Her sense of justice and responsibility are not generic. They emerge from a code she has been exposed to since infancy. She grapples with questions. We do not give her answers. We do not have them. She struggles alone, intellectually and often emotionally.

Ella plans to enlist in the IDF after high school. I support her choice. She believes she will be serving the principles that define her, and that define the people who serve as their custodians. I believe that much of world Jewry is still defined by these principles, but I wonder for how long. How much of world Jewry will stand up for them today? Do we still have the critical mass to preserve our legacy? If not, what cause will Ella be serving?

What I do know is that whatever mass we have is dwindling quickly. If we continue in this direction, I doubt Ella's children will serve, or even identify with their people. Amber and I endowed Ella and her sisters with the tools to define their own lives. They can choose to be Jewish. They can choose to be something else. If we continue to ignore our legacy, or to behave in a manner that abrogates it, we will find fewer and fewer people like Ella making the Jewish choice, until there are none.

I have a Palestinian business partner who, over the years, has also become a close friend. We spend time with each other's families and visit each other's homes often. I trust this man, in business and in friendship. I was once traveling in the West Bank with one of his associates, whom I will call Imad. It was late summer, and Imad and I were in his car, on our way from Ramallah to a business that he managed a few miles out of town. I had a good rapport with Imad, and we spoke freely about the politics of Palestinians and Israelis doing business together. Imad knew my background and accepted it. He shared my sense for the subtleties of national allegiance, in and out of conflict. Our own allegiances were tested by an incident on that short drive.

The road from Ramallah to Imad's business passes through an IDF checkpoint. I had driven on the road a number of times before, and the checkpoint was usually unmanned. It sat at the crest of a hill, and consisted of three concrete barricades in the road, the first on the right, the second on the left, and the third on the right. A vehicle approaching the checkpoint would have to drive slowly in order to slalom between the barricades. On the side of the road, there was a guard shed and a watchtower, which commanded a view of traffic coming from either direction, and of the surrounding hills. When Imad slowed to negotiate the barricades, I noticed that the checkpoint was manned that afternoon. It was about two o'clock, and ours was the only vehicle there.

As Imad wove through the barriers, a female soldier came out of the guard shed and casually motioned for us to pull over. When we had stopped, she turned around and disappeared back into the shed. We waited in the air-conditioned car. Two soldiers, immigrants from Ethiopia, smoked cigarettes in the watchtower, uninterested in us. Eventually, the female soldier sauntered out of the shed with a clipboard. She approached the car and motioned for us to get out. She must have been nineteen years old. She had clearly drawn a short straw to have been assigned this duty. "Have a seat on the curb," she said in Hebrew, looking down at her clipboard. We sat on the hot curb. She did not ask for identification. She took a look inside Imad's luxury car and rolled her eyes, jotted something in her clipboard, and turned back toward the guard shed. I looked up at the Ethiopian soldiers in the watchtower. They were still smoking cigarettes, chatting.

The car stood idling. Imad and I waited in the sun, wondering what the soldier was checking. A few minutes passed, and no other traffic approached. I became impatient. There was clearly not much work for these soldiers on a day like today. It was hot. We were late for our meeting. It seemed we were being detained unnecessarily. I took off my jacket. Imad continued the conversation we had been having in the car. I followed his lead. I was his guest here.

I heard laughter on the watchtower, and looked up to find that the young woman had joined the two male soldiers for a cigarette. I imagined they were laughing at us. I felt for the wallet in my jacket, trying to remember if I was carrying my reserve officer identification. I wanted these soldiers disciplined. There was no security value in detaining us like this. This was an abuse of power.

Beyond the frustration and the heat, I felt ashamed for the IDF, and for Israeli society. If we behave in this way toward the people with whom we are trying to make peace, can we really be surprised if they doubt our sincerity? I found I did have my ID. I could walk over to the tower with it and get each of the soldiers' names and serial numbers. I knew exactly with whom I would speak in the Military Police. I thought about recording my interaction with the soldiers on my telephone, to remove any doubt about the nature of this infraction. I thought about ways of contacting the soldiers' commanding officer directly.

Then I reminded myself that I was Imad's guest. This was his turf. I was riding in his car, from his office to his business. If anyone was going to extricate us from this situation, it would have to be Imad. I am sure he recognized the situation's awkwardness as clearly as I did. To these IDF soldiers, I was a Palestinian businessperson. I certainly look the part. To Imad, who actually knew me, I was a lieutenant colonel in the IDF, just being a friend, temporarily casting my lot in with his. So we sat there sweating, waiting for the young woman to finish her cigarette and whatever else she planned to do. I admired Imad's equanimity and wondered how much of it was calculated to put me at ease. Finally she appeared again, without her clipboard. With a look of feigned surprise that we were still sitting on the curb, she waved us back into the car. "*Yalla*, get out of here."

I kept my mouth shut and got back in the car with Imad. We drove on in silence. I thought of apologizing, but that seemed inappropriate, even disingenuous. We were too intimate for trite formalities. Imad finally came to my rescue.

"You know, I am in favor of the checkpoints. They have to go away at some point but, for now, they are effective. They reduce violence. If a young idiot gets to Tel Aviv with a bomb, your government immediately clamps down, and things become much worse, for business, and for everyone. This way, at least it is quiet."

"I appreciate you saying that," I told him. "I am not sure that particular checkpoint added to our security or to yours."

Imad smiled at the road ahead. "Every society has its great kids, its normal kids, and also its bad kids. You draft the entire population in the army, so we get to meet all three. You know it is no different for the Americans or the British in Iraq. This poor girl is at the peak of her power. Perhaps school was not easy for her socially. She might go back to a difficult life after the army. But for this short time, she is the boss. This is her hilltop. She is enjoying a very crude and simple taste of authority. This is probably the only one she will ever know. Most kids at the checkpoints are better but, believe me, there are also worse."

Imad was expressing a view that I shared. I am sure that Israel's political and military leadership did not have this sort of conduct in mind when they drafted Israel's checkpoint policy in the West Bank. I know that even the right wing of the Israeli government is sensitive to the point that the people we are fighting today are the same people with whom we hope to live in peace tomorrow. The Americans and the British would eventually leave Iraq, but we would be neighbors with these people forever. Avoidable humiliations are tremendously counterproductive—to our own interests. I know that our leaders appreciate this. They also appreciate that kids like this young woman, exposed to constant tension, danger, fear, and rage during their formative years, come home changed. Violence and coercion become everyday instruments in their emotional tool kits. These instruments feature in their interactions with their communities and with their own families. Our leaders are aware of these long-term costs, and of the diminishing value that accrues to those who pay them, but they ignore both in the interest of parochial short-term gain. The Jewish People demands little of its leaders, but individual Jews, in America and in Israel, are beginning to vote with their feet. The breaking point will arrive without warning.

How will Ella react if she finds herself in situations like this one? Will she continue buying the whole package, as I did, understanding that you cannot pick and choose? And if she serves alongside people like the young woman Imad and I met, will she reject their behavior on principle or accommodate it out of loyalty? Checkpoints like these occasionally come under attack by suicide bomber or sniper. Soldiers are wounded and sometimes killed. A unit's members must rely on one another and fight together in order to survive combat. How long will Ella be able to bear the tension between shared fates and conflicting values before her own emotional tool kit becomes compromised? Can we, as parents, regard that compromise as anything but the sacrifice of our child?

And what will Ella's sacrifice accomplish for her generation of Jews? Will she be able to ignore being cursed by Ultra-Orthodox men on a public bus for wearing a uniform they consider immodest? Should she ignore it? By the time Ella completes her service, well over half of Israeli elementary schoolers will be Ultra-Orthodox and Arab Israelis, communities that categorically reject her vision of Israel and will not serve alongside her. When Ella is in a position to weigh the rising cost of service against its declining value in terms of the principles she is serving, will she continue buying the whole package?

If she returns the package, as many will, and goes back to America, will her Jewish identity remain as strong as it is today? Her generation of American Jews is much smaller than mine, and far less affiliated. Without Israel and without a strong Jewish community, organized around a compelling Jewish identity, will Ella not seek a different compass, one less compromised?

I use Ella's experience to highlight the considerations facing many Jewish teenagers today, but it should be clear that she and her sisters are far from representative. Ella and Mia have begun to think through questions like these. They are better equipped to answer them than many of their peers in America and in Israel are. They are familiar with Jewish tradition, and they value it. They speak English and Hebrew. They feel as comfortable in New York City as they do in Tel Aviv. By the time Jews like Ella and Mia begin struggling with these questions, a large swath of their generation will already have unconsciously answered "no." In Israel's case, that will include the segment that is most critical to the country's physical survival. In America's, it is a group so large that its "no" will finally and permanently break the Jewish story's chain. Unless the Jews can collectively define their lowest common denominator, organize around it as a community, and draw value from it as individuals, we might already have met the last generation of Judaism as we know it.

Looking out from Zippori at the yellow hills of Galilee, in the final days of the final revolt, Yehuda Hanassi could not have known the breadth and span of his people's approaching Diaspora. He may have imagined it lasting a generation or two. He may have envisioned it stretching a few hundred miles from north to south, from Babylon in the east to Rome in the west. How would he have reacted had he been presented with the reality of eighteen hundred years of Diaspora, spreading from Sydney to Montreal, from the Russian steppe to the Argentine pampas? Could he have envisioned this small and scattered people, with little communication between its isolated outposts, and no leader to direct them, remaining tuned to the common code he had originally authored? Could he have foreseen the survival of Jewish identity after so many evolutions of practice and belief, long after the dissolutions of Persia, Babylon, and Greece and the fall of those who rose to replace them? Could he have imagined his minute people, the scattered remnants of a small province of Rome, rising to contribute so uniquely and so potently to the story of humanity at large?

Looking back from 2017, we custodians of the Jewish story may appreciate its astonishing span. We may recognize, in retrospect, its specialness, which Yehuda Hanassi could not have imagined. But hindsight obscures its sheer improbability. If Rabbi Yehuda, and all of the successive generations that preserved our fragile legacy for so long, could ask us one question, perhaps it should be *Who are you to end it?*

EPILOGUE

In researching and writing this book, I shared its ideas with people I consider thoughtful and well versed in Jewish history. I also consulted with many non-Jewish analysts of the sociology of different diasporas, including the Chinese and Irish diasporas. These people's guidance has been invaluable. I experienced a diversity of thoughtful challenges to my ideas. A number of these reactions will surely resonate with some readers, so I will summarize them and respond.

1. We are not facing an existential problem. The Jewish population has expanded and contracted repeatedly over the millennia, having persevered through radically varied circumstances. If we are indeed in a contraction, it will work itself out, as all others have.

This assumption has worked well in the past. It may continue working in the future—until it stops, as it has for more than 99 percent of the nations that have inhabited the earth. The fact that circumstances *have* not yet conspired to end Jewish history does not mean they *will* not. Some of the factors on which our survival depends may not be clearly visible to us. We will not necessarily know when these factors change. We will almost certainly not find the answers if we are not asking the questions. In this sense, it may be prudent to examine, understand, and attempt to govern some of the factors on which our survival depends.

One of these factors might be *critical mass*. The invisible logic underlying the model of the constantly vacillating world Jewish population might work regardless of the absolute number of Jews in the smallest phase of the cycle. But it might not. There may be a quantitative threshold below which we cannot recover. The notion that we can allow our numbers to dwindle indefinitely in the certainty that some force will inevitably emerge to replenish our stock is a dangerous assumption. If we are wrong, we will find out only after we have crossed the threshold of inevitability. This is akin to the flawed gambling strategy of doubling each successive bet at the blackjack table in order to win the equivalent of your first bet. In the theoretical world, the logic works. The gambler eventually has to win. He starts by betting, say, $100 on his first hand. If he wins that hand, he has done what he set out to do. He has won the equivalent of his first bet—$100. If he loses the first hand, he is still in the game. He just plays a second hand, doubling his bet to $200. If he wins the second hand, he comes out $100 ahead, having lost $100 in the first hand but gained $200 in the second. If he loses the second hand, he is still in the game. He just puts $400 down on the third hand. If he wins the third hand, he ends up $100 ahead, having lost $300 on the previous two hands but gained $400 on the current hand. If he loses, he puts $800 down on the next hand. Eventually, statistics say, he *has* to win a hand and, in doing so, net the $100 of his original bet. As long as he stays in the game, the odds are in his favor. Of course, in the real world, he could run out of money before being dealt the inevitable winning hand, in which case he is now out of the game—for good. He is finished. The Jews may have sat down at the blackjack table with more chips than the Assyrians or the Phoenicians, but eventually anyone can run out of money. It is foolish to be cavalier when considering irreversible outcomes.

It is also important to remember that laissez-faire has not always worked out so well for us, even though we have survived as a people. This is a lesson I took from Zvi Nussbaum's family in the Warsaw ghetto. Is survival enough of a goal? Is survival despite gas chambers, autos-da-fé, and pogroms necessarily superior to extinction through acts of love? Is it not better to be captains of our own destiny if we can, to both survive and prosper spiritually? Is this not the ambition of Zionism itself?

As I complete the writing of this book, old fault lines between streams of Judaism have reopened. Knesset disputes around a Conversion Bill and a surprise Israeli cabinet decision to renege on a long-negotiated agreement regarding access to the Western Wall for pluralistic Jewish worshippers have reignited familiar political battles within Israel. More dramatically, the Wall debate has suddenly broadened a dangerous battlefront between American Jewry and the Israeli government. American Jewish reaction has included canceling meetings with the prime minister of Israel, threats to withhold long-standing philanthropic donations to Israeli charities, and a de-

clared boycott of Israeli government representatives visiting the
Unites States by American Jewish communities. This episode
may pass, or it may escalate. Either way, we ignore it at our
mutual peril. The challenges this book raises are real. The
threats are only mounting. The longer we wait to face them, the
more we risk crossing the invisible threshold of irreversibility.

*2. The problem you identify is real, but your solutions are too
radical.*

The best outcome that could emerge from this book is a public debate on the future of the Jewish People in light of the
new realities we face, a debate that should have taken place
ninety years ago. I am eager to see an alternate plan, or to see
this one modified. Only if we chart a course can we hope to
steer it and, when necessary, amend it in the face of emerging obstacles.

One obstacle should be clear to all of us: We cannot impose Jewishness on the Jews. The world itself is no longer
imposing Jewishness on the Jews. Nor can we impose Israel
on Israelis. We are all increasingly free to identify and associate as we like. The most productive segments of Israeli society have options. If and when they choose to exercise those
options in sufficient numbers, Israel will lose the critical
mass and quality of human resources required for its survival.

3. It is okay if the Jews disappear.

This is a personal position that each reader needs to stake for
himself or herself. I find it difficult to argue against it. The

non-Jewish world has remained accessible to me. It embraced me many years ago and for some reason has never stopped. I remain in the tribe not because I feel unwelcome or uncomfortable elsewhere but because I find genuine value in my Jewishness. I feel a deep commitment to my people, but I cannot put forward a compelling set of *objective* reasons that we *must* survive as a people. When the alternative to existence was extermination, as in the Holocaust, we were compelled to struggle for our survival as individuals. Survival as a people was a by-product of individual struggles. Today, the threat to the survival of the Jewish People in America has little to do with our survival as individuals. So why fight it? For most of us, there is no answer in divinity. We simply do not believe in the God of scripture. Survival is worth the struggle only if we can establish the secular value, to ourselves or to humanity, of the existence of a Jewish People.

It is important to keep two points in mind, however:

a. As we have noted, extinction is irreversible. Until we are convinced beyond doubt that it is an acceptable outcome, responsibility dictates that we prevent it.

b. Although American Jewish extinction will likely be a benign phenomenon on an individual level, this is unlikely to be the case for Israel. Israel's neighbors will note Israel's accelerating mediocrity, facilitated by continued inaction and by the quickening departure of Israeli excellence for foreign shores. These neighbors have never acquiesced to Jewish sovereignty. Unlike Jewish America's, Israel's end is likely to be violent, a catastrophe composed of millions of individual tragedies.

4. I care about my people's survival, but I feel conflicted on the issue of Particularism. Many of my closest relationships are with non-Jews. My spouse is not Jewish. I do not wish for my people to return to isolated ghettos. I embrace Universalism. **On the other hand,**

5. There is no survival without Particularism. Like it or not, separation from the other is the only formula that has worked over the ages. Our liturgy refers repeatedly to our differentness and even celebrates it. We have always sought to separate ourselves physically from others. Our very dietary laws have prevented Jews from breaking bread, and thereby forming attachments, with non-Jews for over two thousand years. Of course, non-Jews have been complicit in this segregation. The intent of ghettos was to ostracize us, but they ultimately have saved us. Today, isolated Ultra-Orthodox Jewish communities are the only segment of Jewry that is growing.

Points 4 and 5 constitute diametrically opposing views that have defined the tension that guides this book. That tension has been present throughout my life, and throughout the history of the Jewish People. This is not a new struggle. In perhaps his most noted passage, Rabbi Hillel begins as a Particularist. More than two thousand years ago he wrote, in *Pirkei Avot*, "If I am not for myself, who will be for me?" But he continues, as a Universalist, "If I am only for myself, what am I?" Like many other defining questions in Judaism, this question must be struggled with. People will arrive at different conclusions, most of which will represent some balance between the two imperatives. Judaism would traditionally trust the Crowd to guide us more than it would trust any individual.

6. *Why you? There are plenty of experts on Jewish Peoplehood who might have written this book. Indeed, there are plenty of books on the subject already.*

I wrote this book not as an expert, but as a concerned member of world Jewry. I wrote it after having read much of the literature that touches on its subject. It is not meant to replace that literature, but to support it, and to provide a new and personal window through which greater numbers of Jews might be able to view the problem and contribute to a debate around its solution. This debate is urgent, and the numbers are important. We are crossing thresholds that will become visible only in retrospect, and from which there may be no return. I wrote it in the spirit of the third and last of Hillel's interrogatives: "If not now, when?"

APPENDIX

Jewish World Endowment Assumptions

SOURCES OF INCOME

1. Jewish family incomes average $110,000 in the United States, $70,000 in Europe, and $55,000 in Israel.
2. Jewish populations are approximately 6 million in both Israel and the United States and 2 million in the rest of the world.
3. The average Jewish family would have one child enrolled in the program at any given time. (This average includes families yet to have children as well as empty-nesters.)
4. Five percent of proceeds collected would not be applied to the budget, but placed in a permanent endowment.
5. The endowment would be buttressed by voluntary contributions upon death—a sort of Jewish Giving Pledge. The

average member would eventually (at long-term run-rate) bequeath 10 percent of his or her wealth at death. This amounts to approximately $600,000 in the United States, $240,000 in Israel, and an average of $420,000 in the rest of the world.

6. Jewish life expectancy worldwide is 81 years.

7. The endowment's average financial returns over time would be 6 percent.

8. At full potential, the Jewish World Endowment would generate resources of approximately $13.75 billion. The model assumes that, following financial support at launch from a handful of Jewish families, initial enrollment in the program would amount to 5 percent of Jewish families globally. Of course, higher initial financial support would allow for a smaller starting membership.

USES OF INCOME

SUMMER PROGRAMS

Summer programs are modeled, from a budget perspective, after Birthright Israel, arguably the most successful Jewish identity enterprise in existence today. The cost would be $3,200 per participant per summer. The total addressable market of camp-aged youth is approximately 346,000 (with two classes running simultaneously). The assumption is that 5 percent participation, about 17,000 youth, begins immediately, though it is more realistic that families would begin paying their premiums before their children are of camp age.

Summer camp, provided free of charge, including travel, would be the family's first experience of financial return from participation in the Jewish World Endowment. It would also be the American child's first *guaranteed* encounter with organized Judaism, and the Israeli child's first *guaranteed* encounter with the American Jewish community. Of course, different children would arrive with different levels of exposure, but the camps' mission would be to establish and highlight common denominators, and from that foundation to explore Jewish identity together. This would all be provided within the context of a positive experience, where lifelong friendships are formed, and engagement continues between the summers and beyond.

The first year of camp would introduce the Jewish values of *community, tradition,* and *challenge and dissent.* The very act of coming together from around the world as Jews to spend a summer in one of the two great centers of twenty-first-century Jewish life would be a defining and community-building experience for campers. The young campers would arrive knowing no hierarchy, with Americans and Israelis on the same footing and Orthodox, Conservative, and Reform Jews on the same footing. The curriculum would not be religious per se, but a sampling of the foundations of Jewish nationhood, designed not to impart volumes of knowledge but to instill basic familiarity and to spark curiosity and inspire a life of learning in one or more of the areas covered. Abraham, Moses, and the Babylonian Exile must feature, but Maimonides, Freud, Golda Meir, and Zionism could also be included, with equal defining status.

Summertime has no major Jewish holy days, but campers would become familiar with the basics of Jewish *tradition* and the Jewish calendar. This canon would be communicated both through ceremonies, such as Friday night Sabbath dinners, and through a light academic program. The academic program would be based on the traditional Jewish unit of learning, the *hevruta*, in which campers are broken into small groups to study and debate their subject matter. Campers should come away expert in nothing, but comfortable with the exercise of cracking open questions thoroughly and honestly, comfortable in an intellectual world of abstraction, with no absolute right answers and no absolute intellectual authority, empowered to question as individuals, and equipped with the tools of nonhierarchical intellectual sparring. They will have been exposed to the Jewish value of *challenge and dissent*.

Traditional learning opportunities would also be offered, in appreciation of the academic challenges and pressures faced by high school students. These may include math and language immersion, with different offerings provided at different facilities—for example, American SAT and Israeli Matriculation Exam prep, offered in *hevruta* format.

The second year of camp would take place in the other center of world Jewish life. If the camper's first year was in the United States, her second is in Israel, and vice versa. The values targeted in year two would be *education* and *justice*. Study in *hevruta* would continue, but the issues would be weighted toward the contemporary, in preparation for the following summer's Tikkun experience. By the end of the summer, campers will have applied to multiple Tikkun projects, will have been admitted to at least one, and will have selected one. Preparation for the project would begin at the end of the summer camp session and continue into the school year, with formal deliverables and at a level of intensity that would allow Tikkun projects to feature as a key extracurricular pursuit in college applications in the case of the American campers. Traditional academic support would again be offered for the respective high school matriculation hurdles now looming.

THE TIKKUN PROGRAM

The Tikkun program would cost $3,000 per participant, and it assumes a total addressable pool of approximately 173,000 Tikkun-aged youth.

The Tikkun program would have its own administration, as its challenges are significantly distinct from, and far broader than, the summer camp program's. Its participants would be high school graduates, generally more responsible and independent than the campers, but the nature of activities is more challenging, far more diverse, with much greater geographic dispersion, and necessarily lighter supervision. This requires coordination with summer camp administration regarding applicant suitability, and advance screening of applicants for fit with the programs to which they apply.

In order to strike a balance between the vibrancy and relevance of the program offerings and the consistency of quality within the Tikkun program, the program would be structured with an architecture similar to that of the Apple app universe. Social entrepreneurs would pitch projects that meet predefined criteria to a Jewish World Endowment Tikkun Developers Group. Those projects that are accepted into the program would receive funding from the Jewish World Endowment and would be made available for application by prospective participants during their second year at camp. Some projects will demand significant prerequisites, such as special skills or willingness to travel and live in distant locations. A water management project for villages in Uganda would draw on a specific and narrow pool of applicants. On the other hand, teaching English to immigrants to the United States in a program offered in multiple U.S. urban centers could suit a broader pool of applicants.

Carried out in groups—preferably groups including both Israelis and Americans—the Tikkun projects would cement the sense of common cause and Jewish identity initially cultivated in the summer camps. The primary Jewish value that the projects are intended to strengthen is *justice*. Those who have the ability to repair have a Jewish-inspired responsibility to engage in repair. Whether their project deals with a local Jewish community, Israel, or repair in the wider world, the Tikkun project's aim is to inspire a lifetime of Jewish commitment to social justice through action. Of course, the community-building potential of the Tikkun program is dramatic, and its benefits are critical. The Tikkun project is chronologically positioned as the last opportunity for Israeli and American Jews in their formative years to forge lifelong relationships with one another before the former depart for military service and the latter for university.

UNIVERSITY

University tuition is the biggest financial component of the Jewish World Endowment, but the lightest in terms of administrative burden. A student in good standing with the Endowment (that is, one whose parents have remained current on their premium payments, who has attended summer camp, and has participated in Tikkun) will simply file a claim to have his tuition paid by the Endowment at the beginning of each academic year, as tuition comes due. Payment will be automatic. The act of filing a claim, executed by the student herself, is an annual reminder to the student that her studies are a part of her legacy as a Jew, part of her Jewish identity— her community-provided birthright. As such, she is likely to value it and apply herself seriously.

Annual university tuition assumptions are:

1. $31,200 for private universities.
2. $23,000 for public out-of-state universities.
3. $9,200 for public in-state universities.
4. $3,000 for community colleges.
5. Enrollment distribution between the four types of universities is assumed to be equal, a financially conservative assumption based on current enrollment rates.
6. Israeli, and rest-of-world, tuition rates are assumed to equal United States tuition rates, also a conservative assumption.
7. Years of attendance are assumed to be four, even though most Israeli undergraduate programs are three years in length.
8. There are approximately 691,000 university-aged people in the Jewish world today.

At a 5 percent participation rate, total tuition cost for the Jewish World Endowment would stand at about $570 million, versus $26 million for Tikkun projects and $55 million for summer camps.

Total overhead expense for the Jewish World Endowment begins at $20 million, at 5 percent enrollment, and is budgeted to rise by $10 million for each 5 percent in growth, initially.

From the one-child family's perspective, financial participation in the Jewish World Endowment looks like this:

1. Assume $100,000 in pretax family income when the child turns five years old. The parents' contribution amounts to $1,250 in that year.
2. Assuming household income rises by 3 percent annually, the family's annual contribution in year ten, when the child enrolls in her first year of summer camp, is $1,680 (from an income of $134,392). Cumulative contributions will have reached $16,010.
3. Two years at camp, valued at cost, will return $6,400 of financial value to the family.
4. One year of Tikkun, valued at cost, will return $3,000 of value to the family.
5. Four years of university tuition, at an average of $16,500 per year, will return $66,000 in financial value to the family.
6. When their daughter graduates from university at age twenty-two, the family will have contributed a cumulative $29,268 to the endowment and derived a cumulative $75,400 in financial value from the program.

As she continues on her life's path, the Jewish World Endowment student is likely to look back on the Endowment's role in it. She will have received a basic training in Jewish nationhood and in Jewish values. She will hopefully have followed up on some aspects of these with further study and exploration. She will likely have cultivated a network of life-long friendships, in Israel and in the United States. She will hopefully have adopted social engagement and Tikkun as a habit for life and have found an area in which she remains passionately involved. Finally, she will have had her higher education furnished by the community in which she enjoys permanent membership, because education is a value that her community treasures to the extent that it is considered her birthright. As she grows and finds herself engaged in multiple professional and social frameworks, it is likely (far more likely than it is today) that the Jewish community remains a valuable affiliation for her, one of which she is proud and with which she is grateful to associate. She is likely to engage with Israel if she is American, and with American Jewry if she is Israeli. She is likely to seek other forms of Jewish engagement, such as a synagogue or community center. She is likely to enroll in the Jewish World Endowment when she is a parent. And she is likely to marry a spouse who is Jewish, by birth or by conversion.

The Jewish World Endowment would be bigger than any program currently in existence in the Jewish world, a complement or successor to Birthright, on the order of some of the boldest enterprises in Jewish history. It is obviously ambitious, but a less dramatic effort is unlikely to change the current course and to provide a newly relevant set of organizing principles for Jewish national identity, goal setting, and action.

DISCUSSION QUESTIONS

1. How do you define Judaism? Is it a religion? A culture? A civilization?

2. How would you feel if Judaism were to end? Would individual people of Jewish ancestry have lost something important? Will the world have lost something important?

3. Do you believe a religion can—or should—be crowd-sourced?

4. How would you respond to the survey question

> List up to ten identifiers, principles that in aggregate (not individually) form the de facto pillars of contemporary Jewish identity. Your list must be exclusive enough to distinguish Jewish values from those of other value systems (like American values), but each individual tenet must be inclusive enough to be agreeable to at least 75 percent of adult Jews worldwide (to the best of your knowledge). Of course, your list is not

meant to be an exhaustive guide to Judaism for each individual Jew. Other values might be layered on top of your foundation by Jewish individuals or by Jewish communities. Keeping kosher, for example, might not meet the 75 percent requirement but could still serve as a defining practice to a large minority of Jews.

5. What are your thoughts on the results of the tenets survey? Do the tenets—justice, education, challenge and dissent, ritual and tradition, and community—feel Jewish to you?

6. Is there something unique about the way Judaism expresses these values?

7. Is the Jewish World Endowment something you would be interested in having your family participate in? Are there any drawbacks that you can see to joining?

8. Do you have any additional suggestions for the program?

9. Did you find Tal Keinan's personal story helpful to the argument he puts forth about the future of Judaism or did it detract from the more universal aspect of his message?

10. Discuss his proposal for the role of the president of Israel. Does such a role sound persuasive to you?

11. Throughout history there have been moments when it seemed as if Judaism might disappear, and yet it has survived. What do you see as the future of Judaism if we do not take steps to ensure its survival?

ADDITIONAL RESOURCES

From the Maccabees to the Mishnah by Shaye J. D. Cohen

The Beginnings of Jewishness: Boundaries, Varieties, Uncertainties by Shaye J. D. Cohen

Josephus in Galilee and Rome by Shaye J. D. Cohen

The Wisdom of Crowds by James Surowiecki

Homo Deus: A Brief History of Tomorrow by Yuval Noah Harari

Getting Our Groove Back: How to Energize American Jewry by Scott A. Shay

Payoff: The Hidden Logic That Shapes Our Motivations by Dan Ariely

The Upside of Irrationality: The Unexpected Benefits of Defying Logic by Dan Ariely

Predictably Irrational: The Hidden Forces That Shape Our Decisions by Dan Ariely

The Story of the Jews, Volumes I and II by Simon Schama

A History of the Jews by Paul Johnson

Flavius Josephus: Translation and Commentary, Volume 1b: Judean War 2 by Flavius Josephus, translation and commentary by Steve Mason

History of the Arabs: From the Earliest Times to the Present by Philip K. Hitti

Islam and the West by Bernard Lewis

The Jews of Islam by Bernard Lewis

The Middle East: A Brief History of the Last 2,000 Years by Bernard Lewis

The Pity of It All: A Portrait of the German-Jewish Epoch, 1743–1933 by Amos Elon

Founder: A Portrait of the First Rothschild and His Time by Amos Elon

Herzl by Amos Elon

The Israelis: Fathers and Sons by Amos Elon

The Talmud by Adin Steinsaltz

The Essential Maimonides: Translations of the Rambam by Avraham Yaakov Finkel

A History of the Jews in America by Howard M. Sachar

The Jews of Iraq: 3000 Years of History and Culture by Nissim Rejwan

The Changing Face of Anti-Semitism: From Ancient Times to the Present Day by Walter Laqueur

The Chosen Peoples: America, Israel, and the Ordeals of Divine Election by Todd Gitlin and Liel Leibovitz

Aliya: Three Generations of American-Jewish Immigration to Israel by Liel Leibovitz

Ethics of War and Conflict, edited by Asa Kasher

Would You Kill the Fat Man? The Trolley Problem and What Your Answer Tells Us About Right and Wrong by David Edmonds

Raid on the Sun: Inside Israel's Secret Campaign That Denied Saddam the Bomb by Rodger W. Claire

A Treatise on Money by John Maynard Keynes

John Maynard Keynes by Hyman P. Minsky

Start-up Nation: The Story of Israel's Economic Miracle by Dan Senor and Saul Singer

"Cooperation and Punishment in Public Goods Experiments" by Ernst Fehr and Simon Gächter, *The American Economic Review*, Vol. 90, No. 4 (September 2000), pp. 980–994

"A Portrait of Jewish Americans," Pew Research Center, October 1, 2013, http://www.pewforum.org/2013/10/01/jewish-american-beliefs-attitudes-culture-survey/

"Defaults and Donation Decisions" by Eric J. Johnson and Daniel G. Goldstein, *Transplantation,* Vol. 78, No. 12 (December 27, 2004), pp. 1713–1716

"Vox Populi" by Sir Francis Galton, *Nature,* Vol. 75, No. 1949 (1907), pp. 450–451

Taub Center for Social Policy Studies in Israel: http://taubcenter.org.il/

ACKNOWLEDGMENTS

God Is in the Crowd was a dense and meandering treatise before I met Claire Wachtel. It is Claire, acting as editor and coach, who breathed life into this book, and who gently coaxed my own story into it. If the book stirs passion in its readers, it is because of Claire. Deborah Harris and George Eltman are the first readers who believed in the importance of this book's message, and who looked through its convoluted writing to see a mechanism that could deliver that message. It is Deborah who introduced *God Is in the Crowd* to Claire.

Jay Pomrenze, my friend, mentor, business partner, and intellectual foil, provoked much of my thinking on the science and theology that undergirds *God Is in the Crowd*. It is Jay who introduced me to Deborah. Liel Leibovitz sharpened and then resharpened the core ideas in *God Is in the Crowd* and provided many of the references used to develop them. Chaim Seidler-Feller painstakingly proofread this book for Halachic and Talmudic accuracy. He corrected me gently when I was wrong and, in the process, deepened my understanding of the Jewish Crowd immeasurably.

In the summer of 2017, Claire shared this book with Cindy Spiegel. Cindy's steadfast faith in its mission, along with her insightful editing, and her patient management of its author, drove this process to completion. I thank my Clarity Capital colleagues, Jay Pomrenze, David Steinhardt, Amir Leybovitch, Eran Peleg, Boris Dvinsky, Gilead Halevy, Laurence Schreiber, Jonathan Silber, Yitz Raab, and many others, for years of friendship and discourse, and for teaching me the mathematics, the ritual, the Talmud, the history, and the spirit of the Jewish Crowd. I thank my IAF family for their courage, their example, and their sacrifice, all volunteered more quietly and more humbly than my own. Special gratitude to Yishai for permitting me to share the very personal story of our bond. As always, you have allowed the mission—in this case, my mission—to supersede your individual benefit. I thank my mother, Zipora. From the beginning, you obscured the boundaries that would otherwise have defined me. Thanks to Carl Kaplan of KIEDF, to Tova Dorfman of the Steinhardt Foundation, and to Gerry Schwartz of HESEG, who showed me how change happens, in Israel and in the Jewish world. Amber Keinan shares my powerful but often ambiguous bond with our people. She has supported my struggle with this manuscript for years, patiently rereading dozens of rewritings and silently picking up the slack that I left at home. If this mission proves successful, it will have been for Amber's contribution.

INDEX

ABOUT THE AUTHOR

TAL KEINAN is a co-founder and the executive chairman of Clarity Capital, a global asset management firm based in Tel Aviv and New York. Clarity is the vanguard of the emerging Israel-based financial industry serving global clients. He previously was a partner at Giza LLC, an Israel-based private equity firm active in the technology sector.

Keinan is the chairman of Koret Israel Economic Development Funds, Israel's largest not-for-profit small-business lending and microcredit program, which has provided more than $400 million in credit, supporting fifty thousand new and existing jobs.

Keinan serves on the boards of directors of the Steinhardt Foundation for Jewish Life, the HESEG Foundation, and the Reut Institute. He was also a member of the Ariav Commission, a Bank of Israel–Finance Ministry task force on creating a global financial center in Israel.

He is a Young Global Leader of the World Economic Forum and a member of Dialog US and Dialog Global. He is an executive committee member of the YPO Intercontinental Chapter.

Born and raised in the United States, Keinan immigrated to Israel at the age of twenty. He received his bachelor's degree from Tel Aviv University and holds a master's degree from Harvard Business School.

Keinan served in the Israeli Air Force as a fighter pilot and formation commander. He retired from the IAF reserves with the rank of lieutenant colonel.